The Canadian Iroquois
and the Seven Years' War

D. PETER MacLEOD

DUNDURN
TORONTO

CANADIAN
WAR MUSEUM

MUSÉE CANADIEN
DE LA GUERRE

NORTH-EASTERN NORTH AMERICA
1753-1760

0	50	100	200 mi
0	100	200	300 km

Amerindian territory . . . .
Territory settled by the British . . . .
Territory settled by the French . . . .
Battle sites . . . . ✘
Amerindian settlements . . . . ▲
British settlements . . . . ○
French settlements . . . . ●

Ottawa

River

*Georgian
Bay*

LAKE

HURON

*Lake
Simcoe*

Fort

Fort Toronto ●

LAKE ONTAR

● Fort Niagara

*Lake
St. Clair*

LAKE ERIE

*Chautauqua
Portage*

*Chautauqua
Lake*

Alleghany

Fort Presqu'île ●

R.

Fort Le Boeuf ●

French Creek

River

Ohio

Fort Venango ●

Fort Duquesne ●
✘ Monongahela 1755

River

Ohio

Fort Necessity
✘ ○ 1753
Fort Cumberland ○

River

VIRGINIA

For Don and Jean MacLeod

Editor: Diane Mew
Designer: Sebastian Vasile
Printer: Webcom

Library and Archives Canada Cataloguing in Publication

MacLeod, D. Peter, 1955-
   The Canadian Iroquois and the Seven Years' War / D. Peter MacLeod.

Co-published by the Canadian War Museum.
Includes bibliographical references and index.
Issued also in electronic formats.
ISBN 978-1-55488-977-8

1. Canada--History--Seven Years' War, 1755-1763--Participation, Indian. 2. Iroquois Indians--Wars. 3. Indians of North America--Canada--Wars--ca. 1600-1763. I. Canadian War Museum II. Title.

FC384.M24 2012   971.01'88   C2011-903785-8

1   2   3   4   5   16   15   14   13   12

We acknowledge the support of the Canada Council for the Arts and the Ontario Arts Council for our publishing program. We also acknowledge the financial support of the Government of Canada through the Canada Book Fund and Livres Canada Books, and the Government of Ontario through the Ontario Book Publishing Tax Credit and the Ontario Media Development Corporation.

Care has been taken to trace the ownership of copyright material used in this book. The author and the publisher welcome any information enabling them to rectify any references or credits in subsequent editions.

⋁ FEB 10 2012   *J. Kirk Howard, President*

Printed and bound in Canada.
www.dundurn.com

Dundurn	Gazelle Book Services Limited	Dundurn
3 Church Street, Suite 500	White Cross Mills	2250 Military Road
Toronto, Ontario, Canada	High Town, Lancaster, England	Tonawanda, NY
M5E 1M2	LA1 4XS	U.S.A. 14150

LIST OF MAPS

ACKNOWLEDGMENTS

The more I studied the Canadian Iroquois and the Seven Years' War, the more painfully aware I became of just how little I really knew. This being the case, I relied considerably upon the assistance of friends and colleagues who helped me to make better use of what information I had. Foremost among these friends and colleagues were W.J. Eccles, who first recommended me to the Canadian War Museum for this project, and Fred Gaffen and Diane Mew, who served as kindly, patient, if rigorous editors. All three provided me with invaluable critiques, along with Robert S. Allen, Peter Cook, Cornelius J. Jaenen, Jan Grabowski, Don MacLeod, Jean MacLeod, and Bill Rawling who were generous enough to read over the entire manuscript. Each of these individuals made much-appreciated contributions to this manuscript, both through their own suggestions and by preventing me from making a whole series of egregious errors and amusing solecisms. Bill Constable produced the austerely elegant maps that grace this volume. Jim Brant, René Chartrand, Barry Cottam, H.P. Goodman, Pat Kennedy, Lise Legault, Ian MacLeod, Sasha Mullally, Madge Pon, Theresa Redmond, Nicole St-Onge, Karen Jacobs-Williams, and Margo Yeomans read chapters, answered arcane questions, donated assorted items of useful information, and provided moral support.

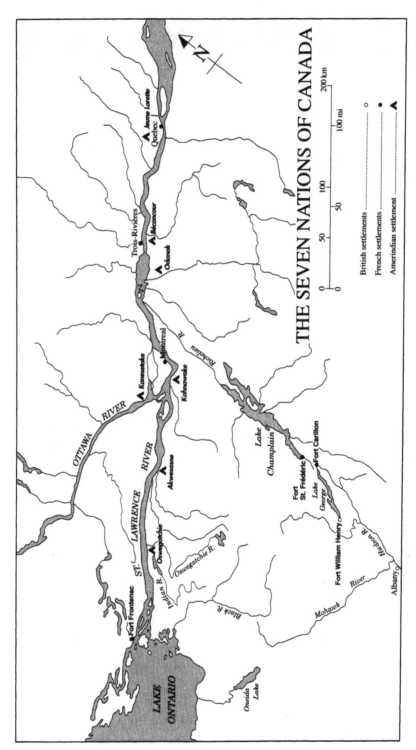

MAP 2. The Seven Nations of Canada, by William R. Constable.

INTRODUCTION

If it had been up to the Canadian Iroquois, the Seven Years' War would never have occurred. Although continuously at war with more distant nations such as the Catawbas, the Canadian Iroquois desired only peace with and among their neighbours in northeastern North America.[1] Yet they lived in a volatile, dangerous neighbourhood. Harmony reigned among the nations of the St. Lawrence valley, but the interests of two of these nations, the Abenakis and the French, were constantly threatened by British colonials. In the mid-eighteenth century, New Englanders pushing north resumed their invasion of Abenaki hunting grounds while Virginians driving west into the Ohio valley threatened French imperial ambitions. Neither the Abenakis nor the French were inclined to stand by passively. The Abenaki response to New England aggression produced a limited, defensive war; Anglo-French imperial rivalry exploded into a general engagement between the two transcontinental empires. The Canadian Iroquois sidestepped involvement in Anglo-Abenaki hostilities, but could not escape participation in the global conflict known as the Seven Years' War.

Between 1753 and 1760 this war threw a cold, dark shadow over the lives of the Canadian Iroquois.[2] Every individual in every Canadian Iroquois community was affected in one way or another. On battlefields as far away as the Ohio valley and as close as Lake Champlain, Canadian Iroquois fighters took part in every major campaign of the war. At home, the war brought both economic dislocation and new economic opportunities, mass death from a devastating smallpox epidemic, and the adoption into Canadian Iroquois families of new members drawn from a rich harvest of British prisoners. In the last years of the war, battlefield and home front threatened to converge as British armies invaded the region occupied by Canadian Iroquois communities.

Just what the Canadian Iroquois thought they were doing fighting another nation's enemies was concisely expressed in September of 1746. In that month, a party of Canadian Iroquois fighters had occasion to explain what going to war on behalf of their French allies meant to them. They "said that they were ... occupied in taking prisoners and breaking heads, thus fulfilling the promises they had given to His Majesty."[3] This statement could be applied just as well to Canadian Iroquois participation in the Seven Years' War. On the one hand, they were fighting to fulfil their obligations as allies of the French, rather than advancing their own national interests. On the other, they were doing so by making war in their own way, without any particular regard for the military habits and aspirations of their European allies. The result was the phenomenon which I have called "parallel warfare," as both parties to the alliance waged a separate war against the common enemy.

This book follows the fortunes of the Canadian Iroquois as they practised their own style of war during each of the major campaigns of the Seven Years' War and the tensions that ensued when waging war according to their own inclinations brought them into conflict with their allies as well as their enemies. It thus portrays the war not just as a military clash between armed opponents, but as a series of cultural confrontations between Amerindian and European military values and customs. These confrontations, which occurred in almost every campaign of the war, most frequently centred on Amerindian seizures of prisoners after surrenders had been negotiated between Europeans and Amerindian refusals to take part in assaults on fortified positions.

It further portrays the war as one in which the French were defeated but the Canadian Iroquois were not. The final chapters cover the intricate diplomatic manoeuvring of the last year of hostilities, as the Amerindians turned from fulfilling their obligations as allies of the French to protecting their interests by negotiating a new alliance with the British.

Definitions

The Canadian Iroquois who performed these feats of war and diplomacy were the men and women of the four communities of Akwesasne, Kahnawake, Kanesetake, and Oswegatchie. These communities were located along the upper St. Lawrence River, hard against the westernmost French parishes of Canada. This placed them within territory that many Mohawks consider to be an extension of Kanienkeh, their homeland and hunting grounds. For these Amerindians, the island of Kawenote Teiontiakon (the Montreal archipelago), "the place where it divides," represents the point where Mohawk territory ends and the lands of other nations begin.[4] In this book the region occupied by the four Canadian Iroquois communities and the intervening tracts will be designated northeastern Kanienkeh. However, readers should be aware that the word "Kanienkeh" does not appear in the European documentation generated by the war and that the meaning of the term here has been stretched to encompass the Onondaga community of Oswegatchie. It is used here as the best available Amerindian term for this region.

Northeastern Kanienkeh was settled by Amerindians from the Iroquois League. This League, known to Europeans as the Six Nations, was composed of the Mohawks, Oneidas, Onondagas, Cayugas, Senecas, and Tuscaroras.[5] In this book they appear as the League Iroquois, League Mohawks, and so on.[6] In the later seventeenth century significant numbers of Catholic Mohawks and other Catholic Iroquois left the communities of the League and came to the upper St. Lawrence, where they established the towns near Montreal that were ultimately located at Kanesetake and Kahnawake. At Kanesetake the Iroquois lived alongside Algonquins and Nipissings, who called it Oka. The remaining Canadian Iroquois communities were founded just before the Seven Years' War, when Catholic Onondagas from the Iroquois League relocated to Oswegatchie in 1749 and Mohawks from Kahnawake settled at Akwesasne in 1755.

The residents of these communities are collectively designated in this book as Akwesasnes, Kanesetakes, Kahnawakes, and Oswegatchies. Kanesetakes is used to refer only to the Iroquois residents of Kanesetake. The Algonquins and Nipissings of that community are invariably distinguished from the Kanesetakes in contemporary European documents and have been treated as a separate group in this book. Although they took an active part in the conflict, there are very few references to Akwesasnes in French documentary records of the Seven Years' War. This is probably because the French grouped the Akwesasnes with the Kahnawakes in their accounts of the war. British documents, however, treat the Akwesasnes as a distinct community.

Akwesasne, Kanesetake, Kahnawake, and Oswegatchie were numbered among the Seven Villages, Seven Castles, or Seven Nations of Canada - the Amerindian communities of the St. Lawrence valley.[7] In addition to the Canadian Iroquois, the Seven Nations included the Abenakis of Odanak and their satellite community of Bécancour, the Algonquins and Nipissings of Kanesetake/Oka, and the Hurons of Lorette.[8] Although in 1755 a Kahnawake identified the members of a war party from Canada by saying: "We are the 7 confederate Indian Nations of Canada,"[9] this expression did not come into common use among Europeans until the British era. It is used here as a collective label for the Amerindian communities of the St. Lawrence valley.[10] On occasion, to avoid repetition, Canadian Amerindians is used as a synonym for Seven Nations. Among the Seven Nations, the Abenakis of Odanak and Bécancour were the most important allies of the Canadian Iroquois. Material obtained from documents relating to the Abenakis and other First Nations appears in this book whenever it can illuminate some aspect of the Amerindian military experience that they shared with the Canadian Iroquois.

During the Seven Years' War, the Canadian Iroquois generally acted in concert with their Amerindian allies. Consequently, in some chapters they will appear as Seven Nations, Canadian Amerindians, or even (when serving with warriors from the Great Lakes or Ohio valley) simply Amerindians, whenever it is impossible to separate their actions from those of their allies who were present at a given event. The words "the allies," on the other hand, always signify the coalition formed by the Canadian Iroquois and their Amerindian and French partners. Onontio was the ceremonial title accorded the governor general of New France by Amerindians. Great Onontio was the king of France. British refers collectively to residents of Great Britain and its colonies. Residents of individual British colonies are referred to by the names of these colonies, those from the British Isles are called metropolitans.

The troupes de la marine or colonial regulars were the garrison of New France. Organized in independent companies and controlled by the Ministry of Marine and Colonies, they were composed of soldiers recruited in France and officers drawn from the Canadian noblesse. The troupes de terre or metropolitan regulars were the battalions of the French regular army sent to Canada to reinforce the garrison after the outbreak of the Seven Years' War. Militia, in this book, applies exclusively to the Canadian militia, composed of the entire adult male population of Canada. Their British counterparts, provincials, were men serving in units raised by colonial governments.[11]

During the French era, the expression "Canada" could denote either the St. Lawrence valley or the whole of the territory occupied by the French and their allies north of Louisiana and west of Acadia. In this book it is used to designate the St. Lawrence valley, the region occupied by the Seven Nations and the French.

Sources, Limits, and Looting

Before proceeding further, the reader should be warned that writing a history of the Canadian Iroquois in the Seven Years' War based upon French and British documents is rather like writing a history of Canada in the Second World War based exclusively upon German and Russian records. It is not impossible, but the sources place definite limits on what can be achieved. In these documents, activities which took place beyond the vision of literate Europeans remain invisible, Amerindians appear only in the company of Europeans, and events which were of crucial importance to their participation in the war often take place off stage and out of sight. This gives a misleading impression of a war in which Europeans dominate the centre and Amerindians are relegated to the periphery of events.

In hope of at least partially redressing this inherent bias and placing Amerindians rather than Europeans at the centre of the action, I have attempted wherever possible to separate European observers from their observations. For example, in the French account of an acrimonious confrontation between the Canadian Iroquois and François-Charles de Bourlamaque on 24 July 1759, the Amerindians come to Bourlamaque and make their protest against his discourtesy and lack of respect for protocol. Thus, although it is the Amerindians who are initiating events, Europeans remain at the centre of the action, the dominating hub around which everything else revolves. However, instead of remaining with the French as they watch the Amerindians approach, I have attempted to follow the Amerindians as they hold their private council, then go to meet with the French to inform them of the results. Accordingly, in this manuscript, the incident begins with the Canadian Iroquois reviewing Bourlamaque's performance as an ally. Once they reached a consensus, the Amerindians send a delegation to meet with their French ally and inform Bourlamaque of their concerns. Bourlamaque then responds to their remarks.[12] As a result, instead of occurring as they came to the attention of literate Europeans, events appear here as they were experienced by Amerindians, and it is the Amerindians who encounter the French "other" rather than the reverse.

Among the invisible yet crucially important Amerindian activities were the internal politics of Canadian Iroquois communities. All Canadian Iroquois groups, and in particular the Kahnawakes, were divided into factions holding different opinions on what course of action with regard to the Anglo-French conflict would be best for their communities. Yet only the most distant echoes of these controversies appear in contemporary documents. Readers, however, should bear in mind that Kahnawakes such as Joseph and his brother (who appear in chapter 8), one of whom served with the allies, the other in Rogers' Rangers, represented factions which exercised significant influence in Canadian Iroquois communities throughout the war.

These factions, along with Canadian Iroquois communities as a whole, were led by strong-willed, capable individuals who played crucial roles in determining the extent and nature of Canadian Iroquois participation in the Seven Years' War. Nevertheless, these leaders are for the most part reduced to near-anonymity in French and British documents. Most critically, the importance of clan mothers, who possessed considerable economic and political power within Canadian Iroquois communities, was blithely over-looked by patriarchal European scribes. Those references that do exist show clan mothers meeting in council with their male counterparts to take decisions regarding peace and war and joining in delegations to confront Onontio and the French leadership in Montreal, but only hint at the real influence wielded by these women. A vital component of Canadian Iroquois leadership is thus perforce almost entirely absent from this book.

The male component of Canadian Iroquois leadership, the war chiefs, village chiefs, and prominent warriors, are only slightly better off. Although references to these leaders abound, European writers most often speak of "the chiefs" or "a chief" rather than identifying prominent Amerindians by name. When named individuals do appear in the documentation, they generally do so only once or twice. Chiefs such as Ad'yadarony or Collière merit a presence in records of the war as prominent and sustained as that accorded European generals. Instead, they flash into sight for an instant, then simply disappear. European documents thus provide a very incomplete portrayal of Canadian Iroquois chiefs in action, and any account of the par-ticipation of the Canadian Iroquois in the Seven Years' War suffers in conse-quence.

Rather than producing a history peopled by named Europeans and largely anonymous chiefs, warriors, young men, and women of the council, I have attempted wherever appropriate to alleviate this disparity by eliminat-ing the names of minor European characters and replacing them with descriptions. Thus, when 130 warriors from the Seven Nations receive news of the outbreak of Anglo-French hostility on 15 June 1754, they do so from "a French officer" instead of Michel-Jean-Hughes Péan.[13] Reducing a number of Europeans to equivalent anonymity does not directly address the lack of documentary references to individual Amerindians, but does at least promote a somewhat greater balance between numbers of named Amerindians and Europeans.

Since French records of Amerindian war parties are much less detailed than in previous wars, this book also passes over much of another major component of Amerindian wartime experience - the numerous small raids which they conducted against British colonies. These raids were employed by the French as a strategic instrument to knock the British colonials out of the war. "Nothing," wrote the governor general of New France in 1756, "is more likely to discourage the people of these [British] colonies and make them desire the return of peace."[14] In the event, however, partisan warfare proved tactically successful but strategically ineffective. Raiders terrorized the colonial settlement frontier, but did not affect the real centres of British power, which were located on the eastern seaboard and in the metropolis. Partisan raids diverted British resources into the construction of chains of ineffective frontier forts, but neither influenced the outcome of the war nor provide much insight into Canadian Iroquois-French relations. Nonetheless, more information on these raids in French documents would have provided the basis for a more rounded portrayal of Canadian Iroquois military activity during the war.

Furthermore, readers should bear in mind that many of the speeches by Amerindians that appear in this book are in fact paraphrases by Europeans. These Europeans generally heard the original statement through the medium of an interpreter, then condensed what might have been a long, eloquent discourse into a few words.

Finally, in contemporary French and British documents, words such as looting, pillaging, and robbery are universally employed to cover an important aspect of Amerindian military activity. Except when they appear in quotations, expressions of this nature have been replaced by the acquisition, collection, or gathering of matériel. These are not meant to be coy euphemisms. Looting, pillaging, and robbery carry the connotation, not just of crime, but of unofficial enterprise, wholly separate from the achievement of national objectives in war. Yet for Amerindians, acquiring matériel was a legitimate and recognized goal of war. Ranking just below the taking of prisoners, it was as valid and significant to Amerindians as the capture of a fortress to Europeans. This point was made by an Abenaki warrior in 1757 who informed a priest that "I make war for plunder, scalps, and prisoners. You content yourself with a fort."[15]

This pursuit of culturally specific military objectives by Amerindians and Frenchmen during the same campaigns of the same conflict serves as a reminder that the Seven Years' War was not simply a French war in which Amerindians served as incidental auxiliaries. It was also a Canadian Iroquois war, waged for objectives as important to the Canadian Iroquois as Louisbourg or Quebec to their uncomprehending French allies.

Place Names

Many places in North America were known by a variety of names during the Seven Years' War, and some names changed following the capture of forts by the British from the French.

Akwesasne = Saint-Régis
Fort Carillon = Fort Ticonderoga
Fort Georges = Fort William Henry
Fort Lévis = Fort William Augustus
Fort St. Frédéric = Fort Crown Point
Kahnawake = Sault Saint-Louis = Caughnawaga
Kanesetake = Oka = Lac des Deux Montagnes
Les Cèdres = The Cedars
Lydius = Fort Edward
Odanak = St. François = St. Francis
Oswegatchie = La Présentation
Oswego = 1. the British trading post on Lake Ontario (1727-1755). 2. the cluster of forts composed of the trading post, known as Fort George, together with Fort Ontario and Fort Oswego (1755-1756). 3. Fort Ontario (1759-).

Measurements Used in Contemporary Maps[16]

1 (linear) arpent = 58.47 metres
1 fathom = 1.83 metres
1 pas (pace) = 81.20 centimetres
1 toise (fathom) = 1.949 metres
1 yard = 91.44 centimetres

Quotations and Translations

The spelling in English quotations has been modernized, except where this would distort the meaning or reduce the charm of the original expressions. All quotations from French documents were translated by me. I have followed Cornelius J. Jaenen in translating the expression "Sauvages," used almost invariably by the French when referring to Amerindians, as "Natives." In the seventeenth and eighteenth centuries, Frenchmen frequently used the numeral 8 to stand for "ou" or "ouáh" when writing Amerindian words.

CHAPTER 1

THE HOME FRONT

In December of 1757 a Kahnawake hunter named Tontileaugo struck his eight-year-old stepson following the commission of some childish misdemeanour. For an Iroquois this was a most unusual, not to say reprehensible, act. The boy's reaction passed unrecorded, but his mother felt that, regardless of the provocation, to strike a child was intolerable. When Tontileaugo next went out to hunt, she gathered up her son, her two horses, and her other possessions, which were legally separate from those of her husband, then set out to return to her mother's family. Immediately he discovered their absence, Tontileaugo set out in pursuit. When he caught up with his family, husband and wife reconciled. But they chose to continue on to spend the remainder of the winter with her mother's family, rather than remaining at their hunting camp.[1]

This incident is of no relevance whatever to the participation of the Canadian Iroquois in the Seven Years' War. It is included here to remind the reader, and even more, the writer, that the Amerindians involved in this conflict were more than simply anonymous actors in a historical drama which has been recreated across the printed page. They were *people*. Real people with human feelings and human failings, and possessed of private lives that transcended their ethnicity and their participation in historical events. These lives were interrupted between 1753 and 1760 by the Seven Years' War. This war, for the Canadian Iroquois, took place against a background of daily economic and social activities, which combined an efficient economy with a vigorous community life that provided a good deal of satisfaction for its members.

The foundations of the Canadian Iroquois economy rested upon a combination of agriculture and hunting that varied with the seasons. This traditional economic cycle was integrated with the festivals of the Catholicism they had adopted in the seventeenth century. Shortly after All Souls Day (1

November) Canadian Iroquois towns were largely abandoned as the greater part of the population broke up into small groups and moved out to hunting camps of log cabins or bark huts for the winter hunt. During this season, men were the primary producers, but all family members had important economic roles. While the men hunted deer, along with bear and racoon, children gathered nuts to make up any shortfall in game, and women processed hides and pelts, and reduced bear fat into oil for transport in containers made of deerskin. Families remained in their winter camps until either Christmas or Candlemas (2 February), when they returned home laden with meat and oil for future consumption.

After a brief sojourn in their towns, Canadian Iroquois families set out again on the day after Ash Wednesday (mid to late February). This time the hunters harvested the pelts of beaver and marten, which would be used for clothing or traded to the French. In the late winter and early spring, families turned to the production of maple sugar. Men, women, and children constructed bark containers, tapped maple trees, and refined the collected sap into sugar. The sugar was transported back to the village for consumption in the spring and summer. In the spring, once more at home, women assumed the role of primary producers, as they set to work first planting, then harvesting the year's crop of maize, beans, squash, pumpkins, peas,

Caughnawaga Indians Snowshoeing, by Amelia Frederica Dyneley and Mary Millicent Chaplin, c. 1850. NAC C-040310

and other vegetables. Women were also responsible for caring for livestock, including cattle, pigs, horses, and chickens. While the women farmed, men continued to hunt and, especially at Oswegatchie and Akwesasne, engaged in fishing on a large scale.

Commerce of one form or another represented another important component of the Canadian Iroquois economy. The proximity of French farming communities and the town of Montreal as well as the close personal ties that existed between the Canadian Iroquois and their neighbours facilitated an extensive trade with the French. This commerce was for the most part the province of women. They traded a variety of products manufactured in their communities, including moccasins, clothing, snowshoes, and canoes, whose quality was acknowledged and appreciated by the French. These items, along with furs and hides, were taken by Canadian Iroquois traders to neighbouring French communities, where they exchanged them for European products or cash.

A second venue for commercial activity was the Lake Champlain corridor that linked Montreal with New York. Here, the Canadian Iroquois aggressively exploited their position at the intersection of the French and British trading systems. This location, combined with their freedom to travel, provided the Canadian Iroquois with access to manufactured goods from New York and allowed them to earn income by transporting goods for Albany and Montreal merchants. Although this trade involved passing over borders set by European governments, the Canadian Iroquois acknowledged neither these borders nor the right of Europeans to control their movements. In the course of the eighteenth century, the French authorities formally acknowledged the right of the Amerindians to cross colonial boundaries and participate in this commerce.[2]

The Canadian Iroquois thus possessed an efficient economy that exploited a wide variety of resources and activities. There might be shortages in winter, if game could not be found, or in summer, between the consumption of last year's produce and the harvest of the season's crops. But shortfalls in production produced temporary hardship rather than starvation, and could in any event often be made up through trading with the French.[3] Something of the strength and efficiency of this economy can be seen from the response of the Oswegatchies when presented with the opportunity to sell provisions to the new British garrison of Fort William Augustus (formerly Fort Lévis) in 1761-62. They supplied the garrison with "very great quantities of fish and in the course of the winter furnished them with fifteen thousand weight of venison, a prodigious quantity."[4]

This economic activity supported a vigorous social life. Indeed, to some British prisoners, life among the Canadian Iroquois appeared to consist of one long party. Wrote one such captive, during a period when the seasonal round brought an entire community together: "They have no such thing as regular meals, breakfast, dinner, or supper, but if any one ... would go to the same house several times in one day, he would be invited to eat of the best."[5] After days spent in visiting, nights were passed in singing and dancing to the music of drums and flutes. A description of one of these dances in August of 1755 gives some idea of the sheer vitality and exuberance of Canadian Iroquois social life:

> This evening I was invited to another ... dance ... The young men stood in one rank, and the young women in another, about one rod apart, facing each other. The one that raised the tune, or started the song, held a small gourd or dried shell of a squash in his hand, which contained beads or small stones, which rattled. When he began to sing, he timed the tune with his rattle; both men and women danced and sung together, advancing towards each other, stopping until their heads would be touching together, and then ceased from dancing, with loud shouts, and retreated and formed again, and so repeated the same thing, over and over, for three or four hours, without intermission. This exercise appeared to me at first irrational and insipid; but I found that in singing their tune they used ya ne no hoo wa ne &c, like our fa sol la and though they have no such thing as jingling verse, yet they can intermix sentences with their notes and say what they please to each other, and carry on the tune in concert. I found that this was a kind of wooing or courtship dance, and as they advanced stooping with their heads together, they could say what they pleased in each other's ear, without disconcerting their rough music, and the others, or those near, not hear what they said.[6]

This vitality carried over into Canadian Iroquois participation in the communal rituals of Catholicism. These ceremonies were most noted for the harmony and beauty of the singing of the congregations. A Jesuit priest at Kahnawake in 1735 reported that when his parishioners came together to worship, "all the prayers are made in song." He compared the voices of the men who sang the first verse to "one hundred Franciscans in a choir" and the voices of the women who responded to those of a large community of nuns. However, he added, "neither monks nor nuns have ever sang as well as our Iroquois men and women, they have voices that are equally sweet and full, and hearing so precise that they never miss a half-note in all the hymns that they all know by heart."[7]

The Canadian Iroquois, in short, lived what was, by any definition, a good life. The experiences of two British prisoners, one living with Tontileaugo's family, the other with a French family, bear comparison. The first, while conceding that he and his adopted Kahnawake family were eating well on fresh corn and wildfowl, which "with us was called good living," could not resist lamenting that this fare was "not equal to our fat, roasted and boiled venison when we went to the woods in the fall, or bears' meat and beaver in the winter, or [maple] sugar, bears' oil, and dry venison in the spring."[8] This second-best fare was consumed in days and weeks of continuous casual visiting during the day and parties in the evening. The second captive, living with a French family, found himself set to work mowing hay "called up with the sun to go to work [and given] a little soup[,] sour milk & but a very little meat to eat & what was very poor warm river water to drink."[9]

Yet however pleasant and however efficient their lifestyle might be, the Canadian Iroquois could not avoid the impact of the Seven Years' War. When they went to war on their own account, against the Catawbas and other "southern Indians," the fighting occurred at a comfortable distance from their homes. The absence of small parties of warriors leaving for a few months of excitement and adventure did not seriously affect the economy. Losses were small and disruption of community routine minimal. This was not the case in a major intra-European war. Rather than limited numbers of warriors away on a venture comparable to an extended hunting trip, at one time or another the Anglo-French war mobilized virtually the entire adult male population of Canadian Iroquois villages. Scouting parties and minor raids kept small groups of warriors continually in the field. A major French campaign swept Native communities clear of adult males as men "from sixteen to sixty" years of age were brought into the fighting zone and out of the Amerindian economy.[10] In July 1757 a Delaware characterized French recruiting by declaring: "For every old man who is able to walk or a young boy who comes among you, you immediately give him a hatchet and say here child, take this and go and kill the English."[11]

Participation in these campaigns was not, however, confined to men. Women frequently accompanied the larger military expeditions and, as in the hunting camps, performed essential domestic functions. According to a seventeenth-century French observer, women on campaign "light the fire and are charged with the task of making the kettle boil and doing all the rest of the housekeeping."[12] This form of participation in military expeditions was a traditional activity for Amerindian women, which dated back to the pre-contact period and would persist until the end of Amerindian warfare. In time of war, Amerindian women thus fulfilled a support role similar to that provided by the Canadian Women's Army Corps during the Second World War.[13]

Yet their roles went beyond cooking and sewing. On at least three occasions during the Seven Years' War, proximity to the fighting drew women into combat. On 8 September 1755, as an allied army pursued the survivors of a defeated British-League Iroquois force, women from the Seven Nations contingent encountered enemy stragglers and killed a promi-

A View of the Lake of Two Mountains with the Indian Village (Kanesetake) on its North Shore, anon, c. 1830. In this rendering of Kanesetake in 1830, and each of the following two images of Canadian Iroquois communities in the nineteenth century, the towns themselves may have changed, but the physical setting remains the same. NAC C-003825

nent chief.[14] Following the surrender of Fort William Henry on 10 August 1757, Amerindian women were active in taking prisoners from the British garrison. Although their opponents were armed soldiers in the midst of their battalions, the women "captured them ... not one but two or three at a time," then led regulars and provincials off into captivity.[15] On 21 August 1759 a party of Amerindian women provided the only resistance to a British landing at Pointe aux Trembles, west of Quebec, and were credited by the French with driving off the invaders.[16] The weapons available to women became progressively more formidable in the course of the war. In 1755 women were described as "having no fire arms" and armed only with spears and bayonets.[17] By 1759 they were carrying muskets. When the British landed at Pointe aux Trembles, the women "fired on them, and put them to flight."[18]

For both those who went to war and those who stayed behind, the Seven Years' War quickly became a pervasive element in their daily lives. First and foremost among non-combatants was concern over the safety of fighters and grief over deaths and injuries. European observers among the Canadian Iroquois passed over this aspect of the war in silence. However, the narrative of Titus King, a prisoner of the Abenakis of Odanak, gives some indication of the depths of Amerindian feeling regarding fatal casualties. During the campaign of 1755 on the Lake Champlain frontier, King noted in his journal that the forty Abenaki fighters taking part in this campaign had expected to return home in August. In the latter part of that month, when neither the warriors themselves nor news of their fate had arrived, the women of the community "began to be uneasy ... [and] afraid the English had killed their [men]." These fears were confirmed when word came that ten warriors had been killed outright or mortally wounded in the battle of Lake George. King, "waked out of my sleep by the crying of the old ... [woman] & three young ones," observed that "this was a sorrowful day among them."[19]

The fatal effects of the war also manifested themselves in the very homes of Amerindians. For the Canadian Iroquois, the most devastating losses were not casualties of battle, but victims of the smallpox epidemic that broke out in their communities in September of 1755. In the course of the war, thousands of soldiers were dispatched to North America from Europe, where smallpox was endemic. Some of these soldiers were infected with this disease and unwittingly passed it on to the much more vulnerable colonials and Amerindians. The impact of this epidemic on Canadian Iroquois communities was devestating. Two hundred adult males died among the Kahnawakes and Kanesetakes, a further hundred perished among the Algonquins of Kanesetake.[20] Women and children would have died in proportionate numbers. Documentary references to these losses are vague. But they are enough to demonstrate that something horrifying happened to the Amerindian communities of Canada in 1755 as a result of the war, and very probably killed more people among these communities than the war itself.[21]

Yet even as losses from combat and disease reduced the population of their communities, the Canadian Iroquois were also engaged in absorbing numbers of British captives who were adopted into Amerindian families. Lacking the ubiquitous racism of the Europeans with whom they shared the continent, Amerindians took in members of European and other First Nations without reservation. Once captives passed through the ritual of adoption, Canadian Iroquois were ready to accept them as full and equal members of their families, clans, communities, and nations. A captive who joined Tontileaugo's family was told in the course of the ceremonies that accompanied his adoption that:

> you are taken into the Caughnewago nation, and initiated into a warlike tribe; you are adopted into a great family, and now received with great seriousness and solemnity in the room and place of a great man; after what is passed this day, you are now one of us by an old strong law and custom - My son, you have now nothing to fear, we are now under the same obligations to love, support, and defend you, that we are to love and defend one another, therefore you are to consider yourself as one of our people.[22]

These adoptions meant that the membership of families and communities was constantly changing as men, women, and children were taken in. New family members were like small children, who had to be introduced to a new lifestyle and culture, taught new skills, a new language, and even the simple courtesy that their previous upbringing had not, in Amerindian eyes, provided. Consequently, Canadian Iroquois families during the war devoted considerable time and effort to caring for and educating these new members of the family. Moreover, as Catholics, they also sought to convert their largely Protestant captives to Catholicism.

Evangelization is now frequently and fashionably considered to be an activity through which European missionaries attempted to impose an alien faith on Amerindians. In the St. Lawrence valley during the Seven Years'

War, however, Amerindians worked hard to evangelize Europeans and in the process became some of North America's most successful missionaries. Evidence for the activities of these Amerindian evangelists comes from the narratives of unsympathetic captives who rejected their ministrations and returned to British America. These writers portrayed evangelization as a purely religious endeavour, an attempt by depraved servants of the anti-Christ in Rome to suborn virtuous Protestants. Robert Eastburn, who lived among the Oswegatchies in 1756, conveyed something of this attitude when he declared that "the pains the papists take to propagate such a bloody and absurd religion as theirs, is [sic] truly amazing!"[23]

It would appear, however, that the conversion of captives by Amerindians was directed much more at bringing them into full membership in a community than compelling them to renounce Protestantism. In the northeastern woodlands, traditional Amerindian religion was concerned with day-to-day life rather than dogma. For Iroquoians, according to Bruce Trigger, religious practices were first and foremost "the dances, customs, and ceremonies that bound a people together and promoted friendship, solidarity, and goodwill among them."[24] Among the Canadian Iroquois, a good many of these customs and rituals were provided by Catholicism. Consequently, to remain outside the society of Catholics was to remain outside the mainstream of life in Canadian Iroquois communities. Conversion thus became an essential part of the integration of adopted sons and daughters into their new families and communities. This integration was a syncretic process, which combined traditional Amerindian rituals with Catholic sacraments. Robert Eastburn's experience at Oswegatchie provides a clear example of this process in action.

Eastburn was a trader who joined a patrol to investigate reports of Amerindian and French activity near the British outpost of Fort Williams. The patrol was promptly ambushed and Eastburn and every person in it killed or taken prisoner. When the Amerindian fighters returned to Canada, the captives were taken on a tour of Canadian Iroquois communities which ended when Eastburn and a number of other prisoners were brought to Oswegatchie.[25] Upon arrival at their new homes, Eastburn and his comrades unwillingly took part in a number of traditional Amerindian rituals that converted them from captive enemies to members of Canadian Iroquois families. They were compelled first "to dance and sing the prisoners song,"[26] then to run the gauntlet. The latter ritual could range from a token formality, as "each Indian only gave us a tap on the shoulder"[27] to the comprehensive beating experienced by Eastburn: "the Indians gave a shout, and opened the ring to let us run, and then fell on us with their fists, and knocked several down."[28] This hazing was followed by solemn formal adoption, again according to traditional rites, as Eastburn was first wept over, then initiated into a new family.

Next came evangelization. This began on the day after Eastburn's adoption when members of his family asked him "to go to mass with them." Eastburn, evidently something of a philistine when it came to choral music, refused, but they persisted in their invitations for several days. In his narrative, Eastburn makes only one reference to the reasoning used by his family to convince him to go to mass. In place of overtly religious arguments, they simply said that "it was good to go to mass." When Eastburn continued to resist, "they seemed much displeased with their new son." With persuasion proving ineffective, his family resorted to discipline: "I was then sent over the river, to be employed in hard labour, as a punishment for not going to mass." This consisted in fact of building a fence for an elderly Oswegatchie couple, who liked Eastburn and treated him very well. As the work progressed, "the old man began to appear kind, and his wife gave me the milk and bread when we came home, and when she got fish, gave me the gills to eat, out of real kindness; but perceiving I did not like them, gave me my own choice, and behaved lovingly."

Yet however successful Eastburn might be as a fence-builder, he persisted in his adamant rejection of Catholicism. Instead of joining his family and community at mass, he slipped off by himself to pray according to his Protestant inclinations. These frequent absences provoked alarm among a number of Oswegatchies, who suspected some intrigue. A bilingual captive, however, explained that Eastburn was simply praying in private. The tolerant Oswegatchies accepted this explanation and allowed Eastburn to continue to worship undisturbed. That he was practising Protestantism did not disturb them, once their concerns about his unexplained absences were resolved. Nonetheless, Eastburn's continued rejection of conversion made him unacceptable as a member of an Oswegatchie family. After a few weeks, his Oswegatchie mother finally conceded defeat, and acknowledged that her son was not going to become a Catholic. She offered to allow him to leave the village and live among the French at Montreal, where she had found a place for him to live.

Eastburn thus became one of many captives who could not or would not adapt to life among the Canadian Iroquois. Like Eastburn, these reluctant adoptees generally found themselves treated with kindness and understanding, as wayward children rather than recalcitrant prisoners. They were released by their families and turned over to the French, who treated them as they would any other prisoner. Eastburn, however, refused his adoptive mother's offer of release. This refusal was not the product of any kind of sentiment or gratitude. Eastburn was planning to escape with three other captives. Another prisoner at Oswegatchie, Ann Bowman, had managed to bring one hundred and thirty dollars with her into captivity, which Eastburn's three friends hoped to use to finance the escape. Accepting his mother's offer would have trapped Eastburn in Canada.

The Oswegatchies met with more success with other British prisoners, who already felt themselves to be part of the Oswegatchie community and to owe more loyalty to the Oswegatchies than their former compatriots. Unfortunately for Eastburn, this group included Ann Bowman, who informed a priest of his intentions. The four aspiring conspirators were arrested and sent under guard to Kahnawake. Eastburn was later moved to Montreal, where he remained until his release on 23 July 1757.[29]

Yet when given a choice and sufficient time to adapt, many British captives found they preferred to remain with their new families and new lives. British children were particularly ready to join Native communities. Titus King lamented "how quick they will fall in with the Indians' ways ... in six months time they forsake Father & mother forget their own land refuse to speak their own tongue & seemingly be wholly swallowed up with the Indians."[30] One French officer noted in 1757 that "the greatest part [of the adopted prisoners] remain and find that life as good as another." He estimated that one in fifteen members of Seven Nations communities were adopted prisoners.[31] These former prisoners settled down, converted to Catholicism, married, and became productive and respected members of the community. So for many people, Amerindians and Europeans alike, the involuntary movement of individuals brought about by the Seven Years' War presented unexpected opportunities to find love, happiness, and family life with partners who would otherwise have been inaccessible.

The Seven Years' War also affected the economies of Canadian Iroquois communities, since the mobilization of adult males meant that they ceased to function as producers for months at a time, year after year. The continuous presence of small war parties in the field during the winter and major expeditions in the winters of 1755-56 and 1756-57 kept scores of hunters from the winter hunt, reducing the amount of dried meat available for consumption in spring and summer. Large-scale campaigning took place in the summer. This was a delicate time from an economic perspective, when stored produce from the previous harvest and the winter hunt was running out and the new crops were not yet in. Living among the Abenaki at Odanak, Titus King found that in the "month of July the Indians with whom I lived told [me that th]eir victuals was all gone."[32]

These costs of military participation were at least partly balanced by the logistical support provided by the French crown to Amerindian fighters and their families. Detailed records of these expenses for the Seven Years' War were not preserved, but a statement of expenditures from September 1746, during the War of the Austrian Succession, gives some idea of the scope and scale of such support.

When warriors in the field could not contribute to the support of their families, the French crown stepped in. Beaumain, a chief at Kahnawake, received seven metres of fine cloth and three metres of flannel "to clothe his family which he cannot do." Some families also received provisions, usually for a limited number of days. Five families from Kanesetake received food for three days, consisting of eleven kilograms of bread and seven kilograms of beef.[33] An unspecified number of Algonquin and Nipissing families from the same village received 2,758 litres of maize and 166 kilograms of bread.[34] With their families thus provided for, fighters setting out on military expeditions could expect to be properly clothed, armed, and equipped. Four Abenakis, then living at Kahnawake, received from the French an assortment of goods "to put them in a state to go to war." This included two muskets, two coats, two blankets, four shirts, four pairs of mitasses, 245 grams of vermilion (face paint), one kilogram of tobacco, and one litre of spirits.[35] Upon returning from the war zone, Amerindians received further provisions to see them home. Warriors from Kahnawake received two days rations, those from Kanesetake, three.[36]

During the Seven Years' War, as economic pressures increased, French contributions on this scale were not, according to one Kahnawake delegation, always sufficient to provide warriors in the field and their families at home "with enough to live on." Under these conditions, Amerindians sought larger quantities of essential supplies from the French. In January of 1759, for example, the Kahnawakes demanded supplies of grain and manufactured goods from French stocks in Montreal on the grounds that they needed them to survive.[37]

French officials considered this support to be enormously generous. In 1756 the governor general blamed rising military expenditure in the colony on the need to supply the Amerindians who were consuming extraordinary amounts of weapons, equipment, and provisions, all furnished and paid for by the crown. The Amerindians, he declared, had to be equipped and re-

St. Regis (Akwesasne) Indian Village on the St. Lawrence River, by William Henry Bartlett, 1838. NAC C-040312

equipped several times during a campaign, since they were continually claiming to have lost their previous outfits. Moreover, they continuously travelled back and forth between the frontier and their homes, each time compelling the French to provide them with provisions for the trip.[38]

The governor general, along with other French officers and officials, ignored the costs of war to Amerindians in terms of forgone production and the wear and tear inherent in military operations. Fighters might leave in new clothing, bearing gleaming weapons and provided with new equipment. But as a missionary among the Ojibwas observed in 1860, "when they return from the wars their clothes are torn, their moccasins worn out, perhaps their entire flotilla expended."[39] With clothing in rags, equipment broken, weapons damaged, munitions expended, and provisions consumed at the end of each campaign, Amerindian fighters needed continuous logistical support if they were to continue to fight. Nor did French support entirely relieve the costs of forgone production. By 1756 a British captive was reporting "that the French Indians were very scant of provisions." The flexibility of the Iroquois economy was such that in the early years of the war, shortages of provisions could be at least partially made up through purchases from habitant neighbours.[40] But French assertions to the contrary, the Canadian Iroquois escaped neither the human nor the economic costs of participation in the Anglo-French war.

Nonetheless, if the war meant hardship for Native communities, somewhat alleviated by support from the French crown, it also presented economic opportunities. The limited surviving evidence suggests that many Amerindians did indeed seek to benefit economically from the war. Women who engaged in manufacturing found a large new market for their products and responded by producing goods needed to equip metropolitan French soldiers for campaigning in Canada. In 1756, for example, these artisans were making beaver hats for French officers, which they traded at a rate of two hats for a blanket.[41] Men too sought out new economic opportunities. Those of the Canadian Iroquois who travelled to the Ohio valley in 1753 and 1754 went in search of remuneration rather than battle. In place of serving as warriors, they expected to act as commercial hunters, who would receive a monthly wage to procure game for French soldiers and militiamen.[42] The outbreak of Anglo-French hostilities brought them into the field as active combatants, but hunting for food to sell to French soldiers remained a source of income throughout the war. In 1757, for example, French regulars performing repairs at Fort St. Jean north of Lake Champlain were approached by two Amerindian families who camped nearby and proposed "to hunt and to make a good profit from their game" through sales to the French.[43]

Another potential source of war-related income came from handling freight. On the portage at Fort Presqu'île, the French paid Amerindians six livres per packet for portaging military cargo.[44] This activity was dominated by the local Delawares, but men of the Seven Nations may have become involved in freighting as well, either there or at other sites along French lines of communication that extended from Montreal to Fort Duquesne.

Some communities were also able to take advantage of French need for their cooperation to compel them make cash payments on specific occasions. In 1754 the Abenaki of Odanak coolly blackmailed Father Onontio for an unspecified sum. Invited to join the expedition to the Ohio, they informed the governor general that they were building houses and needed money to finance the completion of this project. Only after the governor general agreed to make a large cash donation, in addition to the customary presentations of matériel, did they finally agree to go.[45] In 1759 the Oswegatchies profited from the need of their French allies for land for military purposes when they sold the right to build Fort Lévis on an island in the St. Lawrence River just east of their community. The Amerindians further sought and received compensation for the crops that were destroyed when the ground was cleared for construction of the fort.[46]

Probably the most useful economic activity associated with the war, however, was the trade in prisoners. Sensationalist accounts beginning during the war and continuing up to the latest film version of *The Last of the Mohicans* give the distinct impression that all captives of all Amerindians faced a prolonged close encounter with a variety of red-hot implements of torture. In fact, captives of Canadian Amerindians found themselves treated either as potential members of the family and community or valuable commodities who could be exchanged for cash or matériel in Canada. Enemies who attempted to surrender could be and were killed in the heat of battle, but they were much more valuable alive and well.

A preference for capture over outright killing was a longstanding Iroquoian tradition.[47] For however unreservedly meritorious the killing of an enemy might be for a warrior, a dead enemy simply lacked much of the intrinsic value of a living prisoner. During Anglo-French conflicts in the mid-eighteenth century, the relative desirability of prisoners over scalps was enhanced by their respective market values in Canada. A live captive could be sold for between 120 and 140 livres, as opposed to a mere 33 for a scalp.[48] Under some conditions, prisoner bounties could be much higher. In 1755 a French deserter from the garrison of Fort Carillon informed the British that eight Abenakis and Canadian Iroquois, reconnoitring in the vicinity of Fort Edward and Fort William Henry, had been "promised 1000 livres as a premium if they obtain[ed] a prisoner."[49] African-American captives had a higher market value than Europeans, since they were considered to be property that could be alienated permanently rather than people whose labour could be purchased for the duration of the war, but would have to be returned home one day. This quirk of unmitigated racism raised the price of an African-American prisoner to between 600 and 1,500 livres.[50]

Prisoners, in short, were big business, and not to be cast away lightly for the sheer amusement of burning them alive. Instead of a feral barbarian intent on mayhem, captives of Canadian Amerindians were much more likely to be faced with a cheerful opportunist like the Abenaki fighter who, following the birth of a child to a prisoner, "clapped his hands with joy, crying 'two moneys for me! two moneys for me!'"[51]

Canada was an ideal locale for warriors who harvested prisoners rather than furs, since it was near the war zone and contained two major markets for prisoners. First there was the French crown, which made frequent purchases of individual prisoners for intelligence purposes and would on occasion engage in mass redemptions of captives. The mechanism for redemption by the crown could be quite sophisticated. In one case, Amerindians from the Great Lakes secured about 160 prisoners in a preliminary skirmish during the 1757 campaign. Since taking these prisoners fulfilled their goals for going to war, the members of the successful war party decided to return to their homes rather than proceeding on with the allied army to Fort William Henry. Some did, but most were persuaded to turn over their prisoners to the French. In return, they received written receipts. At the end of the campaign the Great Lakes fighters travelled to Montreal and cashed in these receipts, receiving the same price per prisoner as those who had brought in members of the garrison captured during and after the siege.[52]

A second market for captives was found among private individuals. Affluent officials and officers might ransom prisoners for the sake of charity or ethnic and professional solidarity; farmers and artisans would redeem captives for the sake of their labour. Disposing of these captives, however, could involve Amerindian vendors in making the rounds from town to town and from farm to farm in search of a buyer, sometimes unsuccessfully.[53] As a sideline to the prisoner trade, Amerindians also sold the goods that had been seized from prisoners or acquired in raids or battles to Canadians. During and after major expeditions, impromptu markets sprang up in French military camps and outside French towns where vendors and buyers came together.[54]

On the other hand, the war temporarily interrupted the carrying trade between Montreal and Albany. With the Lake Champlain corridor a theatre of war, extensively fortified and patrolled by both sides, commercial traffic between Montreal and Albany was cut off and the Canadian Iroquois thus deprived of a useful source of income and British goods. Nonetheless, it was not long before the imperatives of commerce proved stronger than those of war. By 1757 the Oswegatchies, while continuing to participate in the war alongside the French, had also opened up a new trade route to German Flats, the westernmost New York settlement on the Mohawk River. This trade, conducted by League Oneidas, was judged by the British to be "very considerable ... so that the pernicious trade formerly carried on from this town [Albany] with the Cagnawaga Indians, is like to be revived under another dress at the German Flatts."[55]

Overall, if the war did involve serious economic dislocation for the Canadian Iroquois, it also provided new economic opportunities. The extent to which gains and losses balanced one another is impossible to determine from the existing evidence. What is apparent, however, is that the Canadian Iroquois responded to the economic challenges of the war with characteristic energy and determination.

Finally, as the Seven Years' War drew to a close, war impinged directly upon the Amerindian communities of the St. Lawrence valley. In 1759 a close ally of the Canadian Iroquois received a shattering blow when the Abenaki village of Odanak was raided and destroyed by the British. Already refugees from their former homes in what was now northern New England, the Abenakis became refugees once more. In November of 1759 they relocated to Akwesasne, where they would remain for a decade.[56] Other displaced persons came from Quebec in 1759, when the entire population of the Huron community of Lorette responded to the capitulation of Quebec and subsequent British occupation by withdrawing to Montreal.[57] In 1760 the war reached northeastern Kanienkeh and members of Canadian Iroquois communities themselves joined the ranks of refugees. With three British armies closing in on northeastern Kanienkeh and Montreal, the

The village of La Chine and the Indian Village of Caughnawaga (Kahnawake) on the River St. Lawrence, by John Greaves, engraver W. Walton, December 1826. NAC C-122928

people of Oswegatchie and Akwesasne found themselves directly in the path of the British juggernaut. Many chose to flee to the supposed safety of Kanesetake, out of the British line of march.

So by the last weeks of the war, Canadian Iroquois families were sheltering numerous refugees produced by the fighting, and some had become refugees themselves. More generally, the destruction of Odanak provided a warning as to how the Amerindians of Canada might be treated in the event of a British victory, a victory that seemed a virtual certainty by late August of 1760. They had seen one allied community destroyed, another evacuated, and could be excused for wondering what might happen next.

The Canadian Iroquois in 1754 were a people whose generally happy, comfortable, productive, and intensely social lives were interrupted by the outbreak of a major war. Canadian Iroquois society responded to war much like any other society. Its members suffered danger and privation, while at the same time seizing new economic opportunities. They took part in that conflict not just as fighters, but as parents, children, mothers, wives, farmers, hunters, artisans, economic opportunists, refugees, and married men with responsibilities toward their families as well as to their French allies.

CHAPTER 2

PARALLEL WARFARE

Throughout the Seven Years' War the Canadian Iroquois fought as allies of the French, taking part in the French occupation of the Ohio and every major campaign on the frontiers of Canada. Their support was indispensable to France, both because the personnel that they provided supplemented that of the outnumbered French metropolitan and colonial fighters and because of their particular military skills and local knowledge. Nonetheless, although a French soldier and Mohawk warrior might be marching and fighting side by side, they were fighting two very different wars.

The French state made war upon the British to advance the collective interests of the French empire. The government at Versailles considered the activities of the British in North America to be inimical to these interests and responded with armed force. During the Seven Years' War French forces undertook a series of military operations directed against specific objectives whose capture or destruction was expected to influence the actions of the British.

The human instruments of the French state were soldiers recruited from the marginal elements of the metropolitan population and conscripted Canadian militiamen, all of whom served under military discipline. Although individual soldiers and militiamen might have very little interest in the pursuit of imperial objectives, they belonged to a society that was able to channel its human resources into military operations, and the war itself was waged to further the interests of the empire as a whole.

The Canadian Iroquois fought a different war. For the British were not their enemies. The Canadian Iroquois might be allied to groups such as the Abenakis and the French whose ancestral territories or imperial ambitions were threatened by Anglo-American expansion, but their own lands were not at risk until the last year of the war, and their interests lay in peace

Eastern Woodland Indians, middle of the 18th century, by David Rickman. Department of National Defence

rather than war with the British. The Kahnawakes in particular enjoyed longstanding and mutually profitable commercial relations with New York which they were loath to jeopardize. Yet when the time came, they went to war alongside the French.

They entered a war that advanced French interests rather than their own because the French were their allies. Amerindian alliances were intricate matrices of reciprocal expectations and obligations between equals. In the case of the Canadian Iroquois, close to a century of alliance had established a broad range of private, public, personal, official, economic, religious, social, military, and ceremonial bonds between themselves and the French. During the Seven Years' War, when representatives of the Canadian Iroquois spoke of the strength of these bonds, they frequently employed religious imagery, and in particular invoked the ritual of baptism.[1] "The French Priests," said the Kahnawakes in 1755, "by throwing water upon our heads subject us to the will of the Governor of Canada."[2] This phrasing makes baptism appear to be subtly coercive. The Canadian Iroquois did not in fact consider this to be the case, but as allies, felt themselves bound to consider seriously French requests for military assistance and obligated to stand by their allies in time of war.[3]

Yet although the Canadian Iroquois fought in the Seven Years' War at the request of the French, in so doing they surrendered neither their independence nor their freedom to wage war in their own way. Individual Amerindian males engaged in warfare to obtain status and prestige through military achievement and in particular through the taking of prisoners.[4] As we have seen, these prisoners were valuable commodities, who could be sold, exchanged, retained as a source of productive labour, or incorporated into an Amerindian family and community. This value remained constant regardless of whether a trophy had been secured in a minor raid, a major military operation, an exclusively Amerindian operation, or a French campaign.

During the Seven Years' War, the warriors of the Canadian Iroquois conducted themselves as if their presence in the field was an adequate fulfillment of the obligations of their communities towards their allies. Rather than allowing the objectives of the French to dictate their actions, they treated their participation in this war as they would any other military venture, as "an opportunity of distinguishing ourselves, and of getting some prisoners and scalps to show our people that we had been at war."[5]

When the warriors of the Canadian Iroquois took part in the small war parties that were directed against Anglo-American frontier settlements or the garrisons and lines of communications of British forts, they could generally achieve both these personal goals and those of their French allies with relative ease, since they employed purely Amerindian tactics to further a French strategy of terrorizing the Anglo-American frontier. The French, however, also invited their Canadian Iroquois allies to participate in a series of campaigns against British strongholds. During these campaigns, conflicts could and did arise between the French and Amerindian styles of war. Rather than joining with their French allies to achieve the same objectives, Canadian Iroquois warriors conducted parallel campaigns, directed at the taking of prisoners, along with scalps and matériel, within French military expeditions, which were directed at the capture or defence of forts. This pattern of "parallel warfare" characterized most, if not all, major Franco-Amerindian military ventures during the Seven Years' War.

Since there were definite limits to the extent to which Amerindian and European concepts of war could be reconciled, the practice of parallel warfare made the Seven Years' War as much a series of cultural confrontations between allies as battles between enemies. These cultural confrontations imposed a rhythm of their own upon most, but not all, of the allied campaigns in the Seven Years' War. In almost every year of the war, the Canadian Iroquois would begin by accepting a French invitation to join in a military venture. The allies would set off together, but in the course of the expedition the discordance between European and Amerindian military practices and objectives gradually made themselves felt. In the end, the Canadian Iroquois would either withdraw from the field or continue hostilities after the French and British had agreed to stop. This rhythm was particularly apparent in the spring of 1756, when a force composed of

Pierre de Rigaud, Marquis de Vaudeuil, by Henri Beau. NAC C–539

Amerindian warriors, most of whom were Canadian Iroquois, and French militiamen and soldiers took part in a major raid against the British on the New York frontier. In the course of this expedition both the Canadian Iroquois and the French strove to impose their will upon the enterprise, and adjust its conduct and objectives to conform to their ideas of waging war.

When the French component of this force left Montreal in February 1756, its leaders believed that the success of the expedition was vital to the future of the French empire in North America. A victory could not actually win the war for the French, but a defeat might well lose it. In the fall of 1755 the French had learned, through the Onondagas, of unusual activity at the Oneida Carrying Place, a major portage on the water route between Albany and Oswego.[6] To obtain more detailed information, Pierre de Rigaud de Vaudreuil, governor general of New France and commander-in-chief of the French armed forces in North America, sought the assistance of Ou8atory, an Oswegatchie of Oneida descent. Ou8atory discreetly attached himself to the party of a senior League Oneida chief who was visiting Oswegatchie and accompanied him to the Oneida country, within which the Carrying Place was located. He returned in November with news that the British had built two warehouses there to store munitions and provisions.[7] This information was interpreted by the French as indicating that the British were stockpiling supplies and bateaux at the Carrying Place in preparation for a major spring offensive on the Lake Ontario frontier.

An operation of this nature represented an ominous threat to New France. Since waterways in New York opened about two weeks before those in Canada, the British could launch an attack against the small winter garrisons of forts Frontenac and Niagara at a time when the French, locked in by ice, would be unable to respond.[8] Vaudreuil elected to neutralize this threat by striking first to destroy these supplies and bateaux before they could be used to support a spring offensive. To command the French forces involved in this venture, he selected Gaspard-Joseph Chaussegros de Léry, an officer of the troupes de la marine.

Destroying this stockpiled matériel would be a simple and straightforward operation, since the British supplies were not heavily protected. Ou8atory had reported that the eastern warehouse was guarded by one hundred men, while only forty watched over the western entrepôt. Instead of palisaded forts, these men lived in tents and bark huts.[9] Yet actually reaching this target was expected to pose considerable difficulty, because of the distance from Montreal, the alternate thaws and cold of March, and the obstacles presented by several river crossings, which would be hazardous at that time of the year. Vaudreuil was aware that sending an expedition to the Carrying Place carried its own dangers, "but the situation became urgent and I could not defer [it] without running the risk of being forestalled by the enemy at Niagara and at Fort Frontenac." The governor general considered this expedition to be so important that he was willing to risk war with the League Iroquois to achieve the destruction of the munitions and provisions stored at the portage. If a delegation from the League Iroquois attempted to block the path of the detachment and appeared to be acting on behalf of the British, Léry was ordered to inform them that "I [Vaudreuil] will regard them from that moment as enemies, and will make war upon them as upon the English."[10]

Although New France could easily muster a force of Europeans sufficient to overcome 140 men living in bark huts and tents, this expedition could not have taken place without Amerindian cooperation. The territory between Montreal and the Carrying Place was an Iroquois hunting ground, much frequented by Amerindians but unknown to the French.[11] To travel safely through the region, they were wholly dependent upon the services of Ou8atory and other Oswegatchies as guides. The inclusion of Amerindian warriors in the expedition also provided a source of personnel who were

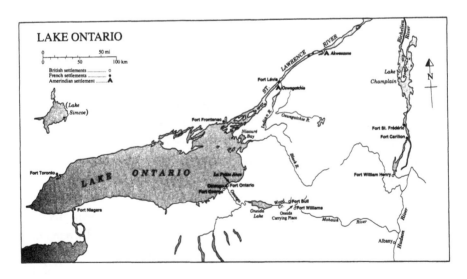

MAP 3. Lake Ontario, by William R. Constable

skilled in North American warfare.[12] Their importance was such that Vaudreuil's orders to Léry contained a clause instructing him to return to Canada if the Amerindians abandoned the expedition.[13]

The Canadian Iroquois cooperated with the French in the planning of the expedition. In a series of conferences with the French, various Kahnawakes, Kanesetakes, and Oswegatchies provided detailed information on the country between Oswegatchie and the Carrying Place which confirmed and amplified that already supplied by Ou8atory. Nonetheless, the Canadian Iroquois remained extremely dubious about the timing of the venture, and "raised many objections to that voyage primarily on account of the difficulty and capriciousness of the season."[14]

Only after considerable persuasion did individual war chiefs agree to accompany the expedition. Among these war chiefs was Missakin who, although an Ojibwa, was the "chief of a band of Iroquois of Sault St. Louis [Kahnawake]." When first approached by Léry on the evening of 24 February, Missakin evinced no great enthusiasm for marching with the French to the portage. Not until the morning of the 25th was he finally convinced by "the words that I [Léry] gave to him in the name of Monsieur de Vaudreuil ... He joined me, along with his band."[15] Other consultations passed unrecorded, but must have been none the less equally reassuring, for the Amerindians eventually consented to accompany the ninety-three metropolitan regulars and 166 militiamen to the Carrying Place. Léry's orders directed him to expect eighteen Kahnawakes, thirty-three Kanesetakes, six Algonquins, and eleven Nipissings. These warriors would later be augmented by three Akwesasnes, three Abenakis from Missisquoi, and sixty-six Oswegatchies.[16]

The Amerindian war parties from Kanesetake, Kahnawake, Akwesasne, and Oswegatchie made their preparations and awaited the French, who left Montreal on 29 February and marched westward along the St. Lawrence towards the rendezvous at Oswegatchie. When the column arrived at successive Canadian Iroquois communities, a council was held at which interested warriors were formally invited to join the expedition and "strike the English together." Two points were stressed by the French during these meetings. First, that the party would be attacking men in bark huts guarding warehouses; second, that the expedition was directed against the British, not the League Iroquois.[17]

Even as Canadian Iroquois fighters were reluctantly consenting to join the expedition to the Carrying Place, other warriors were harrying the Anglo-American frontier. On 9 March, just before the departure of the

A View of Fort La Galette, Indian Castle (Oswegatchie) ...., by Thomas Davies, 1760. The best contemporary painting of a Canadian Iroquois community, made by a British officer who visited that town during the Seven Years' War. National Gallery of Canada 6271

allies from Oswegatchie, a party of Akwesasnes returned from Oswego with nine prisoners. Interrogated by the expedition's English interpreter, they provided Léry with startling new information about the British presence at the Oneida Carrying Place. Instead of the unfortified warehouses that he had been ordered to attack, the munitions and provisions stored at the portage were now defended by two forts.[18] Léry kept this information to himself, and two days later the expedition left Oswegatchie without incident.

Yet if Léry had hoped to conceal the news of the fortifications, he failed completely. On 13 March the Amerindians encountered an Oswegatchie traveller who informed them that the storehouses at the portage had been fortified and the British were on the alert. The Amerindian leaders immediately called a halt, since to proceed farther under these conditions would be both futile and dangerous. This decision brought them into conflict with their French allies.

For French officers such as Léry, a military operation could still be a success if half their subordinates became casualties, providing that it had achieved a sufficiently important objective. This perspective was not necessarily shared by soldiers and militiamen for whom personal survival might take precedence over the achievement of abstract imperial goals. The coercive powers of the French state nonetheless allowed officers to pursue these goals without reference to the wishes of their followers. For Amerindians, on the other hand, no amount of prestige from a military operation was worth the loss of a single life. When Canadian Iroquois fighters went to war, they employed many of the strategies and tactics of the hunt. Successful hunters used stealth and cleverness to assure themselves of the maximum advantage and sought to kill an animal quietly and efficiently. Getting mauled by a bear, lost, shot by accident, or harmed by any of the other dangers incidental to hunting would turn an otherwise successful hunt into a grim failure. When hunters became warriors, they applied the same principles. Their object was to take prisoners, not weaken their communities by sustaining unnecessary losses. Consequently the appropriate action when confronted with a superior enemy force or fortified position was withdrawal, not headlong assault.[19]

Amerindians and Frenchmen brought these contrasting perspectives to bear when they responded to the news of the fortification of the Oneida Carrying Place. The remainder of the day was taken up by negotiations between French and Canadian Iroquois leaders, the first in a series of conferences that would continue throughout the journey southward. During these meetings, Léry spoke for himself, as the authoritarian commander of the French component of the allied force. In this capacity, he expected his soldiers and militiamen to follow his policies and obey his orders, used force when necessary to compel obedience, and considered himself to have failed when he lost control of his troops.[20]

Léry's Canadian Iroquois counterparts, like Missakin and Collière, a "famous chief" of Oswegatchie,[21] on the other hand, first sought to obtain a consensus from warriors who were their equals, then communicated the results of these collective decisions to the French. They spoke in council not as commanders, but as advocates, who could be relied upon to make sure that the views of their compatriots were heard, and their sensibilities respected.[22] In this instance, the Amerindian leaders made it clear that in the opinion of their fellow warriors the original plan was no longer viable, then proposed an alternative that suited their military customs. They suggested that the allies should raid the settlements along the Mohawk valley instead of attacking British forts. From their point of view, this was a reasonable proposition. They had been asked to join in clearing away guards living in bark huts, not to storm forts and risk heavy losses. Now that the target of the Franco-Amerindian force was known to be far stronger than expected, they had every right to reconsider. This ought not to have come as a surprise to Léry, since in each campaign in which they took part, Amerindians seized every possible opportunity to remind the French that they considered the storming of fortifications to be an extremely dubious enterprise.

The Amerindians were thus acting in an entirely customary manner in suggesting that the geographic target of a war party be adjusted in accordance with their particular goals and policies. On many previous occasions, Amerindians had found French officers willing to respond - although not necessarily graciously - to these concerns.[23] In 1756 the war chiefs found the French leadership less accommodating. During the march from Montreal to Oswegatchie, Léry had already rejected a suggestion from his own officers that the expedition be terminated on account of the "very difficult trails."[24] Confronted with a proposition from the Amerindians to divert the expedition away from the forts of the Carrying Place, he elected to treat it as an obstacle, rather than a legitimate response to a changed situation. Having failed to conceal the news of the new fortifications, the lieutenant now sought to delay the moment of final decision. He told the Amerindian leaders that they would know the truth for themselves when they reached the warehouses and that he himself would be "delighted to find many Englishmen there; that Onontio had sent me to fight them."[25]

The Amerindians chose temporarily to accept this postponement of a decision, but reserved the right to reopen the topic at a later date. On 20 March, as the expedition drew nearer to the portage, the Amerindians approached Léry to inquire as to his intentions with regard to the British. The lieutenant once again avoided making a definite answer, declaring that a decision could not be taken until they reached the portage. A day later, they received the following assurance from Léry:

> I assured them that I would not attack the fort, that I had
> not come to give glory to the English and that, if I could

not find an opportunity to fight them without suffering heavy losses, I would return without doing anything; but that it was necessary for me to see the situation there to report to their father [Vaudreuil].[26]

In all of these conferences, Léry never informed the Amerindians of Vaudreuil's plan to forestall a British invasion of New France by destroying the supplies that had been accumulated at the portage. He kept a detailed record of the arguments that he used to attempt to persuade Amerindians to remain with the French, but made no mention of any attempt to explain why it was necessary that the expedition attack the British at the Carrying Place, as opposed to any another location.

Iroquois going on a scout, by Jacques Grasset de Saint-Sauveur, engraver J. Laroque, c. 1796. This frightening caricature reveals much more about contemporary European perceptions of Amerindians than about the Amerindians themselves. NAC C-003165

Some of the Amerindians chose not to debate the issue and simply left the expedition. On 15 March, when word arrived of a fire at Oswegatchie, thirty Oswegatchies returned home to inspect the damage. Other departing Amerindians displayed continued willingness to fight the British; they simply insisted upon doing so only on their own terms. A further nineteen Canadian Iroquois together with four Algonquins formed five war parties which went to Oswego or the Mohawk valley in search of prisoners. Each of these parties was successful, and a total of ten captives was secured.[27]

The majority of the Amerindians reserved judgment and remained with their French allies as they travelled southward.[28] By 26 March the expedition had progressed to within two kilometres of the portage. Although close to their goal, the French were in desperate straits, as they had been without food for two days. However, the scouts who ranged ahead of the allied force throughout the march had discovered convoys of wagons carrying provisions from Fort Williams, at the eastern extremity of the portage, to Fort Bull, at its western terminus.[29] The Amerindian and French leaders held a council and decided to resupply the troops by attacking a convoy on the portage. This attack was entrusted to the Amerindians, who proceeded to demonstrate a higher level of discipline in the presence of the enemy than their French allies. As the warriors lay patiently in ambush, French "officers were obliged to use a degree of force to restrain their famished troops, for fear that musket shots would warn the fort of their arrival."[30] Without firing a shot or raising a war cry, the Amerindians captured nine wagons and ten men. One African-American teamster, however, escaped, and fled towards Fort Williams.[31] With the British about to be warned, Léry decided that this was the time to strike instantly. The Amerindians, on the other hand, decided that this was the time to go home.

At this point, as far as the Canadian Iroquois were concerned, the raid was over. The enemy had been engaged, and prisoners secured without loss. They had done what they set out to do, and saw no need to continue, much less become involved in an attack on a fort. Despite Léry's repeated assurances that he would not expose them to excessive danger, the Amerindian leaders politely but firmly made it clear that they did not intend to become involved in this operation. In their opinion "having secured sufficient food to take us to Oswegatchie and English meat [prisoners], without the loss of a man, it would be against the will of the Master of Life to risk a second engagement."[32]

As a rule Amerindians tended to see European-style war as irrational and unproductive (although in 1757 they would display considerable enthusiasm for the mechanics of siege warfare).[33] The Amerindian leaders considered the frontal assault on Fort Bull proposed by Léry to be so ill-advised as to be suicidal. They informed him that "if I absolutely wanted to die, I was the master of the French, but they were not going to follow me."[34] Amerindian speakers supported their arguments with pointed references to the defeat of the French in 1755 when, contrary to Amerindian advice, Jean-Armand Dieskau had made an unsuccessful frontal assault on a British entrenchment on Lake George.[35]

Yet if the French did have some very odd ideas about waging war, they were nonetheless allies, and the Amerindians were willing to meet their allies halfway. Although they declined to take part in the actual attack on the fort, the Canadian Iroquois would support the French. They first consented to a request by Léry for the services of two warriors to guide the French to their target. Next, they agreed to guard the prisoners and remain on the portage road to watch for any activity on the part of the garrison of Fort Williams.[36]

In the end, three Abenakis, eleven Nipissings, and fifty-six Canadian Iroquois remained on the road, and thirty Canadian Iroquois marched with the 259 French regulars and militiamen towards Fort Bull. On the morning of 27 March 1756 this outpost was occupied by twenty-five soldiers of the 50th (Shirley's) Regiment, thirty-four carpenters, boatmen, and carters, and at least three women.[37] As the allies approached Fort Bull, twenty-four Amerindians became involved in the pursuit of six of the enemy who caught sight of the column and fled into the woods. Consequently only Collière and five other Canadian Iroquois actually took part in the attack.[38]

By 11:00 a.m. they were about nine hundred metres from the fort. Léry had hoped to approach silently and seize the open and undefended gate. But when the allies emerged from the forest into cleared land, the Amerindians, following their own inclinations rather than those of the French, shouted a war cry that alerted the British. The allies raced towards the fort, only to find the gate slammed shut.

A party of regulars began to pound upon the gate, rather ineffectually, with axes, while several militiamen began to attempt to open a breach in the north side of the palisade. In the meantime, the remainder of the attackers seized control of unoccupied loopholes and gaps in the south wall, and fired upon all who showed themselves within. Many of the British sought refuge in the buildings of the fort and were trapped inside by allied fire. Others resisted fiercely. Léry, through an interpreter, called upon the garrison to surrender, but "the fire of the enemy only became livelier and more determined."[39] Among the victims of this fire was Collière, who was shot and killed by the commandant of the fort.[40]

Fighting continued until about noon, when an improvised ram broke down the gate and the attackers fell upon the surviving soldiers and civilians.[41] Of the four men who led the way through the breach, one was a Canadian Iroquois who struck down Collière's assailant.[42] Léry later confessed that "I could not restrain the ardour of the soldiers and Canadians. They killed everyone they encountered. Some soldiers barricaded themselves in the barracks, which were broken open."[43] Once penetrated, the stockade became a trap. Instead of keeping the French out, it trapped the British inside, and prevented them from escaping or putting enough distance between themselves and their assailants to negotiate a surrender. Only "a few soldiers and one woman [Ann Bowman] were fortunate enough to hide themselves from the first fury of our soldiers and Canadians, ... all the rest were slaughtered without daring to make the least resistance."[44] Of sixty-two persons inside the fort at the time of the attack, divided about equally between soldiers and civilians, only three soldiers, one carpenter, and Ann Bowman survived.[45]

With the garrison virtually annihilated, the French turned their attention to the real target of their expedition, the contents of Fort Bull's magazines and warehouses. In all 2,200 kilograms of powder, a large quantity of shells, grenades, and cannon balls, clothing for six hundred men, one thousand blankets, and barrel after barrel of salt pork, biscuit, butter, chocolate, and spirits were destroyed or carried off to provision the detachment for their return to Canada. About one hundred horses were killed or commandeered, and sixteen bateaux and several wagons destroyed.[46] While this looting and destruction was in progress, the powder magazine caught fire and exploded, reducing Fort Bull to smoking debris. Just as the French and Canadian Iroquois were picking themselves up after the explosion, a messenger arrived from the Amerindian force outside Fort Williams with the news that the garrison of that outpost was making a sortie.

Shortly after 10:00 a.m. the teamster who had escaped from the allied ambush staggered into Fort Williams and reported the attack on the convoy. The commanding officer responded to this news by sending out a patrol consisting of a sergeant, fifteen men, and one colonial volunteer - Robert Eastburn - to investigate. In the meantime, seventy-three Canadian Iroquois, Abenakis, and Nipissings had advanced to within about five hundred metres of Fort Williams. When they sighted the patrol, the Amerindians opened fire. Their opponents responded with a single volley then attempted to retreat. Instead, the British fled straight into a bog. A recent snowfall made their tracks clearly visible, and Eastburn and the three other survivors of the brief exchange of fire were easily rounded up by the warriors. The prisoners were stripped of their outer clothing and bound, but not otherwise mistreated.[47]

Thus, at one end of the portage, the occupants of Fort Bull, soldiers and civilians alike, were being massacred almost to the last man and woman by French soldiers and militiamen. At the other, British soldiers who ceased to resist were taken prisoner by Amerindian warriors.

After the two actions, the Amerindian and French components of the expedition reunited. "As soon as they got together," wrote Eastburn, "(having a Priest with them) they fell on their knees, and returned thanks for their victory."[48] Then the allies compared experiences. The French considered the ambush of the patrol to have been a minor action, incidental to their own assault on Fort Bull. This view was not shared by the Amerindians. They complimented Léry for the good fortune, rather than skill or prowess, that had allowed the French to incur so few casualties as they stood in the open and broke down the gate at Fort Bull. At no point did the Canadian Iroquois appear particularly impressed with French tactics or intelligence.[49]

Although French casualties had indeed been remarkably light - one regular killed and two wounded - the experience of the Canadian Iroquois who had taken part in the assault on Fort Bull confirmed the expectations of those who remained behind. Of the six, Collière was killed in the fighting that preceded the storm of the fort and two Kanesetakes and one Kahnawake had been wounded, the latter mortally, by flying debris after the explosion of the powder magazine.[50]

Following the engagements at Fort Bull and on the portage road, Amerindians and Frenchmen returned to Canada without incident and celebrated their separate victories. Each had fulfilled objectives that were incidental to the achievement of those of their allies. The Canadian Iroquois had embarked upon this venture in the expectation of acquiring prisoners. In this they were entirely successful. To the ten prisoners taken by warriors who left the allied force en route, those who accompanied the French to the Carrying Place added at least fourteen more.[51] Like the war party described by a Sulpician priest at Kanesetake in 1746, the Canadian Iroquois of the expedition, upon returning to their homes were able "to deliver their prisoners and the scalps that they had taken, [and] there recount their adventures and their actions."[52] The prisoners were taken on a triumphal tour of Canadian Iroquois communities. The Amerindians who captured Robert Eastburn brought him first to Oswegatchie, then on 11 April to Kanesetake. After a ten-day stopover, the warriors and their living trophy proceeded on to Kahnawake. At each village, said Eastburn, the warriors "when they came within hearing, gave notice by their way of shouting, that they had a prisoner, on which the whole town rose to welcome me."[53]

The arrival of a successful war party with prisoners was the occasion for communal festivities which were vastly more entertaining for residents than prisoners. "As soon as we landed at Conasadauga [Kanesetake]," wrote the involuntary guest of honour, "a large body of Indians came and incompassed us round, and ordered the prisoners to dance and sing the Prisoners song, ... at the conclusion of which, the Indians gave a shout, and opened the ring to let us run, and then fell on us with their fists and knocked several down."[54]

The residents of Kahnawake provided Eastburn with a similar welcome. After a few days in Kahnawake, three young Oswegatchie warriors from his future adoptive family took delivery of Eastburn. The Oswegatchies conducted their reluctant new brother back to Kanesetake, where they remained for another week, then finally brought him home to Oswegatchie and a formal ceremony of adoption.[55] The presence of Eastburn and his fellow prisoners in each of the three communities provided a tangible symbol of a striking Canadian Iroquois victory.

The French for their part returned to Canada convinced that the elimination of a specific physical target had contributed to the safety and security of New France and the French empire. They believed that by destroying Fort Bull and the stores that it contained they had upset the British timetable for a spring campaign on Lake Ontario and bought time for Vaudreuil to prepare a major offensive against Oswego.[56]

The Franco-Amerindian expedition to the Oneida Carrying Place in the spring of 1756 involved members of two societies fighting two different wars. The French had engaged in the storm of a fortified position, which involved a mass rush over open ground towards the target; had remained in the open and under fire for an hour until a breach was made, then embarked upon the entry into Fort Bull and the deliberate killing of their enemies without hesitation or mercy. These tactics entailed the risk, if not, on this occasion, the actual sacrifice, of many French lives to secure a particular physical objective. This risk was justified by the importance of this target to the French empire, and the influence that its destruction might exert upon the British. The Amerindians too held to a particular style of waging war, characterized by refusal to risk unnecessary loss of life. In the words of Tecaughretanego, a Kahnawake war chief, "the art of war consists in

Officer, Compagnies franches de la Marine, middle of the 18th century, by Eugène Lelièpvre. Parks Canada

ambushing and surprising our enemies, and in preventing them from ambushing and surprising us."[57]

Given a sufficiently compelling reason, Amerindians would without hesitation choose to sacrifice their lives in battle. Warriors were generally willing to fight to the death, even when retreat might have been possible, to cover the escape of women and children, to enhance the reputation of their nation as valorous enemies, or simply because they had no other choice. However, in a campaign where their own collective interests (apart from the maintenance of the French alliance) were not at risk, the securing of prisoners without loss to themselves was their paramount goal. The pursuit of this goal justified neither joining the French in attacks on fortifications nor compelled them to strike against the British in any particular location. Instead, the Amerindians fought in their own way, and the five parties who left the expedition and the two ambushes on the portage road all generated prisoners rather than casualties. With these objectives attained, remaining in the field could serve no further purpose. As they told Léry after the attack on the convoy, "the Master of Life has favoured us, here is the food, here are the prisoners, let's return."[58]

The actions and decisions of the French and Iroquois in the expedition to Fort Bull mirrored their respective roles in the Seven Years' War. The French forces in North America were players in a global conflict between empires and in each campaign sought to influence the course of that larger struggle. The Canadian Iroquois, on the other hand, were willing to enter this conflict alongside the French, but had nothing to gain from hostilities with Great Britain, New York, Virginia, or New England. For them, taking part in French campaigns provided an opportunity for individuals to seek prestige without regard for the strategic goals of the French. Under these conditions, Franco-Amerindian confrontations over the conduct of the war were predictable.

For contemporary Europeans, the Anglo-French imperial struggle, with its large armies and tangible victories and defeats, was the more visible of the wars in progress in northeastern North America in the later 1750s. Yet for the Iroquois of the St. Lawrence valley this conflict was only a framework within which they conducted their own parallel war, with very little regard for the military customs and aspirations of the French. Even in the later years of the war, as the possibility of a direct British attack increased, the Canadian Iroquois defended northeastern Kanienkeh by practising their own style of war. As the French fought to capture British strongholds and preserve their own, the Canadian Iroquois continued to fight their own war directed at their own goals for as long as doing so did not endanger their own collective interests.

Viewed from a distance, parallel warfare, as conducted by Canadian Iroquois and the French during the Seven Years' War, bore a certain resemblance to the fur trade. In the fur trade, Amerindians sought exotic items for consumption and redistribution, often in ways that enhanced, rather than supplanted, pre-contact practices and values; Europeans strove to maximize profit and accumulate wealth.[59] In parallel warfare, Amerindians went to war in search of prisoners, scalps, and matériel; Europeans attacked or defended forts. Yet both also managed to find ways of bridging their differences and creating a system within which both parties could hope to achieve their separate goals. This pursuit was never comfortable for either partner. Yet during the Seven Years' War the Canadian Iroquois, other Amerindians, and the French came together to produce a terrifyingly effective military machine that year after year held off a numerically superior opponent until finally overcome by sheer weight of numbers.

CHAPTER 3

THE OHIO VALLEY, 1753–1755

For the Canadian Iroquois, the Seven Years' War began at 11:00 a.m., 15 June 1754, on the portage between Lake Erie and Lake Chautauqua. It was there that a party of about 130 warriors of the Seven Nations travelling from Canada to the Ohio valley were informed that a French envoy to a Virginian outpost had been attacked. This represented a new and alarming development in the complicated politics of northeastern North America. For the first time since the end of the War of the Austrian Succession, French and British forces had clashed directly. A French officer had been killed, and it was most unlikely that the French would allow his death to pass unavenged.

Were the French to retaliate, they would look to their allies for support. Yet many of the Amerindians present on the Chautauqua portage harboured grave reservations about becoming involved in a French vendetta. They had not come to the Ohio valley to make war on the British or anyone else. The Seven Nations had few interests in that region, and those that they had inclined them towards preserving the integrity of the region against *all* Europeans rather than supporting a French occupation.

The Ohio valley had been depopulated in the "Catastrophic Era" that followed the arrival of Europeans in northeastern North America in the seventeenth century, when epidemics and war eliminated or dispersed the original inhabitants. In the first decades of the eighteenth century, however, the Ohio valley once more became a human habitat. Attracted by an abundance of game, League Senecas moved westward and Wyandots and Miamis eastward and southward into the region. These voluntary migrants settled alongside Delawares and Shawnees who had been driven over the

Appalachians following the occupation of their previous homelands by British colonials, and sought a life beyond the reach of Europeans.[1]

The attractions of life in the Ohio valley were such that by the mid-eighteenth century these nations had been joined by a number of Amerindians from the Seven Nations of Canada. By 1753 the residents of the region included Abenaki, Kanesetake, Kahnawake, and Nipissing individuals and families who had established homes and whole villages south of Lake Erie and west of the Appalachians.[2]

Overall, the relationship of the Seven Nations with the nations of the Ohio was reasonably amicable. Although in the winter of 1752 a party of Kahnwakes from Canada had killed a number of Delawares, many other Kahnawakes had married into Delaware families and lived quietly and peacefully in the Ohio region. At least one village was composed of a mixed

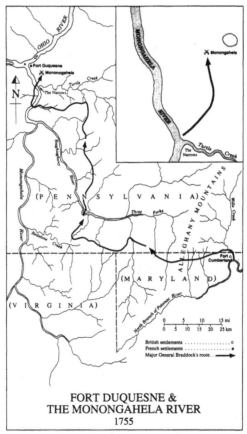

FORT DUQUESNE &
THE MONONGAHELA RIVER
1755

MAP 4. Fort Duquesne and the Monongahela River, 1755, by William R. Constable

group of Kahnawakes and Delawares.[3] So for the Seven Nations, the Ohio valley was not a distant theatre of imperial conflict, but a place where they could expect to encounter friends, relatives, and a way of life much more sheltered from European influence than their own. It was, in short, a region where their interests were better served by peace than war.

Yet if the Seven Nations were not inclined to immerse themselves in a war for the Ohio valley, they were closely allied to the French, who were. It was the French, not the Kahnawakes nor the Kanesetakes, who perceived their interests to be at risk in this region. For the French government, the Ohio valley represented not a refuge, but an enormous, latent threat: a global geopolitical catastrophe waiting to happen. The expansion of British North America towards the Ohio valley produced deep and increasing apprehension among French strategists, as it seemed by the mid-eighteenth century that a familiar Anglo-American pattern was about to be reproduced in this region. British traders, already on the scene, would be followed by speculators and settlers who would displace the original residents, as the Ohio nations shared the fate of the Penobscots and Pequots of the Atlantic seaboard who had been obliterated by British invaders. Tree by tree and hill by hill and valley by valley, the Ohio region would be converted from an Amerindian homeland to a productive unit of the British empire.

Within a generation, this region might harbour a British colonial population comparable to that of all of New France. Lake Erie would become a British preserve, the southern route from Montreal to the west would be severed, and French alliances with the Great Lakes nations would crumble as American traders flooded farther into the west. A vast new market would open for British exports, and the British empire would be one step closer to the Mississippi valley and Spanish America. Unless the British were constrained from expanding farther in North America, Versailles had every reason to fear that France would one day find herself confronted by a British empire that had become an economic and military superpower, capable of dominating the North Atlantic world.[4]

By the mid-eighteenth century this process was already well under way in the Ohio valley. A powerful consortium of Virginian and English land speculators, organized in the Ohio Company, was planning the occupation and settlement of the Ohio valley. Cisappalachian precedents suggested that they would succeed. To prevent this strategic nightmare from becoming reality, the French elected to forestall the Virginians by themselves entering the Ohio valley in force and establishing a chain of fortified outposts. These outposts would allow France - not the Shawnees or the Delawares or the

Miamis, and certainly not the Virginians - to dominate the region. This enterprise was not directed at preserving the Amerindian character of the region, except to the extent that it excluded the Virginians, and did not involve European agricultural settlement.

It was to this venture that Canadian Amerindians were invited to lend their support. Only fragments of information exist regarding the councils which secured their agreement to participate. From these fragments, it would appear that an important concern of the Seven Nations was to avoid entangling themselves in war while continuing to fulfil their obligations as French allies. They had every reason to believe that supporting the French carried the potential for embroiling them in an unwanted conflict, either with the British of Virginia or the nations of the Ohio.[5]

Their concern was not misplaced. The French are frequently credited with practising a kinder, gentler form of colonialism in North America than the British, the Dutch or the Spanish. This was perhaps not entirely evident to the Amerindians of the Ohio in the mid-eighteenth century. In 1749 an ostensibly peaceful French expedition to the region drove whole villages away in flight. During this incursion, the French officially claimed the Ohio valley and referred to the region as French territory in councils with the Ohio nations. In 1752 a community that refused to accede to French demands that they renounce their Virginian trading partners was obliterated by a party of Odawas led by a French officer. So for the Seven Nations, to accompany the French would be to court the risk of war with the Ohio nations; to remain aloof would be to fail in their obligations to an ally.[6]

In the end, the Seven Nations reached a compromise. They agreed to support the French, but not to fight for them. Instead, they came to the Ohio valley as salaried workers, who would lend their skills as hunters to provide food for the French expedition that would actually build the new French outposts. They "would not engage to war with ye English etc. on Ohio, but are employed at so much p[er] month to hunt for ye army."[7] Speaking in 1754 with the governor general of New France, Ange Duquesne de Menneville, the Seven Nations were guaranteed that they were "sent only to work to maintain good relations ... and ... their Father Onontio assured them that they would serve only to respect and maintain the peace" in the region.[8] So in the summer of 1753, as the French built Fort Presqu'île on Lake Erie and Fort Le Boeuf on the portage over the Lake Erie-Ohio valley watershed, about two hundred hunters from the Seven Nations were present. While their allies built forts, the Amerindians hunted for pay.[9]

Yet if this activity was uncontroversial and remunerative, diplomacy was more interesting, albeit on occasion unnerving. Throughout that summer Canadian Amerindians were privileged to watch and learn as their French allies sought to win friends and influence people. In a series of councils, the nations of the Ohio were given the good news that a loving and compassionate Father Onontio had only the best interests of his children at heart. That a Virginian invasion might loom, but the French were there to protect them and to supply them with abundant quantities of trade goods. That the lands which they inhabited were the property of the French crown, as the result of a taking of possession by René-Robert Cavelier de La Salle in 1670. And that anyone who challenged French claims or French actions would be obliterated without mercy. Resistance was futile, as the French would "overthrow them [opponents] with such vigour that those who attempt it will be crushed."[10]

Unimpressed with the hectoring rhetoric of Onontio's emissaries, the Ohio nations would have preferred continued independence to occupation by either Virginians or Frenchmen. Nonetheless, they needed trade goods and the services of gunsmiths. In the absence of the Pennsylvanians and Virginians, who had prudently departed, these could only come from the French. Moreover, they were finding lucrative employment hauling French cargo over portages. So the Ohio Amerindians refrained from any act of active resistance, while observing the developing situation and pondering their options.[11]

The Delawares, however, did protest the presence of the contingent from the Kahnawakes of Canada. The killing of Delawares in the previous winter by a Kahnawake party had not been forgotten, and their inclusion in the French expedition was not appreciated. The Ohio nations consequently expected the Kahnawakes to remain outside their territories until they had suitably adjusted their relationship with the Delawares through the appropriate rituals of condolence and peace. Instead, the Kahnawakes continued southward with their allies. Not until July did a Kahnawake delegation come to Venango "to make the Delaware's satisfaction." By then, many of the Delawares had reached a temporary accommodation with the French occupation and the ceremonial reconciliation was facilitated by the good offices of Custaloga, the leading Delaware at Venango.[12]

In the meantime, the French invasion of the Ohio valley was in the process of coming apart. Three forts had been built, but plans to construct a fourth at the forks of the Ohio were deferred to the next year. To continue would have been impossible. By the end of summer French logistics were overstrained and the health and morale of the French component of the expedition was cracking. In the blazing heat of summer, overworked soldiers and militiamen fell victim to exhaustion, malnutrition, and disease. Their officers lost all enthusiasm for the venture and devoted their energies to seeking reasons to justify returning to Canada.[13]

The Canadian Amerindians had also had enough. In the fall of 1753 they approached the French commander and took their formal leave. Not a single warrior of the Seven Nations remained with the French in the Ohio, "because they were weary and they wanted to return to their village[s]." Upon their return to Canada the Amerindians met with a cold reception from the governor general, who considered their departure from the Ohio valley to be tantamount to desertion. There is no indication that the Seven Nations were impressed by his bluster, although delegations continued to meet with Duquesne until he granted a "pardon."[14]

The collapse of the French expedition allowed the Virginians to regain the initiative in the Ohio. In March 1754 a Virginia outpost was under construction at the forks where the Monongahela and Allegheny rivers meet to form the Ohio. The new French commander in the region, Claude-Pierre Pécaudy de Contrecoeur, who had recently arrived with a second expeditionary force, responded quickly to reports of the British initiative. He marched south with six hundred Frenchmen, arrived on 17 April, and ordered the forty-two Virginians to surrender. Within an hour, France had acquired a new western stronghold.[15] Using tools purchased from the Virginians and logs and squared timbers prepared by the British colonials, Contrecoeur's force set to work building a new fort on the north bank of the Monongahela River. This fort, named Fort Duquesne, became the headquarters for the French occupation of the Ohio.

Contrecoeur's commander-in-chief considered the successful occupation of the forks of the Ohio to be a signal military victory. In language that would have appalled the Seven Nations and made a mockery of his frequent declarations of pacific intentions, Duquesne fulsomely congratulated Contrecoeur. "The English," he wrote, "have retired with their ... shame" and left Contrecoeur "master of the battlefield." This action, continued the gleeful governor general, "restored tranquillity in a colony that you have torn from the hands of a greedy usurper."[16]

His counterpart in Virginia also considered this expulsion an act of war and used it to justify subsequent military actions in the Ohio, where the destruction of Fort Duquesne became the primary objective of the British in the region. "The breach," wrote the ingenuously outraged governor of Virginia, "was begun by the French in taking our fort." He assembled his own army under the command of George Washington, who was ordered "to march over the Allegheny mountains, [and] if they should think it practicable, to endeavour to dislodge the French from the fort."[17]

Back in Canada, in the spring of 1754 the Seven Nations were once again approached by the French to contribute to the Ohio occupation force. Once again they consented, after seeking and receiving assurances that they would not be required to engage in military operations. All together, about 130 Abenakis, Algonquins, Canadian Iroquois, Hurons, and Nipissings assembled for the journey west. Those present included Missakin, who would take part in the expedition to Fort Bull in 1756. The Amerindians were accompanied by a number of respected French officers, including Louis Coulon de Villiers, whose younger brother was already serving in the Ohio.[18]

Travelling west from Montreal up the St. Lawrence River, Lake Ontario, and Lake Erie, this body of Amerindians and Frenchmen reached the Chautauqua portage at 6:00 p.m. on 14 June 1754.[19] The next morning, at 11:00 a.m., they encountered a French officer heading north bearing shattering news: at a time when Britain and France were officially at peace, fighting between British and French forces had broken out in the Ohio valley and Villiers' brother, Joseph Coulon de Villiers de Jumonville, had been killed.[20]

Now aware that they were entering a theatre of war, the Canadian Amerindians continued along the portage. The next day they set out in canoes across Lake Chautauqua, then proceeded down the Allegheny River toward the forks of the Ohio. At 8:00 a.m. on 26 June the fighters from Canada reached Fort Duquesne, where they found their French allies busily engaged in preparing for war with Virginia. Contrecoeur, now commandant of Fort Duquesne, had organized a detachment of five hundred Frenchmen and eleven Amerindians which was to march against the Virginians the next morning.[21]

Later that day the Seven Nations attended a council with the French to discuss the possibility of their agreeing to accompany this expedition. The chiefs and warriors listened with habitual courtesy to Contrecoeur's declaration that he, like them, had come to the Ohio valley only to keep the peace and maintain good relations. His response to a military incursion from Virginia had been the dispatch of an emissary to ask the intruders to return peacefully to their own country. Contrecoeur's envoy, however, had been treacherously attacked and brutally murdered. This left the French with no alternative but to strike back. Contrecoeur asked each nation in turn to accept a wampum belt and axe which symbolized his invitation to join with the French in their noble enterprise.

This invitation posed a problem for the Canadian Amerindians. Some were inclined to accept, others to hold to their original intentions and avoid fighting. The formal reply to Contrecoeur was made by a Canadian Iroquois chief. He reminded the commandant that Onontio had asked them to come to the Ohio valley only to keep the peace and that they had received solemn assurances from the governor general that this would be their sole role in the region. Yet in making this declaration, the Canadian Iroquois chief was not speaking for the warriors. While their leaders hesitated, they accepted the axe and the wampum and began their ritual preparations for war. At this point, the council adjourned and the chiefs met in private and sought to reach a consensus. Two hours later the council reconvened. This time the Abenakis, Algonquins, Hurons, Kahnawakes, Kanesetakes, Nipissings, and Oswegatchies all agreed to fight. The chiefs requested that the departure of the expedition be deferred by one day to allow them to make the necessary preparations.

The divisions among the Amerindians, however, had been smoothed over, not resolved. About ninety of the Seven Nations fighters at Fort Duquesne wished to go to war, while forty preferred to remain at peace. Discussions continued during the night, but both sides held firm. Finally, they decided that those who wished to fight would fight and those who held to their original goal of "working to maintain good relations" would remain at the fort.[22] Thus, with considerable discussion and division, came the faltering beginning of the participation of Canadian Amerindians in the Seven Years' War.

The day of 27 June was passed in making new moccasins and drawing rations, powder and shot from the French quartermaster. The next morning the allied force of about one hundred Amerindians and six hundred Frenchmen departed at 10:00 a.m., some by land, others in canoes.[23] Missakin's party, who found themselves lacking some necessary items, remained at Fort Duquesne to equip themselves and did not rejoin the main body until 29 June.

Although a minority, the Amerindians quickly took control of the expedition. When Villiers, who had been appointed by Contrecoeur to command the French militiamen, attempted to choose a route, he was overruled by the fighters of the Seven Nations. They preferred to take the advice of a Seneca chief from the Ohio area who proposed following the Monongahela

River. He recommended this route on the grounds that it led past a store-house built by Virginia traders, which might have been reoccupied by Jumonville's assailants if they had continued towards Fort Duquesne.

Led by the Seneca chief, the allies travelled upstream along the Monongahela until 30 June when they reached the Virginian storehouse, which proved to be abandoned.[24] Here the expedition left the river and struck out overland. The chiefs accepted Villiers' suggestion that they leave the canoes and reserve provisions at the storehouse guarded by twenty militiamen, along with five Amerindians who were ill.

Although the exact location of the Virginians had yet to be determined, the allied force was now within striking distance of the enemy. On 1 July ammunition was distributed and parties of scouts sent out in search of the British colonials. The next morning one of the Amerindians who had been left behind at the storehouse rejoined the column. He brought with him a British deserter who informed the allies that the Virginians had retired to a fort. On 3 July the weather changed for the worse, to the dreary overcast skies alternating with heavy rain that would persist for the remainder of the campaign. Nonetheless, the march continued; towards noon the expedition

The restored entrenchment and stockade of Fort Necessity. Photograph by W.J. Eccles

reached the site of the attack on Jumonville and his party and saw the four corpses that remained. The allies halted while the bodies were buried, then Amerindians and Frenchmen joined in prayer over the graves. In a dramatic speech on the site of his brother's death, Villiers spoke to the Amerindians of his brother and the revenge that he hoped to obtain with their help. Missakin and the other chiefs promised their support.

At about 3:00 p.m. Amerindian scouts returned and reported that they had located the British fort. The allied force advanced cautiously towards the site, so as to come as close as possible without being discovered. But lack of local knowledge caused some confusion, as the leading elements of the column blundered unexpectedly out of the forest. They saw before them a large open meadow, covering about sixty hectares and lying between ranges of hills. Within the meadow stood Fort Necessity.

The heart of Fort Necessity was a circular palisade 16 metres in diameter surrounding a small hut, 4 metres square and covered with bark and animal skins, that was used to store munitions and provisions. The stockade lay at the northeast angle of an entrenchment shaped vaguely like a diamond, with sides ranging from 15 to 30 metres in length and a long axis of about 50 metres running from northwest to southeast. This unimpressive fortification, begun on 2 July and still incomplete when the allies arrived, consisted of a trench and earthwork which was described by one of Washington's soldiers as "a little entrenchment round them [the garrison] about two foot deep."[25]

Out in the open, the Amerindians and Frenchmen came under fire from nine swivel guns emplaced along the entrenchment. At the same time they sighted the Virginians and South Carolinians advancing across the meadow in line of battle. Rather quaintly, Washington appeared to be preparing to fight a miniature European-style battle in the midst of the North American forest. This was an interesting development. Standing upright in a field waiting to be shot might have been very effective in Europe, but was hardly the tactic of choice in the forests of North America. The British colonials, given time to reflect, apparently agreed with this assessment.

As soon as the main body of the allies heard the firing, they advanced quickly towards the entrenchment, shouting war cries as they ran. The response of their enemies was equally prompt. Before the allies could fire a shot, the British colonials executed a smart about-turn and fled back to their entrenchment. The allies advanced to a wooded hill about 60 metres from the fort, then took cover among the trees and opened fire. The

Virginians and South Carolinians of the garrison replied with musketry and swivel guns. Thus began the short inglorious siege of Fort Necessity.

The task of the assailants was greatly facilitated by the location and layout of Washington's stronghold, which might have been expressly designed to be attacked rather than defended. Fort Necessity was located in an open meadow, conveniently placed about a musket-shot from the high ground to the southwest. This allowed any attackers to fire down on the entrenchment from behind the trees, without exposing themselves to the annoyance of return fire. Moreover, with only about 60 metres of entrenchment and 20 metres of palisade facing the allies to the south and west, only a fraction of Washington's force could actually confront their assailants.

Once the Virginians and South Carolinians were back inside the fort and the Amerindians and Frenchmen had taken station at the border of the forest, both sides settled into an exchange of fire that dragged on throughout the afternoon. The allied sharpshooters were the more effective. In the course of the day, seven hundred allied fighters lost three killed and seventeen wounded. The defenders lost thirty killed and seventy wounded out of three hundred.[26] Other British casualties were self-inflicted, as

Fort Necessity as the Amerindians and French would have seen it during the siege. Photograph by W.J. Eccles

Washington lost control of many of his troops who chose to desert the firing line and make war upon kegs of rum instead of the allies. So popular was this activity that by the end of the action half of Washington's soldiers were drunk.[27]

Although it involved a fort, this engagement was not quite a siege. It was more a battle between British colonials hiding in a water-filled ditch behind a muddy earthwork and Amerindians and Frenchmen hiding behind dripping trees, all soaked and miserable as they fired back and forth in the rain. Without cannon, the allies could not force the issue, except by charging across the open meadow against a fortified position, inviting British colonials to cut them down. The defenders could not attack the allies, since this would have meant a charge across the same field followed by a mêlée in the forest, another novel way to commit suicide.

The European commanders might have been willing to continue indefinitely, but by the late afternoon the Amerindians were losing patience. Wet, uncomfortable, and thoroughly fed up, the warriors were willing to stand by Villiers in avenging Jumonville, but totally lacked the desire of the French to do so by taking this particular shabby little fort. As the firing continued, the chiefs reached a consensus that the warriors had had enough and that they would all leave the next day. A delegation was dispatched to inform Villiers of this decision.

At this point, with the Amerindians unwilling to continue to assist their quixotic allies in this masochistic venture, the French decided to invite their opponents to talk. Washington and his officers agreed. Following lengthy negotiations over the exact terms to be accorded the garrison, articles of capitulation were signed later that evening. Under this agreement, the South Carolinians and Virginians were to be allowed to return in safety to Virginia, taking with them their personal effects, provisions, weapons, and ammunition. They were granted the honours of war, and permitted to retain their flags and one symbolic cannon. In return, Washington surrendered, acknowledged responsibility for the death of Jumonville, and promised that the survivors of his escort would be released. Two members of the garrison, including Captain Robert Stobo, commander of a company of Virginia provincials, would serve as hostages for their safe return.[28]

As far as the Europeans were concerned, this capitulation ended the campaign. The French considered it to be a modest triumph. A fort had been attacked by a force of Amerindians and militiamen and secured with minimal losses. An important diplomatic and propaganda victory had been secured, and the Virginian advance thrown back beyond the Appalachians.

The Amerindians, on the other hand, were not at all impressed with this result. A political and strategic victory for the French empire was neither here nor there as far as they were concerned. For the Amerindians, regardless of agreements made between Europeans, the campaign would continue until they too had obtained a satisfactory outcome. To do so, they needed to take some prisoners, along with whatever matériel they could obtain from their defeated enemies.

So the next morning when the Seven Nations watched a French detachment take possession of Fort Necessity and the garrison begin to leave, the warriors took action to achieve success on their own terms. Ignoring the French, they advanced towards the British position, intent on continuing the engagement. Once there, they confronted the two hundred fit and armed soldiers of the garrison, still in organized units and accompanied by their officers. The one hundred warriors relieved the Virginians and South Carolinians of their baggage and possessions, and killed two of the wounded and three soldiers who lay sleeping in a drunken stupor. Instead of resisting their outnumbered assailants, the British colonials panicked and fled, leaving behind a flag and the one canon that the terms of the capitulation allowed them to carry off. The Amerindians immediately set off in pursuit. Twelve kilometres from the entrenchment, one party caught up with the fugitives, and secured ten prisoners. A second group took six more.

When the first party of Amerindians returned to Fort Necessity with their trophies, they were met by Villiers, who considered these captures to be a violation of the articles of capitulation. After some discussion, the now-triumphant warriors allowed themselves to be persuaded to release their prisoners. The Amerindians further agreed to join six militiamen in escorting the liberated captives back to the disorganized mob of fleeing British colonials. After leaving Fort Necessity, however, they killed and scalped three of the British. The remaining seven were stripped of their clothing and allowed to proceed under the escort of the militiamen. The Frenchmen, who had protested but not attempted to intervene during the killing, did not care to proceed alone. They abandoned the released prisoners and returned to Fort Necessity with the warriors.[29]

The second party of Amerindians kept their prisoners to themselves and brought them to Fort Duquesne when the expedition returned on 7 July. Two of these prisoners were presented to the commandant as a courtesy. Stobo vigorously protested the continued detention of the four remaining captives as a violation of the articles of capitulation. Contrecoeur, who had already unsuccessfully attempted to ransom the Virginians, informed Stobo that "they were the Indians,' and he could not get them from them."[30]

Shortly after the engagement at Fort Necessity, the fighters of the Seven Nations returned to Canada, taking with them their four prisoners. Prior to their departure, a delegation of chiefs approached Contrecoeur and sharply criticized French security at Fort Duquesne. In particular, they warned him against allowing Ohio Amerindians unrestricted access to the fort. They repeated this criticism to Duquesne himself upon their return to the St. Lawrence valley.[31] In giving this warning, the chiefs of the Seven Nations demonstrated a firmer grasp of the principles of security than their allies. For Robert Stobo, now a resident of Fort Duquesne, had chosen to expand his role from hostage to spy. Provided with ample opportunity to observe the activities of the French, he drew up a detailed map of Fort Duquesne along with a plan for its capture. Stobo then arranged for this material to be carried to Virginia by Delaware messengers.[32]

The remainder of 1754 passed without any further major confrontations in the Ohio, but in 1755 both France and England sent reinforcements of regular troops to North America and prepared to take the offensive. The British planned to attack French positions in Acadia, Lake Champlain, Lake Ontario, and the Ohio valley. The French, who received larger reinforcements but had fewer total resources, limited their ambitions to a single offensive against Fort Oswego on Lake Ontario. In other sectors, they remained on the defensive.

For the third year in a row, the Seven Nations were approached by the French and asked to send contingents to the Ohio valley. Once again, they agreed to support their allies. On 12 May twenty-two Hurons and twenty-two Kahnawakes left Montreal for the west. They were followed by eighteen Kanesetakes and six Oswegatchies, and on the 28th by twenty-one Nipissings. At Fort Duquesne the various contingents joined one hundred Seven Nations fighters who had wintered in the Ohio.[33]

The names and personal histories of the Canadian Iroquois who served in the Ohio valley in 1755 remain shrouded in anonymity, with one exception, a young Kahnawake warrior named Atiatonharongwen. Born in 1740 in Saratoga to an African-American father and an Abenaki mother, Atiatonharongwen became a Kahnawake following an Amerindian-French raid on that town in 1745, during the War of the Austrian Succession. In the course of this attack, he was seized by a French officer who planned to make him a slave. His mother resisted, calling out "He is my child!" When the officer replied "No, no, he is a Negro and he is mine," she appealed to several nearby Kahnawakes. The warriors confronted the officer and successfully insisted that he restore the child to his mother. Mother and son then accompanied the fighters to Kahnawake. Once there, Atiatonharongwen converted to Catholicism and learned to speak French fluently while working for the local Jesuit priest. At the same time, he took an interest in public affairs that was unusual for one of his age, and regularly attended Kahnawake councils. In 1755, now a thoroughly assimilated adolescent, Atiatonharongwen took his place among the warriors who travelled to the Ohio to fight for Onontio.[34]

In the early summer of 1755, as Atiatonharongwen and his fellows arrived at Fort Duquesne, the survival of the French presence in the Ohio valley appeared increasingly problematic. By 21 June both allied scouts and a British deserter had reported to Contrecoeur that a major offensive against Fort Duquesne was imminent and that a British army was already on the march. Contrecoeur responded with a series of attempts to harass this army, beginning with an effort by four Abenakis against the rearguard, but each one failed.[35] The British, commanded by Major-General Edward Braddock, took careful precautions against surprise and ambush. Their advance was slow, on account of the need to hack a road out of the forest, but nonetheless relentless. Each day, this army drew a few kilometres closer to Fort Duquesne, and each day, the prospects for a continued French occupation of the Ohio valley grew dimmer.

By the beginning of July, Braddock's force of about fifteen hundred regulars and provincials accompanied by a powerful artillery train was within striking distance of Fort Duquesne.[36] The size of this army was deceptive, given that it was largely composed of virtually untrained Pennsylvanians and Virginians serving with provincial units or recruited into "regular" battalions. This was not, however, apparent to the Amerindians and Frenchmen at Fort Duquesne. Since an army this strong could be expected to overwhelm the defences of the fort, the best possibility for a successful resistance lay in marching forward to engage the enemy in the forest before they reached the forks of the Ohio.

With only a very limited number of French soldiers and militiamen at hand, the success or failure of this venture would depend entirely upon the willingness of Amerindians to support the French. Should this support be secured, it would mean a major engagement between European soldiers and Amerindian warriors in the heart of the North American forest. By a quirk of competitive European imperialism, a region that had for so long been a refuge for Amerindians from the Europeans was about to become a European battleground.

On 7 July scouts reported that Braddock's army was thirty kilometres away, marching in good order and heading straight for Fort Duquesne. The Amerindian scouts fired on the rear of the column and inflicted some casualties, but failed to delay the British.

At Fort Duquesne, opinion among the assembled Amerindians regarding the wisdom of confronting Braddock was mixed. A vocal minority was forthrightly pessimistic. One spokesperson for this group told the French commandant that given these odds, "you evidently want to die, and to sacrifice us [too]."[37] Most, however, were willing to fight with some confidence of success. Their opinion was expressed by an English-speaking Delaware in conversation with a Virginian prisoner who declared "that Braddock's army was advancing in very close order, and that the Indians would surround them, take trees and (as he expressed it) *shoot um down all one pigeon.*"[38]

MAP 5. The Battle of Monongahela
Although this map is not as clear as it could be, one can see, from right to left: the Ohio River, Fort Duquesne, the route of the allied army to the battlefield, the allied forces in a crescent formation enveloping the British column, the ford over the Monongahela River, and Braddock's route to the battlefield. Note that Braddock crossed the Monongahela a short distance above Turtle Creek (not shown), then recrossed it at the ford, instead of marching parallel to the Monongahela as indicated by this map. French map of the Battle of Monongahela. Untitled, anon. NMC 7755

In the end, the cocky and confident prevailed over the prudent and politic. When the Amerindians from the Seven Nations and Great Lakes met in council with Contrecoeur and his officers on 8 July, every nation but one agreed to stand with the French. The exception was the Potawatomi contingent from Detroit, which remained silent and deferred making a decision. Preferring unanimity, the other nations postponed their departure until the following day. Patience was rewarded when, overnight, the Potawatomis fell into line. With an allied force committed to fight, local Shawnee and League Seneca warriors announced their willingness to join them as well. Most Ohio Nations, however, reserved judgment, and awaited the outcome of the battle before committing themselves.[39]

On the morning of Wednesday, 9 July, Amerindians and Frenchmen drew powder and shot then marched out to meet the enemy. In all, the allied army that assembled in front of Fort Duquesne mustered 637 Amerindians, including about 230 from the Seven Nations, 117 colonial regulars, and 146 militiamen.[40] This force, formidable as it might be, had no intention of confronting the British head on. Instead, the allied leaders apparently planned to lay an ambush for Braddock. The exact site would depend upon the movements of the British, but the key location for the allies was the area surrounding the intersection of the Monongahela River with Turtle Creek which, like Fort Duquesne itself, was located on the north bank of the Monongahela.

From their last reported position, to the east of Fort Duquesne, the British could follow the north bank of the Monongahela through an area known as The Narrows, "a very difficult pass, on the right side entirely commanded by high ground & on the left hemmed in by the Monongahela,"[41] then cross Turtle Creek and continue westward to Fort Duquesne. Alternatively, they could bypass The Narrows by looping south across the Monongahela, then fording the river again just west of Turtle Creek. Here, the Monongahela might have been "not much more than knee deep" but it was about 300 metres across and its banks rose "above 12 feet perpendicularly high above the shore."[42]

Either The Narrows or the western ford would have made excellent sites for an ambush where surprise and an advantageous position would give the heavily outnumbered allies the edge that they needed. British observers described the first as so rugged that it "would have taken a days work to have made passable" and said of the second that "if the enemy should have possession of it, they would not be able to get over without a great loss."[43] An army at Turtle Creek would be in a position to manoeuvre as necessary to lay an ambush either at some point along The Narrows or at the ford. But only if it got there first. With Braddock known to be close by and coming up fast, the allies had to reach Turtle Creek before the British. They set out quickly, moving "on the run"[44] down a path that led northeast along the bank of the Ohio River for a short distance, then turned sharply inland, leading towards the ford and The Narrows, preceded by a party of scouts. The campaign had become a race.

A race the allies were destined to lose, and lose badly. At 1:00 p.m., about two kilometres short of Turtle Creek, the Amerindians and Frenchmen entered a lightly wooded area: "an open wood free from underwood with some gradual risings, this wood was so open that carriages could have been drove in any part of it."[45] Here, allied scouts encountered three horsemen, the leading element of the vanguard of the British army. One horseman fired a single shot in the direction of the allies, then "turned round his horse [and] cried, the Indians was upon us."[46]

With this encounter between the British and allied forces, the advancing Anglo-American settlement frontier crashed headlong into the Franco-Amerindian resistance. At this historic moment, everyone within sight of an opponent whipped round and ran in opposite directions. The allied scouts hurried back to the main body, a short distance behind, and made their report. The allies now divided. Large parties of Amerindians broke away and flowed around the left and right flanks of the British advance guard.[47] Some went to ground and opened fire. Others continued to move eastward, working their way towards the rear of the elite grenadiers who led the British advance.[48] As they manoeuvred through the trees, the Amerindian fighters encountered two British flanking parties, each of a sergeant and ten men, which they cut off and overwhelmed.[49]

The Amerindians had reacted instantly to the sighting of the British and before long had gone a fair way towards surrounding the advance guard. Yet their movements through the forest took time, and in this interval the French regulars and militiamen facing the head of the British column found themselves in difficulty.

Simultaneous with the beginning of the Amerindian flanking movements, the French regulars and militiamen lunged directly forward towards the head of the British column. Advancing quickly, the Frenchmen soon caught sight of the British advance guard and fired an ineffective volley from out of range. As they came within musket range of the British, the French in turn became the targets of a series of heavy and accurate volleys from British grenadiers drawn up in line of battle. The impact of this fire was devastating. The militiamen were armed adolescents rather than veteran fighters. Under fire for the first time, they panicked. About one hundred of these young men, together with two cadets from the colonial regulars, fled at the first volley, shouting "Sauve qui peut!" This deteriorating situation was exacerbated when the French commander was killed by the third volley. Shaken, deprived of its leader, and facing a resolute enemy, the allied centre faltered and stalled.

As the French stumbled, the two six-pounder field guns that accompanied the British advance guard came into action, and volleys of musketry were supplemented by salvos of grapeshot. This further rattled the allied centre. Amerindians deeply disliked facing artillery, and as grapeshot whistled through the trees and their French allies wavered, numbers of those Amerindians positioned near the French began to give ground and withdraw. One Amerindian was so shaken by the first shock of battle that he fled back to Fort Duquesne. Arriving at 4:00 p.m., he announced that the allies had been defeated. The French too began to fall back.

For long minutes, it looked as if the French element of the allied army might crack altogether, and that the British grenadiers might smash their way through to Fort Duquesne. But the moment passed.

The Fall of Braddock, by C. Schuesselle, engraver J.B. Allen. Although a purely imaginative reconstruction, this engraving catches something of the chaos and confusion of the disintegration of Braddock's army. NAC C-002644

Under steadily increasing fire from the Amerindians to the right and left, the British failed to press their ephemeral advantage. The surviving French officers brought the troops and militiamen under control. Ceasing to fall back, they took cover and opened fire on the British. Amerindians and Frenchmen perceived that, however great the noise that the field guns might make, the actual salvos of shot were passing over their heads and harming only the trees.

As the allied centre stabilized, the British began to learn the limitations of grenadier tactics in a forest. Formed in line, standing upright, they had gained a fleeting ascendancy over the French, but now presented a conspicuous target to enemies who had "always a large mark to shoot at and we having only to shoot at them behind trees or laid on their bellies."[50] The field guns were silenced by the Amerindians who "kept an incessant fire on the guns & killed ye men very fast."[51]

While the French regulars and remaining militiamen maintained the pressure on the head of the column, the Amerindians continued to work around both sides of the British force, always remaining under cover, pouring a withering fire into the British ranks. The Amerindians of the allied left seized a hill overlooking the rear of the advance guard, which forced the enemy to draw back and abandon the guns.

The engagement between the allies and the advance guard lasted for about one hour before the British withdrew after suffering very heavy casualties. One British participant estimated that about two thirds of the men in the advance guard were killed.[52] As they retreated, the survivors of the advance guard encountered the main body of British troops, which was moving forward and preparing to engage. The two bodies collided. The result was muddle and confusion from which Braddock's army would not emerge intact.

For the next two to three hours the British army gave a convincing imitation of a complete and utter shambles. It ceased to advance, and remained at the foot of the hill occupied by the Amerindians on the allied left. Lashed by the fire of an invisible enemy, the beleaguered army became an enormous, passive target, whose soldiers fired away their twenty-four rounds of ammunition "in the most confused manner, some in the air, others in the ground."[53] Officers lost control of their troops and proved unable to organize an effective counterattack. So great was the confusion and the fear, that bodies of soldiers who attempted to advance upon the allies found themselves fired upon by both sides.

That the British held out as long as they did was as much the product of the circumstances of the battle as the courage of the beleaguered regulars and provincials. Over a thousand soldiers, however distressed and inept, formed too powerful a body for the allies to charge and disperse, even if they had been so inclined. Moreover, ineffective as it might have been in harming the allies, the firing of the British does appear to have provided a measure of safety for Braddock's soldiers. The repeated discharge of their muskets would have generated a dense cloud of black powder smoke over their position, into which the Amerindians and French would have been firing more or less at random, hoping to hit something. The dense concentration of huddled British soldiers ensured that, on occasion, they did.

Only at the tail of the column were the British able to mount a successful defence. Here a very small number of Amerindians, forming the tips of the wings that enveloped Braddock's army, had worked their way around

The Burial of Braddock, by H. Pyle, *c.* 1850. A romantic reconstruction, featuring an improbably sedate ceremony and a finely crafted coffin. NAC C-007220

to the wagon train and cattle herd that followed the army. They were fended off by the British rearguard, who kept open the line of retreat to the ford.

After two to three hours the Amerindians began to press heavily upon the rear of the main body of British troops: "they begin to inclose us more and more till they had nigh inclosed us in ... they had surrounded all but a little in the rear, which they strove for with all their force. But our men knowing the consequence of it preserved the pass till we retreated."[54]

While some British soldiers fought to keep open the passage to the ford, others began to desert the main body and make their way towards the rear. With the army finally breaking apart, those men who remained under discipline were ordered to withdraw to join the rearguard at the wagon train, to attempt to cover the removal of whatever ammunition and provisions could be salvaged. When they reached the wagons, the British survivors found that the drivers had already fled with the horses, immobilizing the supply train. Rather than rallying, most of the remaining soldiers on the field "went off by tens and twenties."[55] A very small group which remained "stood about these wagons for some little time without any fire."[56]

As these soldiers waited for orders, the Amerindian left wing came up to join those warriors who had been harassing the rearguard and the French advanced to the front through the wreckage of the British stand. The allies opened fire on the wagon train and the last remnants of Braddock's army fled down the path towards the ford,[57] followed by a force of Amerindians who killed many of the British as they struggled across the Monongahela River. The remaining Amerindians roamed the battlefield collecting prisoners, scalps, and matériel, including a considerable amount of gold and silver specie. They then returned to Fort Duquesne "overloaded with the spoils of the English," leading captured horses laden with matériel and twenty prisoners, including seven women or girls.[58]

In all, British losses totalled 456 killed and 520 wounded, out of a force of 1,469.[59] Allied casualties amounted to twenty-two killed and sixteen wounded out of 891.[60] With the allied force scattered over a two-kilometre battlefield and the British in flight, the French officers decided to withdraw with the wounded to Fort Duquesne, leaving the field to the Amerindians and the dead.

The French had intended to reorganize and prepare for another engagement, in the event that the British reformed and resumed the attack. On 10 July, however, the Odawas of Michilimakinac and the Odawas and Potawatomis of Detroit announced their intention to depart. They were followed two days later by the Wyandots. Displaying uncharacteristic consideration for the needs of their allies, the fighters of the Seven Nations stayed until scouts returned with word that the British had left for good. By 26 July only two Kahnawakes and two Abenakis remained at Fort Duquesne.[61]

Monongahela was the greatest Amerindian battle of the Seven Years' War. It represented an Amerindian rather than a French victory, in an engagement where French forces were limited and concentrated in a single area of the battlefield, and their contribution was eclipsed by the numbers and effectiveness of the Amerindians.

Of all the major campaigns in which the Seven Nations took part, Monongahela was the one which allowed the Amerindians the greatest freedom to practise war in their own way. In the course of the engagement, Amerindians reacted instantly to a surprise encounter, rapidly gained the ascendancy over a numerically superior, more heavily armed enemy, and won a sharp, decisive victory. This victory presented an awesome demonstration of the potential power of Amerindian warriors. Under the right conditions, an Amerindian force could obliterate a European army, reducing whole regiments to shattered, fleeing rabble. Thanks to the presence of the Amerindians at Fort Duquesne and their willingness to fight alongside the French, an army that could have walked over the garrison and shelled the walls of the fort to rubble was swept away as if it never existed.

As a result of the support of their Amerindian allies, the French prevented the British from establishing themselves in the Ohio valley. Yet this victory proved transient. With the outbreak of fighting all along the Anglo-French frontier in northeastern North America in 1755, the Ohio valley was quickly relegated to the margins of a general war. Since the French presence in the Ohio depended upon the continued flow of supplies from Canada, its fate would be ultimately be determined by events in the east.

As for the nations of the Ohio, they still had no great desire to see their territory studded with French outposts. Nonetheless, once the French had demonstrated that they could hold out in the teeth of British opposition, these nations were temporarily willing to tolerate Onontio's garrisons and accepted French logistical support in their own war against the British to protect their lands against encroachment. This successful war devastated the western agricultural frontiers of Virginia and Pennsylvania between 1755 and 1758, and temporarily ended with the British forced to agree to respect Amerindian territorial claims beyond the Appalachians. The terms of this agreement, however, were soon violated and continued colonial expansion caused the Ohio nations to resume their war against the British in 1763.[62] The withdrawal of local Amerindian support and the deteriorating situation on the borders of Canada left Fort Duquesne vulnerable to a British expedition in 1758. The fort was evacuated on 24 November, and the French never again returned in force to the region.[63]

The Battle of the Monongahela effectively ended the large scale-participation of the Seven Nations of Canada in the war in the Ohio valley. Their remaining campaigns would be fought on the Lake Ontario, Lake Champlain, and Quebec frontiers.

CHAPTER 4

LAKE GEORGE, 1755

When they came to the Ohio valley, the Canadian Iroquois not only entered a new arena of overt Anglo-French conflict, they also left behind a region already at war. For back in Canada, their Abenaki allies were engaged in making war upon the English of New England and New York.

Fighting on the Abenakis' southern frontier had began in 1750, with the murder of an Abenaki chief, and continued as New Englanders steadily encroached on Abenaki lands. The Abenakis, refugees from the ethnic cleansing of the Connecticut River valley by New Englanders, now fought to preserve their remaining territory against the relentless northern expansion of British America. From time to time the Abenakis received military assistance from the Hurons of Lorette and the Algonquins of Trois Rivières, together with logistical support from the French. But the war against New England remained very much an Abenaki war, waged to protect Abenaki interests.

In 1754 this conflict had escalated dramatically when the Abenakis invaded New York. They came in response to requests for assistance from the last Amerindians of Schaghticoke, on the upper Hudson River. Constant pressure on their land base from British settlers had forced generations of Schaghticokes to seek safety in Canada. Now a series of murders by Europeans drove them to ask the Abenakis for help in seeking revenge. An Abenaki war party obligingly raided northern New York and rescued the surviving Schaghticokes, who removed to Odanak where they were absorbed into the Abenakis.

The French attempted unsuccessfully to restrain the Abenakis and prevent the war from spreading to New York in 1754, and only began to provide armed support for their Abenaki allies after the outbreak of violence in the Ohio valley. When the French entered into open war with the

British in 1755, they joined the Abenakis in a conflict that had been in progress for five years, and would continue until the end of the intra-European conflict made further resistance impossible. The Canadian Iroquois also remained aloof from the Anglo-Abenaki war and the Kahnawakes had gone so far as to attempt to mediate between the combatants. Only when they agreed to support the French in making war upon the British were the Canadian Iroquois drawn into the Abenaki war as well.[1]

Just when the Canadian Iroquois finally decided to fight against the British is uncertain. But at some point in 1754 or 1755 the Seven Nations formally committed themselves to go to war alongside the French. This decision was not made by the fighters in the Ohio valley who agreed to join Villiers in avenging the death of his brother. Instead, it was the product of long and careful discussion and deliberation, particularly among the Kahnawakes.

Until September 1755 the position of the Kahnawakes remained somewhat equivocal. On the one hand, they had provided armed support to the French in the Ohio valley in two engagements and had also agreed to take part in a major campaign in the Lake Ontario region. On the other, Kahnawakes had also been in touch with the British of New York and the League Mohawks, to whom they gave assurances that their community would not participate in an Anglo-French conflict.

Indeed, as the Seven Years' War began, the British had every reason to hope that the Kahnawakes might remain neutral. The Kahnawakes enjoyed longstanding and mutually profitable commercial relations with New York which hostilities would interrupt. A decade earlier, this community had responded to news of the outbreak of the War of the Austrian Succession by sending a messenger to the British at Albany with word that "the Sachems of Caghnawaga [Kahnawake] were inclined ... not to meddle with the war but to live in peace and keep open the path [to Albany]."[2] The New Yorkers, however, did not respond to this overture and the Kahnawakes entered the War of the Austrian Succession on the side of the French.

Even so, as Canadian Iroquois warriors were returning from Fort Necessity in August of 1754, there was a Kahnawake delegation in Albany, which agreed to remain at peace with New York.[3] In June of 1755, when William Johnson, the superintendent of northern Indians, consulted the League Mohawks regarding the attitude of the Kahnawakes, he was informed "that those Indians have at present a more favourable disposition towards the English interest than for many years past."[4]

Sir William Johnson, anon. NAC C-021368

During the first half of the 1750s the neutralist faction had been strong enough to keep the Kahnawakes out of the Anglo-Abenaki war and to undertake diplomatic initiatives aimed at maintaining good relations with Albany. Nonetheless, intervention on behalf of the French was not without powerful advocates, among them those who had brought the Kahnawakes into war alongside the French in the War of the Austrian Succession and gained approval for the dispatch of armed contingents to the Ohio valley.

The question of war in 1755 was resolved by discussion between members of these groups. On one side were those who spoke of the religious ties that linked them to the French and their obligations as allies. On the other were proponents of neutrality. Among these was Tecaughretanego. A prominent war chief who made his reputation fighting the Catawbas,

Tecaughretanego "had all along been against this war, and had strenuously opposed it in council." He believed that since no Kahnawake interests were at stake in the Anglo-French war they should not get involved. Summing up this position, Tecaughretanego said "if the English and French had a quarrel, let them fight their own battles themselves, it is not our business to intermeddle therewith."[5]

In the end, the interventionist faction prevailed. Consequently, when a party of League Mohawks came to Kahnawake with a message from Johnson "in order to prevail on them [the Kahnawakes] at least to stand neuter between the French & us," the delegates met with a polite but unequivocal refusal. Speaking to the League Mohawks, the Kahnawakes made reference to the ritual of baptism that symbolized their alliance to the French and recommended that the Six Nations themselves remain neutral in the Anglo-French conflict.[6] In their reply to Johnson, Kahnawake orators said nothing of animosity or grievances on their part against New York, New England, or the British empire as a whole. Instead, they spoke of their close relationship with the French and their obligation to support an embattled ally, declaring that "the French & we are one Blood & where they are to dye we must dye also. We are linked together in each others Arms & where the French go we must go also."[7]

Representing themselves and the French as being of "one blood" and walking arm-in-arm made for a very strong statement of commitment to the French alliance. Linked arms were a traditional Iroquoian diplomatic metaphor, whose meaning was explained by Kiotseaeton, a chief of the League Mohawks, at a conference with the Algonquins and French in Trois Rivières in 1645. After linking arms with an Algonquin and a Frenchman, Kiotseaeton said of this gesture: "Here is the knot that binds us inseparably; nothing can part us ... Even if the lightening were to fall upon us, it could not separate us; for, if it cuts off the arm that holds you to us, we will at once seize each other by the other arm."[8] Nonetheless, the strength of this declaration did not indicate an unlimited commitment on the part of the Kahnawakes to either the French alliance or the French war effort. Events in the coming campaign would demonstrate that the Canadian Iroquois placed definite boundaries on their willingness to cooperate with the French.

Now formally at war with the British, in the summer of 1755 the Seven Nations of Canada were preparing to send a contingent of warriors to Lake Ontario to assist their French allies in besieging Fort Oswego, New York's outpost on that lake. On 4 and 6 August the Kahnawakes and Kanesetakes received a visit from Vaudreuil, who had succeeded Duquesne as governor general and had come to solicit their support. The Canadian Iroquois gave him a favourable response.[9]

The Kahnawakes agreed to join with the remainder of the Seven Nations in taking part in the Lake Ontario venture. Yet they themselves were convinced that the most immediate threat to Canada lay elsewhere. Their commercial contacts with Albany gave the Kahnawakes an intimate knowledge of events in New York, and since October of 1754 they had

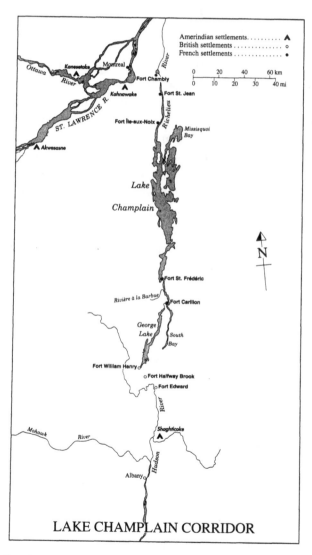

MAP 6. The Lake Champlain Corridor, by William R. Constable

repeatedly warned the French of preparations for a British expedition against Fort St. Frédéric on Lake Champlain. This advice had been discounted by Duquesne, whose scouts found no evidence of these preparations and in any event considered that "the English of this continent are not warlike enough to conduct sieges."[10] Not until a new governor general took office and victory in the Ohio led to the capture of Braddock's papers did the French finally take the Kahnawake warnings seriously. These documents, which reached Vaudreuil by 5 August, revealed, among other things, precise details of the British plan for the capture of Fort St. Frédéric.[11]

Vaudreuil immediately cancelled the expedition to Oswego and redeployed allied forces to defend the Lake Champlain frontier. Between 10 and 20 August the army left Montreal, and by 1 September the entire force was assembled at Fort St. Frédéric. The allied army consisted of 760 Canadian Iroquois, Abenakis, Algonquins, Hurons of Lorette, and Nipissings, and a small group from the Great Lakes, along with nearly three thousand French regulars and militiamen.[12] To command the French element of the allied army, Vaudreuil appointed Jean-Armand Dieskau. A Saxon serving in the French army, Dieskau had been sent to Canada as the commander of the metropolitan battalions that reinforced the colonial garrison in 1755. His appointment did not prove to be one of Versailles' better decisions.

In the Ohio valley, the Seven Nations had dealt with officers from the troupes de la marine such as Léry and Villiers who were, for the most part, born in Canada, reasonably competent, and generally familiar with Amerindian military and diplomatic practices. Dieskau, on the other hand, was a German, just off the boat from Europe, who would have found it easier to establish a rapport with Braddock than Missakin or Collière. Regardless of his merits as a European soldier, Dieskau quickly proved to be a source of concern and frustration for the Seven Nations contingent. This friction began with his plan for dealing with the British and continued until the last moments of the campaign.

When word arrived on 27 August of three thousand British troops camped at Lydius, on the Hudson River at the head of the portage to Lake George, Dieskau decided to advance and await the enemy at Carillon, between Lake George and Lake Champlain. No sooner had this movement been completed, however, then a party of Abenakis brought in a prisoner who revealed that the British had advanced to the head of Lake George to build a fort, leaving only nine hundred men in the camp at Lydius. In response to this intelligence, Dieskau decided to forsake passivity and make a quick strike south against the small, vulnerable garrison of Lydius. To this end, he assembled six hundred Amerindians, six hundred militiamen, and two hundred metropolitan regulars, including the grenadiers of La Reine and Languedoc.[13] This flying column departed from Carillon on 5 September.

With Dieskau in command, the Lake George campaign afforded the Seven Nations a marvellous opportunity to see the German genius for war in action. They were evidently not impressed. The Amerindian chiefs had not been consulted regarding Dieskau's plan of action and once he attempted to implement it, they quickly made their feelings known. Using Jacques Legardeur de Saint-Pierre, the colonial officer who acted as liaison between Dieskau and the Amerindians, as an intermediary, the Seven Nations raised three principal objections to Dieskau's plan. First, as believers in the military principle of concentration of force, they informed Saint-Pierre that the general was most unwise to leave more than half of the army at Carillon and thus invite defeat in detail. Second, they disapproved of the proposed route. Dieskau had originally intended to outflank the British at the head of Lake George by travelling southward up the lake, then striking inland. The

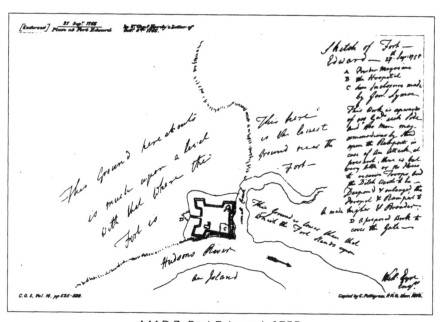

MAP 7. Fort Edward, 1755
A sketch of Fort Edward," 27 September 1755, by William Eyre, NMC 7756

Amerindians considered this to be a frankly stupid idea. Given that the British were building a fort on Lake George and transporting supplies between Lake George and Lydius, they suggested that it might be even easier to bypass the British if they travelled by way of Lake Champlain, and left their boats at South Bay at the head of that lake. Third, they objected to Dieskau's failure to provide a small force to guard the canoes and boats when the overland march began. This would leave the vessels exposed to capture or destruction by the British, which would endanger the safe return of the army.

Saint-Pierre passed their comments on to Dieskau, then returned with the general's response. Dieskau had declared that he had brought enough men to defeat the enemy and would send for two hundred men from Carillon to guard the canoes, and that the army would travel south along Lake Champlain to South Bay. The Amerindians remained unimpressed with a commander who left half of his fighters behind at Carillon when he went to war on the Hudson. Dieskau responded to their concern by lying, as he announced that the remainder of the army would presently join them.[14]

After this faltering start, the allied army set out on 5 September. By the seventh, the column was within striking distance of Lydius, and the Seven Nations found themselves faced with another plan that did not accord with their ideas of how to make war.

When scouts returned from the Hudson River, they reported that the southern end of the portage to Lake George at Lydius was now defended by a fort. The trading house of John Hendricks Lydius, a former resident of Montreal who carried on an extensive trade with the Kahnawakes and Abenakis, was now Fort Edward. Built under the supervision of a professional military engineer, it consisted of a palisade "in the form of a square with three bastions." Although the ditch and rampart were still under construction, the engineer considered that behind these defences "3 or 400 men will be able to resist 1500 ... if cannon is not brought against it."[15] The scouts further reported that the bulk of the British force at the Hudson River was camped in fifty tents outside the fort, and that traffic continued on the road between Lydius and Lake George.

This information made Dieskau decide that the British at Fort Edward were unaware of the allied march and vulnerable to a swift approach and attack. Once again, he made his plans without consulting his allies, and furthermore failed to consider the implications of the presence of a fort for the Amerindians. Some time later the chiefs were invited to a formal council by Saint-Pierre and informed that Dieskau had decided to attack the new

British fort on the Hudson. Their response was unequivocal: "They refused all unanimously to go to attack a fort."[16]

The Canadian Iroquois bluntly refused to participate and began to consider turning back and returning to Montreal. The Algonquins and Nipissings were equally pessimistic. Their orators expounded at great length regarding the risks to which an attack on a fort would expose their warriors and predicted that attacking Fort Edward would lead to defeat. Only the Abenakis were willing to proceed farther. The Abenakis were unique among the Seven Nations in that they were already at war with the British of New England when Anglo-French hostilities began, and were fighting to defend their own interests rather than provide assistance to an ally. They may have considered the northern expansion of New York implied by the establishment of a military presence at Fort Edward and Lake George to be a threat to Abenaki lands in the Lake Champlain valley.

In any event, the Abenakis set about influencing the other Amerindian nations. An Abenaki orator made a dramatic speech to the Canadian Iroquois requesting that they not abandon their allies from Odanak. This intervention turned the tide in the debate and all of the nations agreed to continue. The Canadian Iroquois placed themselves at the head of the column, and the whole army continued southward towards the Hudson.

By sunset the allied force was camped about four kilometres from Fort Edward and had received new intelligence. Shortly after the end of the day's march, scouts intercepted a mounted courier from Lake George. A letter found on the courier warned of the presence of a French army in the area and ordered the commander to withdraw the garrison into the fort. Another group of Amerindian scouts sighted twelve wagons on the road, heading south. They attacked and seized the wagons, but captured only three of the teamsters. The remainder swam the Hudson River and escaped. All of this evidence led the allies to believe that the garrison of Fort Edward had been warned of their presence.[17]

Appalled Amerindian chiefs soon discovered that Dieskau had not changed his intentions in light of this new information. Informed in council that Dieskau planned to attack at dawn, they requested an hour's recess to consult among themselves and confer with the warriors. After two hours of intense discussion, the chiefs returned and announced that they were not going to attack the fort. The Abenakis, Algonquins, and Nipissings portrayed themselves as willing to proceed but constrained by the wishes of the Kahnawakes who "refused absolutely." The Kahnawakes, "since they were considered by the other Natives to be the oldest and the first," could not be overruled and that was that.[18] Whether this was in fact the case is impossible to say, but given the absolute unwillingness of Amerindians to become involved in attacks on forts under any circumstances, this explanation sounds more than a little ingenuous.

At this point, the Kahnawake chiefs received a visit from Dieskau. All that would be required of them, he said, would be to make a diversion, safely out of musket range of the fort, which would allow the regulars and militiamen to undertake the real attack. The Canadian Iroquois apparently found this less than convincing, but difficult to refute directly. They promptly changed their line of argument and now informed Dieskau "that they had resolved not to act against the English in territories that belonged to them by right," but would follow him against the English within French territory.[19] This position represented something of a departure for the Canadian Iroquois, who had cheerfully participated in numerous attacks on locations deep within New York during previous Anglo-French conflicts. They remained unmoved when Dieskau attempted to counter their argument with a claim that Fort Edward was constructed on French territory. Finally, conceding defeat, Dieskau then asked them what they would be willing to do. The chiefs replied that the army at Lake George was camped within French territory, and would make a suitable target.

The general council then resumed. Dieskau gave the Seven Nations "the choice to go the next day to the fort [Edward] or to march against that army [at Lake George]." Faced with choosing between an army and a fort, the Amerindians not surprisingly opted for the army. All present agreed to march for Lake George the next morning.[20]

At dawn Amerindians and Frenchmen turned north, marching in three columns, with the regulars in the centre on the road, the Amerindians to the left, and the militiamen on the right. This formation kept the army together, but at the cost of some heavy going for the warriors and militiamen who were compelled to make their way through the forest. By about 10:00 a.m. the allies were about five kilometres from Lake George. At this point, scouts reported British troops marching south along the road and two prisoners revealed that the British force consisted of about one thousand men and that they appeared to be unaware that the allied force was so close.

On hearing this news, Dieskau decided that he had been presented with a golden opportunity to ambush the British column, and immediately ordered a halt. The regulars were ordered to station themselves across the road; the militiamen lined the sides of the road, concealed within the forest; the Amerindians took a position just beyond the militiamen, about 230 metres from the regulars.[21] According to Dieskau's plan, the British would walk past the Amerindians, past the militiamen, right up to the regulars. The regulars would open fire first. Then the militiamen would attack from the sides and the Amerindians would sweep across the enemy rear. Dieskau's intention was to create "a cul de sac into which ... [he would] lure the English." If all went according to plan, "not one of them would have escaped."[22]

The Seven Nations were not pleased with Dieskau's grand design. The exact details of their objections were not recorded, but they had at some point extracted a commitment from the general that he would "rely on them to attack the enemy in the woods."[23] Dieskau's unilateral decision to stage an ambush and his issuing of orders regarding deployment without prior consultation violated this agreement. Nonetheless, the Seven Nations complied with Dieskau's request. Within minutes of the redeployment, the British column approached. The Anglo-Americans were careless and marching without advance guards or flankers, directly towards Dieskau's cul de sac, perfect targets for an ambush.

But as the Amerindians at the head of the ambush caught sight of the British, there was a new and disturbing development. The New York and New England provincials that they had expected to encounter were not alone. They were accompanied by a contingent of League Mohawks, along with some Oneidas. Theyanoguin, a leading League Mohawk chief, was riding next to a New England colonel at the head of the column.

This created a very awkward predicament for the Canadian Amerindians. The Seven Nations were at war with the British, not the League Mohawks, and had no desire whatever to fight fellow Amerindians. Caught between loyalty to their allies, which meant fighting the British, and to their own interests, which inclined them towards peace with the League Iroquois, they needed to clarify the situation and decide who was fighting whom.

As the League Iroquois and the British drew near, a Kahnawake fighter shouted out a challenge. He asked the Mohawks to identify themselves and was told by Theyanoguin that they were League Iroquois. The ensuing exchange echoed the statements made by League Mohawk and Kahnawake representatives at Kahnawake earlier in the summer, when each asked the other to avoid involvement in the Anglo-French conflict. The Kahnawake replied "We are the 7 confederate Indian Nations of Canada ... and we come in conjunction with our Father the King of France's Troops to fight his enemies the English." This warrior further informed Theyanoguin that the Seven Nations did not wish to fight other Amerindians, then asked the League Iroquois to stand aside from the imminent battle. Theyanoguin in turn asked the Seven Nations to remain neutral.[24]

Neither party was posturing. In the past, Amerindian groups allied to Europeans had gone to some lengths to avoid fighting one another wherever possible. For example, in August 1746, as an Amerindian-French war party was about to attack Schenectady, a delegation of Abenakis, speaking on behalf of themselves and the Canadian Iroquois, approached the senior French officer. This officer was François-Pierre de Rigaud de Vaudreuil, whose brother became governor general in 1755. The Abenakis informed Rigaud that they were alarmed by the possibility that the Odawas, Potawatomis, and Wyandots in the expedition might inadvertently attack League Iroquois who might be visiting Schenectady. Rigaud sympathized with this concern, commenting that "in that they were correct." He readily agreed with a proposal that the target of the expedition be changed.[25]

On the road between the Hudson River and Lake George the situation was more complicated. Although each Amerindian group wished to avoid fighting the other, they were equally determined to fight the French or the English. Circumstances did not permit a prolonged exchange of views. By opening negotiations with, rather than fire upon, the League Mohawks, the Canadian Iroquois had displayed a characteristic tendency to place their own military and diplomatic concerns ahead of those of the French. However willing they might be to fight even fellow Iroquois on behalf of their allies, to offer the League Iroquois a last chance to avoid a fight remained their first priority.

Just who fired the first shot is impossible to determine, but even as Theyanoguin asked the Seven Nations to remain on the sidelines, firing began. A young warrior of the League Iroquois fired at Theyanoguin's inter-locutor, who remained concealed among the trees. Two fighters of the Seven Nations, placed very close to the British, "judging by their behaviour that they had been warned" by League Mohawks, opened fire more or less simultaneously.[26] With the alarm raised, the remainder of the Canadian Amerindians joined the attack. According to Mohawk oral tradition, they "immediately made an impetuous charge rushing down the hill, on which they had been ranged, [then] they mixed in promiscuous fight with the Mohawks, who resisted with much valour."[27] The French militiamen left their positions and rushed up to support their allies. A short, sharp firefight ensued.

Dieskau's planned battle of annihilation quickly came apart. Instead of trapping the entire British-League Iroquois force, the allies engaged only the head of the column. Their attack was devastating - the British commander was killed almost immediately, along with several other officers - but most of the enemy escaped. All of the League Mohawks and a number of provincials at the front of the line of march resisted the Canadian Amerindians and militiamen, but according to one Massachusetts participant, "there was not above 100 of our men [provincials] that fired at all."[28] The rest of the provincials remained frozen in place.

One incident of this engagement illustrates the strength of the personal bonds between Iroquois of different communities that endured despite the war. In the midst of a swirling mêlée, a Kahnawake fighter encountered a Mohawk of the Iroquois League who had been cut off and surrounded. The League Mohawk, however, proved to be an old friend, and "so strong was the band of friendship, that even when meeting in hostile array, - it obliged them to spare each other." Instead of fighting, they exchanged greetings and shook hands. The Kahnawake stood by without interfering as the League Mohawk fought off a pair of less sentimental warriors, then said, with the laconic understatement that can come with translation, "My friend, - We have met in disagreeable circumstances: - Let us then part." The two thereupon went their separate ways to do battle on behalf of their respective European partners.[29]

The combat was brief and the British colonials were quickly forced to give ground. With the van retreating, "a panic took place, & the whole fled in a disorderly manner towards the camp."[30] Only the survivors of the League Mohawks and provincials at the front of the column managed to make a fighting withdrawal "by continuing their fire & then retreating a little & then rise and give them a brisk fire."[31] The League Mohawks were most unimpressed with the performance of the majority of their British allies, and later complained to Johnson, the commander the force at Lake George, "that our people left them exposed to the Enemy in the morning & did not second them."[32]

As the British broke and fled, Saint-Pierre was killed by a provincial. Nearby Amerindians seized his assailant and hacked him to death with axes. At about the same time a group of Kahnawakes, who, according to one French source, were "irritated to have lost several men," rounded up eight League Mohawk and Oneida prisoners and about the same number of provincials.[33] These captives, who had been tied together in groups of three and four, were killed as well. Other Canadian Amerindians turned to caring for their wounded and generally sorting themselves out. To the north, warriors of the Seven Nations continued to pursue. They clung relentlessly to the fleeing enemy until they came into sight of the camp at Lake George and the fugitives reached a safe haven.

At this point, with many of the Seven Nations and militiamen scattered, disorganized, and out of breath, the French regulars reached the site of the ambush. The battle had left them behind, but Dieskau had no intention of allowing the enemy to escape. He planned to march straight for the British camp and launch a frontal assault.

As Dieskau was passing through the site of the ambush, a number of chiefs approached Luc de la Corne, a captain of the colonial regulars, and asked him to inform Dieskau that they needed time to pause and regroup before returning to battle. La Corne attempted to pass on their request, but Dieskau ignored the veteran Canadian officer and continued to advance at speed. Several shouted to their warriors, suggesting that they remain in place. Some complied. Many other Amerindians, in particular the Kahnawakes and Abenakis, together with most of the militiamen, followed the regulars. Those Amerindians who had pursued the British were already outside the camp.[34]

Among the Amerindians who advanced to Lake George were a number of women. Unremarked by European chroniclers during most of the campaign, they travelled with the army and performed their customary role of supporting the warriors in the field. Although not normally expected to engage in combat, the women were armed with spears and bayonets and prepared to defend themselves or attack if the occasion arose. This occurred when they followed the warriors past the site of the morning's engagement and fell in with survivors from the ambush. Theyanoguin himself, unhorsed and attempting to escape to Lake George, encountered these women and was killed.[35]

Dieskau himself reached the clearing that surrounded the Lake George camp at about 11:30 a.m. Since he had not reconnoitred the site, it was only upon emerging from the forest that the regulars discovered that the British position had been fortified.[36] Instead of the exposed campsite that Dieskau expected, the provincials and League Mohawks were sheltered behind an improvised breastwork of wagons and tree trunks, with four field guns in the centre. Nonetheless, Dieskau believed that he had only to crash through the entrenchment to destroy the British army. While the Amerindians and Canadians "directly took tree within handy gun shot," the regulars advanced straight ahead.[37] The French grenadiers marched down

General Johnson's Victory near Crown Point, 1755, anon, 1877. This engraving of the collapse of Dieskau's attack at the Battle of Lake George does not quite manage to convey the suicidal folly of leading a charge of two hundred metropolitan regulars against three thousand provincials sheltered behind entrenchments. NAC C-006488

the road in column six abreast, then advanced directly towards the battery with the intention of seizing the guns. About 100 metres from the entrenchment, they halted, reformed into line, and opened fire.

The British responded with artillery. Standing upright and exposed, the grenadiers of La Reine and Languedoc made perfect targets for the gunners whose roundshot "made lanes, streets, and alleys through their army." Under terrible pressure, the regulars "kept their ground & order for some time with great resolution and good conduct, but the warm and constant fire from our artillery and troops put them into disorder, their fire became more scattered and unequal."[38] The survivors retreated and joined the Canadian Amerindians and militiamen among the trees. The battle settled down to an exchange of fire which lasted until about 4:00 p.m., when Dieskau was wounded and his successor ordered a withdrawal.[39]

As the French withdrew, groups of warriors and militiamen who had not been informed of the order to fall back continued to fire upon the entrenchment. Only when the British attempted a pursuit and threatened to cut off the French retreat did the allied fighters leave off attacking the entrenchment in order to come to the aid of a party of grenadiers from La Reine who were attempting to hold off the British sortie. These regulars were about to be overwhelmed when the Amerindians "fortunately came to their assistance and forced the enemy to retire, without that they would all have been killed."[40] The Seven Nations were thus the last of the allied army to leave the field of what had been a thoroughly unsatisfactory engagement.

Following the retreat from the entrenched camp, many of the Seven Nations and militiamen made their way south back along the road to the site of the ambush where they had left their packs in the morning. There, towards dusk, they encountered a detachment of 210 provincials from Fort Edward and were defeated and driven off in a confused engagement lasting about two hours.[41] Total allied losses in the three engagements amounted to 120 killed and 150 wounded. The British lost 122 killed, 812 wounded, and sixty-seven missing; the League Mohawks and Oneidas thirty-two killed and twelve wounded.[42]

By 11 September the defeated allies had reached Carillon. From there the Seven Nations continued on to Montreal. In council with Onontio, they spoke at length about Dieskau, blaming his temerity and incompetence for their losses and lack of success.[43]

For the Seven Nations, this had been a thoroughly exasperating campaign, in which everything that could go wrong, had. They had won a battle when the British walked into the ambush on the road, only to see their victory thrown away by an impetuous, blundering European whom they would not have considered competent to hunt rabbits, let alone lead a war party. Rather than coming back with prisoners for sale or adoption, they had lost good men who were irreplaceable; rather than returning with the matériel of a defeated enemy, they had themselves lost many of their own personal effects in the British ambush in the afternoon. The only positive result of the campaign for the Seven Nations was that they were rid of Dieskau for ever.

As for Dieskau, he had been taken prisoner and was now a trophy in the hands of the English. Converted by European conventions from a deadly enemy to an honoured guest, he alternately indulged himself in paranoid accusations of treason against the Kahnawakes and little lectures on the correct use of irregular auxiliaries in North America. In conversation with his captors, Dieskau helpfully informed the British, then conducting an inquiry into Braddock's defeat, "that it was a maxim with them [the French] never to expose regulars in the wood without a sufficient number of Indians & irregulars for any attacks that might be expected."[44] He remained silent as to the advisability of forming two hundred men in line of battle to attack three thousand entrenched opponents. With regard to Dieskau's accusations against the Kahnawakes, Johnson wrote: "There is a misapprehension in the Baron's letter when he imagines that the Canadians & Indians forsook them ... they continued at the attack till all was near decided, & the last push was made by some of their Indians."[45]

For the French, the campaign had been an embarrassment but not a serious defeat. Dieskau's overriding goal, after all, had been to defend Fort St. Frédéric, not overrun Johnson's army. For the second time in 1755, a combined Amerindian-French force had successfully defended a strategic position by moving to intercept a British invasion force.

Monongahela had been a brilliant tactical victory, Lake George a blundering tactical failure. But both were successful in strategic terms. Monongahela was an unequivocal strategic victory that threw the British out of the Ohio and back to their starting point. Lake George was a less complete strategic success, in that the campaign left the British firmly in place on the Canadian side of the height of land and thirty kilometres closer to Montreal. Yet the British, who only days before had been cutting wood to build boats to carry an army north to St. Frédéric, now braced themselves against an apprehended second attack. Johnson's provincials had held out in their entrenched camp, but the advance on Fort St. Frédéric would not resume until 1758.

But what had been a strategic success for the French was an absolute failure for the Seven Nations. This was possible on account of their different conceptions of the war. The Seven Nations had suffered casualties and returned without prisoners and matériel, therefore they failed. Whether or not the French fulfilled their strategic goals was incidental in terms of the Amerindian definition of victory. For their French allies, on the other hand, an expedition was a success if it fulfilled its strategic goals, regardless of the losses incurred.

At Monongahela, in contrast, both the French and the Amerindians had succeeded in fulfilling their aims in making war. The Amerindians collected their prisoners and matériel, with minimal loss to themselves; their French allies protected Fort Duquesne and the French presence in the Ohio. This engagement, along with the ambush on the road to Lake George, occurred under conditions which made it possible for both the Seven Nations and the French to succeed according to their own definitions of victory. In battles fought in the forest, Amerindians were free to secure whatever prisoners, scalps, and matériel that they could without interference from the French. The circumstances of battle thus prevented any fundamental conflict between the allies.

Moreover, these were rather conventional operations for Amerindians, involving as they did of a pair of large-scale ambushes. The assault on the camp at Lake George, however, marked an end to this period of conventional warfare for Amerindians. The campaigns of 1756 and 1757 would centre on the sieges of Oswego and Fort William Henry.

Sieges were highly technical operations, dominated by artillery and fortifications and conducted by European specialists. This form of warfare produced a new military environment for the allies that would make simultaneous victories in a parallel war much more difficult to achieve without some disagreement over what constituted legitimate acts of war. The engagement at Fort Necessity, in which the Seven Nations continued hostilities after the French and Virginians had agreed to stop, foreshadowed the fundamental conflicts between two different ways of making war that these campaigns would bring.

CHAPTER 5

OSWEGO, 1756

The campaign of 1755 on the Lake Champlain frontier had not been a happy experience for the Seven Nations. One year later Canadian Amerindians found themselves confronted once again with the challenge of dealing with a senior French officer who had just arrived in North America. This time, however, they did not wait until they were about to go into battle to educate the general regarding their military preferences. Instead, prior to the commencement of the campaign, a senior Nipissing chief explained with great care that Amerindians were not in the business of assaulting fortified positions and obtained a firm commitment that this would not be asked of them.

This explanation occurred on the afternoon of 6 August 1756, at a general council on the shores of Niaouré Bay (Sackett's Harbor). At this meeting, leaders of the Seven Nations met with Louis-Joseph de Montcalm, Dieskau's replacement as commander of the troupes de terre in Canada. As the council came to an end, the Nipissing chief rose and explained to the new French commander the conditions under which the Seven Nations would take part in the forthcoming campaign. He asked Montcalm "never to expose the Natives to the fire of artillery and musketry from the forts, since their custom was never to fight against entrenchments or stockades, but in the forest where they understood war, and where they could find trees for cover." Montcalm accepted these conditions with good grace, and replied that the Amerindians would be employed "to watch for reinforcements that might come to the enemy, and to keep a good lookout, while the French fought against the forts." This statement was repeated to each of the assembled nations by their respective interpreters. Speakers from each nation then pronounced themselves satisfied with Montcalm's understanding of their position.[1]

Louis-Joseph de Montcalm, Marquis de Montcalm, by Antoine
Louis-François Sergent, engraver Adolphe Varin. NAC C-034178

Niaouré Bay, located just south of the outlet of Lake Ontario into the
St. Lawrence River, was at that time the site of an allied advanced base on
the lake. Constructed in May 1756 by Villiers, it consisted of a small stock-
aded fort that was later augmented by bread ovens, magazines, and a hospital.[2] Amerindians and Frenchmen had assembled there in late July to
resume the expedition against Oswego that had been so abruptly cancelled
in the previous year. Reaching a consensus regarding the Amerindian role
in this operation was essential, since the capture of Oswego would entail a
formal, European-style siege.

Contemporary Europeans tended to view warfare in North America as
peculiar and exotic. During the Seven Years' War many metropolitan soldiers displayed an intense curiosity about Amerindians and their quaint and
colourful ways of war. It does not appear to have occurred to these soldiers

that they themselves, rather than the Amerindians, were exotic intruders who brought with them their own quaint and colourful ways of making war, including siege warfare.

For Amerindians, to take part in a formal siege was to step out of the forest and into a military twilight zone. The Seven Nations were accustomed to the sight of the fortifications that surrounded French towns and the firing of artillery as a part of public celebrations. But formal siege warfare was something new and strange.

Siege warfare in the eighteenth century was the western European equivalent of the Japanese tea ceremony. Its practice involved a series of rigidly prescribed moves and counter moves, with each step succeeding another in exact sequence towards an inevitable conclusion. When correctly followed, all other things being equal, this process led to the surrender of the fort on honourable terms. Besieger and besieged were both players in an elaborate game with very strict rules. And as long as everyone played by these rules, a satisfactory outcome was assured and only a limited number of people would actually get hurt. Siege warfare thus represented a form of ritual encounter that had a good deal in common with the Amerindian battles of pre-gunpowder warfare in North America. In both forms of war combatants were kept relatively safe during engagements and fighting ended once it reached a mutually acceptable point.

Amerindian pre-gunpowder battles took place by prearrangement, between carefully organized bodies of fighters protected by wooden armour and shields.[3] Armed with bows and clubs, two teams of warriors, each in formation behind a standard consisting of a round piece of tree bark painted with a clan or village totem, first indulged in ceremonial insult and posturing, then came to battle in an open field. A typical encounter consisted of an exchange of arrow fire followed by a charge and hand-to-hand combat, and lasted until a few casualties had been inflicted and a few prisoners taken. By Amerindian conventions of the time, this constituted victory for one side and defeat for the other. Since both sides agreed that this was the case, it was possible to fight a major battle without serious casualties.[4]

European siege warfare during the eighteenth century was in some ways startlingly similar. Amerindian armour and shields were replaced by trenches and ramparts, which were as effective against roundshot as wooden armour against stone arrowheads. And just as arrows and blows flew in both directions only until a very small proportion of the defeated army had been killed or captured, a siege continued until a breach had been made in the walls of a fortress. In both cases, hostilities ended with the losing side capable of continued resistance, but accepting defeat according to conventions that allowed a decision to be reached without further bloodshed. In place of ritual challenges and insults between warriors, a European siege featured frequent exchanges of elaborately polite notes between commanders and less formal interchanges between lower ranking combatants. In this case, the resemblance between traditional Amerindian and European siege warfare was so striking that one French participant in an Amerindian engagement noted that the verbal exchanges between Huron and League Iroquois fighters were "such as one is accustomed to at a siege of a city."[5]

A European siege, however, was a much longer and more elaborate ritual than a pre-gunpowder Amerindian battle. First came investment, as light forces isolated the fortress. Next, engineers surveyed the area, decided which side of the fort to attack, and selected sites for support facilities, trenches, and batteries. The besiegers next set to work establishing the infrastructure of siege warfare - artillery parks, magazines, manufactories to produce fascines (bundles of sticks) and gabions (wicker baskets filled with earth), field hospitals, and store and provision depots.

Then came the real beginning of the siege, the establishment of the first parallel, a trench so named because it was parallel to the walls of the fortress. At night, with strong covering parties to the front, workers deployed along a line marked by the engineers with a row of fascines and dug the trench. By dawn, they would be below ground level and safe from the guns of the fortress. From this parallel, communications trenches were pushed forward, zigzagging to prevent the defenders from firing down the length of the trench, to the site chosen for the second parallel, closer to the fortress. Batteries were established along successive parallels, first to sweep the ramparts, then to batter down the walls. These batteries consisted of a parapet of large gabions topped by fascines and pierced with embrasures for the guns. The guns themselves rested on timber platforms and were supplied from magazines located to the rear of the battery. For every move by the attackers, there was a prescribed counter-move by the defenders, generally involving either a sortie by the garrison or counter-fire from artillery mounted on the walls. Yet the progress of a well-conducted siege was generally held by European soldiers to be irresistible.

The construction of the network of trenches and batteries continued until there were guns literally under the walls of the fortress, pounding the ramparts until they produced a practicable breach. At this point, the fun and games came to an end, and everyone became extremely serious. If hostilities persisted, the next step would be one or more assaults by infantry.

These assaults would produce very heavy casualties on both sides, and could be ultimately expected to lead to the victory of the besiegers and the massacre of the garrison and any civilians found within the walls. Rather than risk undertaking or enduring a storm, both sides generally preferred to negotiate.

In other words, once they reached a point where real fighting might break out, everyone stopped. For the commander of a European garrison, to surrender once a practicable breach was effected was an honourable act. To surrender before this condition was met was to court severe censure, but to persist and stand an assault was considered foolish and irresponsible. General agreement among Europeans that a siege was decided once it reached a given point thus made possible to resolve a siege with a minimum of casualties.

Etiquette demanded that the commandant of a fortress begin the process of surrender by raising a flag indicating his intentions. A British garrison would raise the French flag, a plain white ensign; a French garrison would use a red flag or, if available, a Union Jack.[6] In the ensuing parley, the commandant or his representative would present a list of conditions under which the garrison would be willing to yield. Besiegers and besieged generally agreed upon articles that provided for the lives and safety of the garrison and civilians, the protection of personal property and some symbols of respect for the honour of the defenders, which often involved the garrison marching out with a band playing, flags flying, and dragging one piece of artillery.

North American sieges in the interior were much less elaborate than European sieges of first-class fortresses. Elaborate trench networks could be replaced by a single parallel; the guns of one battery might be enough to compel the surrender of a fort that was very small and flimsy by European standards.[7] Nonetheless, participation in a formal siege represented a new kind of war for Amerindians, conducted in a stark, empty landscape, scarred by trenches and dominated by guns poking out between embrasures, a landscape where humans lived below ground level or died. Into this bizarre, artificial world of death stepped the warriors of the Seven Nations, for whom the art of war meant a cleverly contrived ambush. Yet refusal to take part in the campaign would have meant a major breach with the French, since the capture of Oswego was considered by Vaudreuil to be of the first importance for the security of New France. If, in 1755, the capture of Oswego had been desirable for the French, by 1756 it was essential.

For the campaign of 1756 began with Fort Duquesne and the French presence in the Ohio valley in danger once again. This year the threat came not from an army painfully making its way from Virginia toward the forks of the Ohio, but from a fleet of small warships that the British were building at Oswego, on the south shore of Lake Ontario. Fort Duquesne depended for its continued existence upon the arrival of a steady stream of convoys of bateaux that passed over Lake Ontario. These bateaux carried the provisions and munitions that not only supported French garrisons, but enabled the Ohio nations to carry on their independent war in defence of their homelands against encroachment by British colonials. Were this line of communications to be severed by a fleet that controlled Lake Ontario, "Fort Duquesne [would] fall of its own accord."[8] With the loss of free passage over the lake, the French would also be forced to abandon their outposts on Lake Ontario at Frontenac, Toronto, and Niagara, and to prepare for an invasion of Canada by way of the upper St. Lawrence. If, wrote Vaudreuil, the shipwrights of Oswego were allowed to continue unmolested, their ships would soon be "so numerous and so strong that they will give [the British] superiority over Lake Ontario."[9] The best way to counter this threat would be to capture Oswego and destroy its shipyard.

This was eminently possible, since the defences of Oswego were anything but formidable. In 1755 and 1756 Oswego had expanded from a small commercial outpost into a sprawling military installation, but it remained virtually indefensible. Fort George, the original trading post that formed the core of Oswego, mounted only three guns, which "must not be fired for fear of bringing down the wall" and was overlooked by high ground to the east and west. To compensate for these defects, two new forts had been erected on the heights. Yet each new outpost contained flaws that tended to neutralize whatever contribution it might have made to the defences of Oswego. Fort Ontario, to the east, was badly designed and "defenceless against cannon." Fort Oswego, to the west, was "by no means tenable" and considered to be "a work begun only, and what is done does rather more harm than good." So flimsy was its construction that "ever since the spring this fort had been deserted and made use of only to turn cattle in."[10]

Were an allied army to reach Oswego, the capture of the fort and shipyard was almost a certainty. To this end, in July of 1756 there assembled at Niaouré Bay eighty-seven Canadian Iroquois and 173 other Amerindians, mostly from the Seven Nations, and 2,787 French regulars and militiamen.[11] This allied force of 3,047 would confront a garrison of 1,244 soldiers and seamen.[12]

Private, 50th and 51st Foot, c. 1755-1756. Gerry Embleton.
Department of National Defence

Atiatonharongwen, the sixteen-year-old Kahnawake veteran of
Monongahela, was a member of the Canadian Iroquois contingent. His presence was perhaps surprising, given that a few months before he had been
wounded in a skirmish with British rangers while scouting on the Lake
Champlain frontier. This wound healed imperfectly and troubled
Atiatonharongwen for years afterwards, but won him a reputation for
courage that formed the basis for his subsequent rise to prominence among
the Kahnawakes.[13]

Vaudreuil had hoped to assemble a much larger Amerindian contingent for this expedition by inviting the Great Lakes nations as well as
Canadian Amerindians to take part. This invitation, issued by the commandants of French posts in the Great Lakes region, met with a very positive

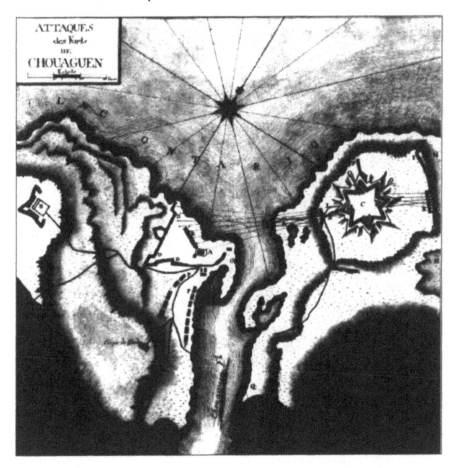

MAP 8. The allied siege of Oswego in 1756.

The cartographer has arranged his notes in such a way that they form a narrative through which the reader can follow the progress of a European siege:

A. Old Oswego

B. Fort George (Fort Oswego)

C. Fort Ontario

D. English entrenched camp

E. Wall constructed by the English after the investment with barrels of pork

F. Houses and magazines burned at the time of the evacuation

G. Shipyard. The French landed during the night of 11–12 August to besiege the forts of Chouaguen.

H. Slope of the hill that, by hiding the French from the enemy, facilitated their approach

response. In the summer of 1756 well over five hundred warriors from the Great Lakes came as far as Fort Presqu'île on Lake Erie. Yet upon their arrival the westerners learned that the smallpox that had devastated the Seven Nations in the previous winter had spread to Fort Niagara. Rather than risk infection, the greater part of the Great Lakes contingent returned to their homes. Only forty Menominees continued eastward to join the allied army at Niaouré Bay.[14]

The Seven Nations began their role as members of a besieging army on 10 August when 150 warriors, together with three hundred militiamen and ninety colonial regulars, travelled to La Petite Anse, a cove two kilometres east of Oswego.[15] That evening they covered the landing of the first division of the army that had crossed the lake in bateaux. The next morning a detachment of Amerindian fighters left the vicinity of the fort and travelled up the Oswego River to watch for British attempts to relieve Oswego. With a numerically superior British force based in New York and the nearest British outpost at the Oneida Carrying Place, outside intervention remained a real possibility throughout the siege. The Amerindian scouts thus performed an essential service, which allowed the complex work of a siege to proceed without fear of surprise.

In the meantime, the remaining Amerindians and a force of militiamen left the cove and marched to a ridge overlooking the first objective of the allied army, Fort Ontario. There, they "made a chain around the

I. Parallel opened the night of 12–13 through the stumps and trunks of trees on the crest of the hill
K. Battery of six guns began on the 13th
L. Road by which the English retired on the 13th at 5:00 p.m.
M. Battery en barbette of nine canon, established during the night of the 13-14th
N. Communication trench from the ditch to that battery
O. Ramps that led into the ditch where the French descended up to the communication trench (to the battery marked K)
P. Battery of mortars and a howitzer began on the 14th
Q. Place where the Natives crossed the river on the morning of the 14th. The English capitulated on the 14th at 10:00 a.m., and became prisoners of war.

fort."[16] With the regulars protected by this line of sentinels, the business of siegework began. An Amerindian selected a route for a road from the landing site to the ridge, where the French planned to establish the first parallel and the battery that would pound Fort Ontario into submission. He was followed by an engineer who blazed trees to mark the route and three hundred workers who began construction. Far to the rear, the second division of the army, carrying the siege train, sailed from Niaouré Bay.

That afternoon the garrison of Fort Ontario opened fire on the allies, first with muskets and later with artillery. Neither the irregulars investing the fort nor the soldiers at work on the road were harmed. The Amerindians and militiamen retaliated with accurate sniping from cover which the French believed had considerable moral impact: "Although their fire did not kill a soul, it tied down the enemy, fearful for their scalps, and gave great confidence to our soldiers."[17]

On the morning of 12 August, Amerindian scouts reported British activity on the Oswego River. A force of two hundred militiamen was sent twenty kilometres upstream to reinforce the Amerindians and investigate further. They found no trace of a British force, and returned to the siege lines in the evening. The spurious report may have been the result of sightings of couriers attempting to carry messages to and from Oswego, for later that day a party of Amerindians intercepted a letter from the commandant urgently requesting reinforcements. With the garrison known to be seeking assistance, the screen of allied scouts was supplemented on the thirteenth by a detachment of Amerindians and militiamen stationed at a portage twelve kilometres south of Oswego.

Also on 12 August, the second division arrived at La Petite Anse, where the guns were landed and taken to the artillery park. While this operation was in progress, French engineers, "covered by the musketry of militiamen and Natives,"[18] marked out the first parallel of the siege works - a trench running inland for about 200 metres along the crest of the ridge 175 metres from Fort Ontario. That night the regulars began to dig the trench. By dawn on 13 August this parallel was sufficiently advanced to allow the besiegers to continue to work during the day and construction commenced on a battery of six guns, which the French hoped to have in place by the next day.

At four o'clock in the afternoon, however, the besiegers noticed that the guns of Fort Ontario had fallen silent. A party of Amerindians and militiamen approached the fort to investigate. Cautiously peering over the stockade, the allied fighters found that the British had abandoned the fort rather than face a bombardment. They were followed at once by a company of grenadiers who took possession of Fort Ontario.

Immediately this outpost was secured, Montcalm gave orders to begin preparations to erect a new battery in front of Fort Ontario. Every fit European in the army set to work and continued for the rest of the day and throughout the night. By dawn the next morning, the guns were in place and the battery was ready to open fire into the rear of the defences of Fort George. While their allies laboured, the Seven Nations passed a quiet night. With the Oswego River between the French and their enemies, the services of the Amerindians as guards against a sortie were no longer required.

On the morning of 14 August, however, the Seven Nations were on the move again. At about 5:00 a.m. all of the Amerindians and most of the militiamen left the siege camp and crossed the Oswego River over a ford three kilometres above the fort. They intended to isolate Fort George from Fort Oswego, then await the arrival of a detachment of regulars and artillery who would travel over the lake at nightfall. When the regulars arrived, the two groups would unite to attack Fort George from the west.

This manoeuvre, wrote Montcalm, "was made in a brilliant and decisive fashion." Under fire from the guns of British warships anchored in the river, whose roundshot passed harmlessly over their heads, the Amerindians and militiamen flung themselves into the rapid current of the Oswego River "some swimming, the others in water up to their waists or up to their necks."[19] Once ashore, the Amerindians and militiamen first advanced northward, parallel to the river, then wheeled to the left and marched westward towards the heights to the west of Fort George. As they marched, the allied fighters saw the garrison filing out of Fort Oswego and returning to the old trading post. When the allies came into musket range of the retreating garrison, they "pointed their guns upon them & killed two of their men." Following this encounter, the Amerindians and militiamen quickly occupied the abandoned fort and "took up the brow of the hill from the river to the lake."[20]

This movement by the Amerindians and militiamen proved to be decisive in bringing the siege to an end. The British had intended to evacuate Fort George and make a last stand in Fort Oswego, but the seizure of this post by the Amerindians and Canadians forestalled this option and left them no alternative but surrender.[21]

A French officer later recorded that "although until then the fire of the besieged had been superior [to that of the allies] at ten o'clock they raised the white flag" and sent two officers across the Oswego River bearing

Capitulation of Oswego, 1756, anon, 1877. This imaginary portrayal of the departure of the garrison from Oswego after the capitulation makes the fort appear to be a sort of medieval castle and the departure itself to be a dignified and orderly procedure. NAC C-000799

a flag of truce to negotiate a capitulation with the French.[22] The British at first asked to be allowed the honours of war, to retain their arms, and be repatriated immediately. Montcalm refused, and demanded that the garrison lay down their arms and become prisoners of war. The colours of the two British regiments of the garrison were to be handed over to the French.[23] Influenced, Vaudreuil later said, by "the frightful cries and threats of our Canadians and Natives," the British agreed.[24] By 11:00 a.m. both European commanders had signed the articles of capitulation. An hour later a French officer took possession of Fort George. The French decided to transfer the garrison across the Oswego River to Fort Ontario in order to guard them against any action by the Amerindians.

With the surrender of Oswego, the French had scored a brilliant success. The ramshackle Gibraltar of Lake Ontario had fallen, and with it both the threat to the supply lines to the Ohio and the danger of an invasion by way of Lake Ontario. Munitions and provisions seized from Oswego would be used to resupply the west and underwrite the next year's campaign. The French forts of Lake Ontario were safe, and henceforth all of Vaudreuil's resources could be allocated to operations on the Lake Champlain frontier.

The Amerindians, on the other hand, had nothing whatsoever to show for their considerable efforts. This was no more acceptable to them than leaving Oswego in the hands of the British would have been to the French, and the warriors moved immediately to rectify this situation. As the French occupied Fort George and prepared to transport the garrison to Fort Ontario the Seven Nations brushed past French sentries, approached the disarmed British soldiers, and began to relieve them of their possessions. About fifteen members of the garrison were taken prisoner. Those who resisted were killed.[25]

One party of warriors invaded the British hospital, the southernmost in a row of buildings that extended southward from Fort George along the river bank which had formerly been occupied by traders. As it was located some distance away from the fort and the French regulars, the Amerindians found the hospital completely unprotected. Amerindians routinely killed prisoners who were unable to walk, since they could not keep up on a march, and made no exception for hospitalized casualties. On this occasion, the warriors forced their way into the building, where "all of the sick and wounded it contained were scalped."[26] Other Amerindians crossed to the east bank of the Oswego, and attempted to harass members of the garrison as they disembarked. These warriors were held off by French regulars, who escorted the British to Fort Ontario. By 2:30 p.m. the last of the disarmed British soldiers had been transported to safety.[27]

The Amerindians did not, however, cease their efforts to secure a victory on their own terms. They were inadvertently assisted in this endeavour by those members of the British garrison who attempted to flee to British-controlled territory rather than remain under the protection of the French. These fugitives were, for the most part, deserters from the troupes de la marine who had taken service in the two regiments of the garrison. When the order was passed down to cease fire, they decided that it would be better to flee than risk arrest and execution at the hands of the French. Some slipped away as soon as the garrison capitulated. Others remained, laid down their arms with the rest of the troops, then made their escape afterwards.[28]

The efforts of Lieutenant-Colonel John Littlehales of the 50th (Shirley's) Regiment to persuade French deserters serving in his regiment to remain were recorded by one Claude Frederick Hutenac. Immediately hostilities ceased, Hutenac approached Littlehales and told his commander that "if you are to give up the fort you must suffer me who am a deserter from the French to make the best of my way because they will have no mercy upon me." Littlehales assured Hutenac that the terms of the capitulation would shield him from French military justice, but Hutenac and several companions chose to ignore their commander's advice and take their chances in the forest: "not caring to trust [Littlehales' advice] ... they all went off."[29] Hutenac and a dozen others eventually reached the safety of a British outpost at the Oneida Carrying Place, but most of the fugitives were hunted down and killed.

The Amerindians left off their pursuit of victory only after a night spent circling Fort Ontario, shouting war cries, and engaging in shoving matches with the "strong guard of regulars [posted] to prevent the Indians from rushing in upon [the prisoners] ... which they several times attempted."[30] By morning the Seven Nations were apparently satisfied with their efforts, for the prisoners were left in peace until they were shipped to Montreal. In Montreal "they were treated in a manner not to leave any room for complaint, and, in the course of the year, most of them were exchanged."[31]

British officers viewed the killings after the capitulation with remarkable equanimity and divided responsibility for the incidents between the Amerindians and their victims. Littlehales, the senior surviving officer of the garrison, noted in his official report that "some of them [the garrison] having gone in liquor fell in to wrangling with the Indians, & several of them were killed, but the number as yet is uncertain." Another officer described them as "murdered by the Indians and their own drunken misconduct."[32]

In human terms, the cost of the campaign to the allies was relatively light. One Amerindian and four Frenchmen were killed and twenty-four wounded, none of them seriously. British losses are more difficult to ascertain, since an unknown number of the garrison either escaped or were killed after the capitulation. Officers of the garrison reported twenty-one casualties during the siege.[33] Estimates by the French regarding the number killed after the capitulation varied from thirty to one hundred and thirty.[34] These killings represented an atrocity for Europeans, but a victory for Amerindians. Once again, Amerindians had displayed a blithe disregard for the conventions and sensibilities of the allies as they sought to achieve success on their own terms.

In the course of the campaign of 1756 the warriors of the Seven Nations had demonstrated that they could play a significant role in the most technical expression of European warfare. Amerindian scouts could give early warning of British movements and the Amerindian contingent of an

Medal struck by the French government to commemorate the fall of Oswego. NAC C-062197 (obverse), C-062198 (reverse)

allied army provided a force that could intervene effectively when such a warning was received. Just as Amerindian-French forces had interposed themselves between British armies and French forts in 1755 at Fort Duquesne and Lake George, during allied sieges Amerindians placed themselves between the engineers and regulars who conducted the siege and potential British relief columns. This role was of the first importance in view of the numerical superiority of the British. A successful siege meant not just reducing the walls of a fort, but avoiding a British counterblow. Amerindians also played a secondary but nonetheless vital role in the siege itself. Screens of warriors protected the regulars who dug the trenches and hauled the guns against sorties from the garrison while Amerindian sharpshooters swept the walls of forts and on occasion even reduced the rate of fire of artillery by killing or intimidating gunners.

Yet if Amerindians could play a role in siege warfare, the events of 1756 also demonstrated that the physical circumstances of sieges created conditions where the fundamental conflicts between European and Amerindian systems of war would emerge and flourish. These cultural conflicts would continue until both components of an allied siege force had fulfilled their reasons for going to war. This would be repeated on a much larger scale in the campaign of 1757 following the capitulation of Fort William Henry.

CHAPTER 6

FORT WILLIAM HENRY, 1757

The Battle of Lake George in 1755 neutralized the British offensive against Fort St. Frédéric but left the British in place at the southern tip of Lake George. There they built Fort William Henry, which became a base from which to launch a renewed offensive against New France at some future date. With Oswego reduced to charred ruins, Vaudreuil now turned his attention to this outpost, which became the target of an allied siege in 1757.

Vaudreuil expected to undertake this siege with the cooperation of the Canadian Iroquois. Yet in the spring of that year he inexplicably chose to go a fair way towards alienating one Canadian Iroquois community by attempting to extend his authority as governor general of New France over the Oswegatchies. Thanks to Vaudreuil, in April 1757 the Oswegatchies found themselves defending their community against a threat that came from their French allies, rather than their British enemies.

Oswegatchie was governed by a council composed of twelve clan mothers, twelve village chiefs, and six war chiefs. On 25 March 1756 a gap had been created among these leaders when Collière was killed in the attack on Fort Bull. Vaudreuil, for reasons best known to himself, decided in 1757 to fill this gap by appointing his own candidate to the position.

He selected Ohquandageghte, a young Onondaga war chief who had recently emigrated to Oswegatchie. Prior to the siege of Oswego, Ohquandageghte had considered that the best interests of the Onondagas lay in association with the British. He wore a British medal, provided information about the French to the commandant of Oswego, and carried trade goods between Oswego and Fort Frontenac. The ease with which the British at Oswego had allowed themselves to be dispossessed, however, so alienated Ohquandageghte that he renounced his British ties and removed to Oswegatchie. At some point he came into contact with Vaudreuil, who was evidently extremely impressed with the young man.[1]

Vaudreuil gave Ohquandageghte a commission which read in part, "We have hereby named and rise him to be head warrior of said village [Oswegatchie], to be & to have in said capacity, all authority & command over the warriors of said village."[2] This was a rather strange thing to do. To put Vaudreuil's action in context, it was rather as if the Oswegatchies had sent a war chief to Montreal to take command of a French regular battalion.

The Oswegatchies were not amused. When Ohquandageghte returned to Oswegatchie from Montreal, carrying belts of wampum from Onontio along with his commission, and attempted to assert his authority, he encountered immediate, total rejection. A sixty-person delegation, which included the clan mothers and chiefs, left immediately for Montreal, taking Ohquandageghte with them.

When they met with the governor general on 26 and 27 April 1757, the Oswegatchie delegates emphatically informed Vaudreuil that they considered neither his candidate nor his action to be appropriate. Ohquandageghte was yet not a Catholic,[3] which in itself made him unacceptable to the Christian Oswegatchies. Moreover, he was a recent arrival from Onondaga, and the Oswegatchies sharply criticized the French for expecting them to place too much trust, too quickly, in the League Iroquois in general and presumably Ohquandageghte in particular. Finally, Vaudreuil had no right whatever to appoint a chief. The Oswegatchies selected their leaders themselves based on their own criteria. The ability to work with the French, who were close allies, was an important qualification for leadership, but it was more important that a chief be acceptable to the Oswegatchies, and at this point Vaudreuil's candidate was not. His attempt to appoint a chief, said a French officer who was present, "appeared to them to be contrary to the rights of a free and warlike people that know only the chiefs that they had given themselves."

Confronted with a flagrant intrusion into their internal affairs, the Oswegatchies strongly reaffirmed their commitment to the French alliance, but unequivocally repudiated any suggestion that this alliance made them in any way subordinate to the French. In making this statement, their speaker referred to the ritual of baptism and the relationship of equality that it established between Amerindians and the French crown: "In causing ourselves to be reborn in the same baptismal water that washed the Great

Louis-Antoine de Bougainville, anon. Bougainville's diary, a priceless source of information about the Seven Years' War, contains a vivid account of the meeting between the Oswegatchie delegates and Vaudreuil. NAC C-100619

Onontio, we have not renounced our liberty, [or] our rights that we hold from the Master of Life." The Canadian Iroquois were allies of the French, but remained members of autonomous self-governing communities. In 1757 this autonomy was recognized, albeit unwillingly, by the governor general. By the close of the conference Vaudreuil had disavowed any intention of imposing a leader upon the Oswegatchies, claiming that he had merely commended the Onondaga chief to their notice as a suitable replacement for Collière. He added that "as soon as he had been baptized" Ohquandageghte would made a good leader.[4]

With the independence of Canadian Iroquois communities from outside interference thus reaffirmed, preparations for the expedition to Fort William Henry continued apace.[5] On 10 and 11 July Kanesetake and Kahnawake were graced with the presence of Montcalm, along with a number of his senior officers.[6] In council in each community, the chiefs of the Mohawks, Nipissings, and Algonquins were informed of the planned expedition to Fort William Henry and asked, in Vaudreuil's name, to take part. The Amerindians agreed, and informed the French officers as to the number of warriors that would be coming.

This conference was a success, but the private opinions of the French officers who attended gave a hint of problems to come. In public, their guest comported himself as befitted a respected allied war chief, consulting with his colleagues and taking part in the appropriate ceremonies. In his correspondence, on the other hand, Montcalm indulged in slighting comments about Amerindians and referred to himself as "obliged to pass my life with them in ceremonies that are as tedious as they are necessary."[7] The Seven Nations would not learn of the true opinions of their ally for another year.

In the meantime, the warriors were off for Lake Champlain. This year the Seven Nations would not be the only Amerindians fielding a major contingent. For the first time in the Seven Years' War, a significant body of warriors from the Great Lakes allies would be taking part in a campaign on the frontiers of New France. By May the westerners had begun to arrive in Montreal. Some encamped there and waited for the campaign to begin, others went directly to Lake Champlain.[8]

Vaudreuil would never have a better chance to take Fort William Henry. Amerindian scouts based at the new French outpost at Carillon had been generating a steady stream of prisoners for sale to the French. Voluble captives informed the French that the British commander-in-chief was about to employ his best regular regiments in a maritime expedition directed at Louisbourg or Quebec. This intelligence led Vaudreuil to take advantage of the temporary British weakness in New York by lunging south to take Fort William Henry.[9] A successful siege would drive the British back over the watershed that lay between Lake George and the Hudson River and clear the way for an invasion of northern New York. So, for the French, the campaign had an important strategic target that would enhance the security of Canada.

For the Canadian Iroquois, on the other hand, this represented the fourth annual invitation to join with the French in an expedition against the British that, if successful, would produce a harvest of prisoners, scalps, and matériel. In July, immediately following the conferences with Montcalm at Kahnawake and Kanesetake, warriors of the Canadian Iroquois travelled with the French general from Montreal to Carillon, where they arrived just in time to witness a major confrontation between the French and the Great Lakes nations, produced by different concepts of what constituted victory in war.

On 24 July four hundred Odawa, Ojibwa, Menominee, and Mississauga warriors, along with one hundred militiamen, encountered a British detachment of 350 provincials on Lake George. After an easy victory, the allies took 161 prisoners, then returned to Carillon with their trophies.[10] On the following day many of the westerners announced their intention of returning home. In taking prisoners, they had fulfilled their goals for going to war. Their campaign was thus over, before that of their French allies had even properly begun.

The French, reluctant to lose four hundred fighters, attempted to persuade the westerners to remain. Following a series of discussions that extended over two days, it was agreed that the prisoners would be placed in the custody of the French for the duration of the campaign in exchange for written receipts and guarantees that the captives would be properly cared for. The warriors, for their part, would stay with the allied army. Only forty Odawas and Mississaugas left with their captives and abandoned the expedition.[11] The remaining prisoners were taken by the French to Montreal on 26 July, the same day that the chiefs of all the nations met in council with Montcalm.

At this council, the chiefs listened to a statement of French intentions regarding the departure date and order of march of the expedition. Following Montcalm's exposition, they withdrew to prepare replies that would be delivered the next day.[12] When the council reconvened, Kisensik, a chief of the Nipissings of Kanesetake (Oka), responded for the Seven Nations. He began with a speech of welcome to the Great Lakes Amerindians, followed by a declaration of solidarity with the French. Montcalm made a formal reply, thanking the Amerindians for coming and asking them not to leave until the end of the campaign. Speakers for each nation responded favourably.

The council then turned to practical matters. The Canadian Iroquois, who were "originally proprietors of this region," consented to act as guides.[13] All agreed that about one-third of the Amerindians would march by land with the advance guard on 30 August and the remainder would follow on the lake with the main body of the allied army. Among the Seven Nations, a council of this nature would normally end with the communal singing of traditional war songs. However, out of courtesy to the Great Lakes nations, who did not share this practice, this concluding ceremony was omitted.[14]

Kisensik's speech of welcome to the western allies was notable as the first time that a representative of the Seven Nations spoke publicly of the possibility that a British occupation of Canada might lead to the loss of Amerindian lands. In 1755 a Kahnawake had described the war as one in which the French crown "makes war against the English."[15] Now Kisensik thanked the western allies for "coming in order to help us defend our lands against the English who want to usurp them."[16] Two years later the western-ers themselves would speak of coming to Canada to "to defend the lands of their brothers the [Canadian] Iroquois" against the British.[17] This concern for their land did not, however, influence the military and diplomatic con-duct of the Canadian Iroquois until late August of 1759, when a British incursion into the St. Lawrence valley had actually occurred and an inva-sion of northeastern Kanienkeh appeared imminent.

The allied army that marched on Fort William Henry was composed of 355 Canadian Iroquois, 1,061 other Amerindians and 6,753 French regulars and militiamen.[18] The advance guard left on schedule, but the Amerindians of this body experienced some difficulties with their French allies during the first day of the march. First, French officers attempted to deploy most of the Amerindians on the right flank. The Amerindians did not find this acceptable and took their accustomed place at the head of the column. Later on, during the night, as the Odawas were engaged in prayer and invo-cation, they were approached by an officious French officer who attempted to restrain them on the grounds that the British might hear. The Odawas replied that the Manitou would prevent their words from reaching the enemy, and were henceforth left in peace.[19]

Back at Carillon, those Amerindians who would travel over Lake George with the main body advanced twelve kilometres and awaited the French. Both the Seven Nations and the western allies then halted and made spiritual preparations for the campaign. The Seven Nations passed the day in confession before their Catholic priests. Those of the Great Lakes sought the same spiritual comfort from the ministrations of their shamans.[20]

On 3 August the advance guard, which now included all of the Amerindians, reached Fort William Henry. As they approached the fort from the northwest, the Amerindians encountered a number of small British outposts and became involved in several minor skirmishes that lasted until the defenders were forced to retire. As the Amerindians pressed forward, the British regulars and provincials were forced to abandon their bivouac southwest of the fort, tear down the tents, burn the huts, and with-draw to an entrenched camp. Beyond the camp lay the road to Fort Edward. Here, the warriors came upon the livestock of the garrison and proceeded

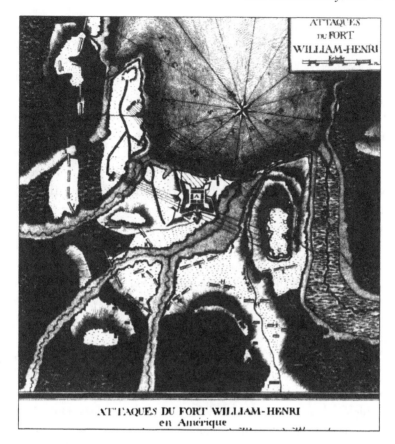

MAP 9. The siege of Fort William Henry in 1757

Rectangles representing French troops are half light and half dark, those representing Amerindians are solid blocks.

A. Fort William Henry
B. Opening of the trenches on the night of 4-5 August
C. Entrenched camp occupied by the English on the arrival of the French
D. Bay where the French landed their artillery
E. Battery of eight cannon and one mortar
F. Battery of ten cannon and one mortar
G. Battery of six guns
H. Position of Lévis during the siege
I. Position of the troops during the siege
K. Their position after the capitulation during the demolition of the entrenchments

Attaques du fort William-Henry en Amérique par les troupes françaises aux ordres du Marquis de Montcalm. Prise de ce fort le 7 Août 1757. Lieutenant Therbu, engraved by Contgen. NMC 7805

to round up over four hundred cattle, sheep, and horses, as well as killing numerous cattle and sheep. When one hundred provincials from the Massachusetts Regiment attempted to interfere with this activity the sortie was thrown back with a loss of nineteen killed and several wounded.

By noon the approaches to Fort William Henry had been secured and the British position surrounded. Shielded by Amerindians who watched the fort and the road to Fort Edward, the regular regiments took up position west of the fort, behind the site selected for the projected siege works. Lieutenant-Colonel George Monro, the commandant of Fort William Henry, was politely asked to surrender. Monro first politely refused, then opened fire on the besiegers with artillery.[21]

Once again, an allied siege had commenced with the investment of the enemy position by Amerindians. This time, in addition to penning in the British and covering the landing of the French, the Amerindians made a major contribution to the allied commissary. Their capture of the livestock of the garrison was, wrote the second in command of the French force, "of great service during the siege to all of the army who, by this means, had fresh meat to eat."[22]

The object of this siege, Fort William Henry, consisted of four bastions linked by curtain walls that formed a somewhat irregular square, about 120 metres across at its widest point. The ramparts were of earth, about 3 metres high, 4.5 metres broad, and faced with heavy logs. Only 450 men actually occupied the fort, which mounted seventeen cannon and three mortars and howitzers. The remainder of the garrison occupied the entrenched camp on a height to the east of the fort. This camp, armed with six field guns, was described by a French observer as "a fortified rock, faced with palisades supported by piles of stones." These positions were held by 2,339 regulars and provincials.[23]

On 4 August the Amerindians and a detachment of militiamen were deployed to contain the British in the entrenched camp and watch for reinforcements on the road to Fort Edward. The warriors in the forest waited "to overwhelm small parties on the Fort Edward road and neighbouring woods, to intercept all couriers and convoys not of great size and to warn us of major movements which might be made at Fort Edward in time for us [the allied army] to be prepared, and not be taken by surprise." Those at the fort and camp maintained "a fire of hell on the entrenchment ... a man could not appear in the open without attracting at least ten gunshots."[24] As for their allies, during the day French engineers and gunners reconnoitred the ground to the west of the fort where they planned to establish the first parallel and two batteries that would fire on the north bastion. Work began that night, shielded from British sorties by a party of Amerindians. Vaudreuil later said of their services that "if they had less inconvenienced the besieged the work [of the French sappers] during the night of 4 to 5 [August] would not have been so considerable."25

Not all of their French allies were this impressed. The next day Montcalm called a council at which he complained that the Amerindians were neglecting "the essential object of scouting" in favour of sniping and watching the progress of the siege.26 However eloquent Montcalm might have been, his credibility was undermined in advance when a party of Amerindian scouts snapped up a courier bearing a letter from Fort Edward promising assistance, should adequate reinforcements arrive in time. Montcalm, once he had finished his little tirade on the subject of scouting, informed the assembled Amerindians of the contents of this letter. The chiefs thanked the French general for the news and assured him that by daybreak they would be ready to comply with his wishes.

The intercepted letter was delivered to Monro under a flag of truce, along with the elaborately expressed good wishes of Montcalm and a hint that he might like to surrender. Monro, equally courteously, told Montcalm that if it was all the same to him, he would keep fighting for a while.27

On the night of 5-6 August the first French battery was completed, an event which the Amerindians had awaited with considerable impatience. For with the French busy digging and hauling, the chiefs and warriors felt that they "were paying the price of the war alone."28 Now, finally, their eccentric, industrious allies began to both play a more visible role in the siege and provide some real entertainment when eight canon and one mortar opened fire at dawn, "to the great satisfaction of the Natives." Such was their interest in the working of the "great muskets" that appreciative Amerindians surrounded the French gunners and seized every opportunity to wield linstocks to apply burning slow match to touchholes to fire off the cannon themselves.29

In the previous year this enthusiasm had either been less apparent or allowed to pass unrecorded, but at the siege of Fort William Henry, Amerindians found that they rather liked siege warfare. Or rather they liked watching their funny, busy allies at work. Firing off the guns might be great fun, but what really impressed them was the art of trench warfare. Here was something new and exciting, worth the trip from Kanesetake or Michilimakinac.

The siege works at William Henry were considerably more complex than those at Oswego and Amerindian observers were able to watch the curious, colourful, antlike French as they constructed a whole network of roads, parallels, communications trenches, batteries, magazines, and depots. But passively watching and learning about new ideas was not enough for energetic young men. After observing for a while, one group of warriors decided to put these new ideas into practice. Borrowing picks and shovels from the French, they dug a communications trench towards the entrenched camp. Work on this trench continued until they were within easy musket range of the enemy outpost. At this point, the warriors dug a parallel, from which they opened fire with muskets on 7 August.

All of this activity produced considerable alarm among the occupants of the camp. The Massachusetts Regiment, expecting an assault, stood "at their posts, with fixed bayonets."[30] About three hundred soldiers from the entrenched camp, who apparently did not fully appreciate the privilege of watching a cross-cultural exchange of ideas and technology in action, rather crassly attempted to interrupt the experiment with a major sortie. After a prolonged skirmish, the Amerindians forced the British to retreat.[31]

This interest in new ideas and new technology was characterized by French observers as a childlike fascination with the achievements of a superior civilization. In fact, French prowess at siegecraft excited admiration rather than awe among the Amerindians. Their allies had one way of making war, were good at it, and thus worthy of respect. But this in no way diminished their high opinion of their own military customs and abilities. As the assembled chiefs informed Montcalm in the course of the council on 5 July, "you have brought into this place the art of war of the world beyond the great lake; we know that in that art you are a grand master, but for the science and the art of scouting, for the knowledge of these forests and the way of making war here we have the advantage over you."[32]

Furthermore, the Amerindians were not the only ones taking an interest in the customs of an ally, and their fascination with the French was returned with interest. If they had found the officers as worthy of attention as the gunners and sappers, Amerindian observers could have noted a typical post-Gutenburg European response to a novel situation - the attempt to convert a new experience into a best-seller. The concentration of metropolitan regiments at William Henry drew a whole swarm of followers of the "and-then-I-said-to-Montcalm-'Wolfe-is-trapped-just-charge-down-the-hill'" school of memoir writing. So as the Amerindians watched the French, a good many metropolitan officers watched the Amerindians, and jotted down

anecdotes and descriptions of their companions-in-arms to fascinate antici-
pated readers at home.

As the allies continued to watch one another, the siege proceeded on
schedule. By the morning of the seventh a second battery of eight cannon,
two howitzers, and one mortar opened fire on the entrenched camp. That
evening, work began on a communications trench leading forward towards
the fort and the proposed site for a new parallel and battery. In the meantime, the fire from the batteries of the first parallel was devastating for the
garrison. Within two days, reported a senior British artillery officer, "the
guns and mortars in the fort, except some 6 and 4 pounders, were rendered
useless." At the same time, firing into the entrenched camp inflicted many
casualties.[33]

The great guns were not alone in hammering the fort. Regardless of
Montcalm's killjoy objections,

> the Natives posted themselves in sight of the embrasures
> of the fort and aimed their gun shots so well that the gun-
> ners abandoned them [the embrasures] without which it
> would not have been possible to work in the marsh. The
> fear that the English have of our Natives who would not
> cede to the grenadiers the advantage of mounting the first
> assault contributed no less than the speed of our
> [siege]works and the favourable circumstances to the
> reduction of the place.[34]

The Amerindians did not allow these diversions to slacken their watch on
the enemy: "each day Native activity and courage multiplied the prisoners
... it was not possible for an enemy to take a step outside the place, without
being exposed to captivity or death, so alert were the Natives."[35]

Secure behind the Amerindian shield, the allied besiegers were
making steady progress. On the night of 7-8 August the French brought
their communications trench to within 200 metres of the fort and began a
second parallel. By the evening of the eighth, the time was fast approaching
when the garrison would be in a position to consider an honourable surrender.

The opening of the second parallel proved to be decisive. With the
greater part of the British artillery already disabled by existing French batteries, the construction of a new set of artillery emplacements caused the
officers of the garrison to decide that the time had arrived to prepare for

surrender. With "no assistance to be expected from Fort Edward, the fort not able to hold out, and our retreat cut off," the garrison could surrender honourably. On the morning of 9 August, at 5:00 a.m., the senior officers met to draw up terms for a capitulation. Two hours later, the white flag was raised over Fort William Henry.[36] A British officer rode out to meet the French and returned with Montcalm's aide-de-camp. The European officers quickly reached agreement on terms.

The garrison of the fort and entrenched camp would be granted the honours of war, retain their weapons and personal effects, and be escorted to Fort Edward by French troops. In return, they agreed not to serve again for eighteen months and guaranteed that within three months all allied prisoners held by the British in North America would be released. The artillery and stores of the forts would become the property of the French crown. Montcalm's envoy raised two other issues. For their own safety, he asked that the British destroy all of their public and private stocks of wine, brandy, and other liquor and that the garrison remain within the entrenched camp until their departure for Fort Edward.[37]

The Amerindians had been relegated to the status of bystanders as these negotiations took place. Only after a final agreement on articles of capitulation had been reached between the Europeans were the chiefs invited to a council with Montcalm. The chiefs were informed of the terms under which the British had agreed to surrender and asked to give their consent and take steps to ensure that the younger warriors would not violate the capitulation. According to the French, the Amerindian leaders assured Montcalm that they approved of all that he had done and that they would "restrain the young men from committing any disorder."[38] In consequence, the capitulation was signed at 11:00 a.m., and Fort William Henry formally surrendered.

Just what was actually said at the council between the chiefs and Montcalm is open to question. The French appear to have chosen to believe that the acquiescence of the chiefs meant complete acceptance of the intra-European accord. Subsequent events suggest that the Amerindians were rather more equivocal. Whatever interpretation was placed upon the words of the chiefs by the French, acceptance of these terms by the Amerindians would have meant repudiating any hope of attaining success in their own terms. In any case, their actions quickly indicated that they placed a very different interpretation upon the capitulation than their allies, and did not consider this agreement to apply to them. Siegecraft was fun to watch but war was war. Successful war meant acquiring prisoners, scalps, and matériel.

This was simply not going to happen if they allowed their rightful trophies of victory to prance merrily away, carrying with them immense quantities of material and escorted by their inexplicably dense - albeit entertaining - allies.

In 1750 one of Vaudreuil's predecessors as governor general had attempted to prevent a war party of Kanesetakes from travelling west to attack the Foxes. The French at the time were meeting with a Fox delegation in Montreal, with whom they hoped to negotiate a peace. When asked to cancel their expedition, the Kanesetakes responded:

> Great Onontio who lives beyond the great lake had ordered that this nation be destroyed, that in consequence of this order Mr. de Beauharnois [the governor general] placed an axe in their hands to strike the Fox, and that since this time, he has not removed it, and thus he is considered to be still [of] the same will.[39]

By accepting the axe, the Kanesetakes had formally declared war according to the metaphors of Amerindian diplomacy. In so doing, they had made a formal commitment to Onontio and their commitment stood, regardless of the actions of the French. The French might have made peace, but that was entirely their concern. The Kanesetakes had not, and until they made a ceremonial return of the axe to Onontio, they remained at war. That the Amerindians conceded the right of their allies to make their own decisions regarding when to fight and when to stop was neither here nor there with regard to their own actions.[40] This reasoning would seem to have been followed in 1757. As they had in 1754 and 1756, the warriors continued hostilities after the French had agreed to stop fighting, and persisted until success had been achieved according to their own definition of victory.

Following the signing of the capitulation, a traditional European military ritual occurred as French grenadiers took possession of the fort and relieved British guards at the gates, the powder magazine, and the provision stores. The 442 regulars and provincials of the garrison left the fort without incident, carrying their weapons and personal effects. They marched to the entrenched camp, where two hundred French regulars had taken post in order to secure the safety of the British. The British and French expected that the garrison would depart the next morning, accompanied by a French escort.

The Amerindians, however, continued to wage their own war against the British. Even as French grenadiers were acting out their part in the ceremonial relief of the guards on the gate, Amerindians entered the fort through embrasures. Once within, they killed the sick and wounded soldiers who had been left behind and engaged in extensive gathering of matériel.[41] They then turned their attention to the entrenched camp. Here the warriors confronted British troops who remained in organized units, retained their weapons, and were located within a fortified position. Yet when the warriors began to enter the camp in the early afternoon, they found the British incapable of defending themselves. Once inside, the Amerindians began to collect the possessions of members of the garrison: "They soon got over the works, and began to plunder many small things, as brass kettles &c. &c. They were all this day very troublesome, stealing the baggage of the officers & what they could lay their hands on."[42] Some of the British resisted, others attempted to buy off the Amerindians with rum or money. Most remained passive.

When the French regulars detailed to protect the British proved inadequate to the task, Montcalm himself, together with a number of chiefs and senior officers, hurried to the entrenchment and attempted to calm the situation. His intervention cannot have been very effective, since the disturbances lasted into the evening.

The incidents in the entrenched camp must have been relatively minor, for they did not prevent European officers from engaging in customary courtesy visits. That afternoon, wrote a French engineer, "many of us went to visit, in the camp, the English officers, who, according to custom during a suspension of arms," entertained their guests to the best of their ability under the circumstances. The engineer, out of professional curiosity, asked for a plan of the fort and entrenchments and received one from an obliging British colleague.[43]

With the situation tense, Monro and Montcalm first decided that the British should march at midnight, rather than waiting until the morning of the ninth as they had planned. The garrison paraded and had actually began to march out the gate when word arrived of an Amerindian ambush on the road. This warning proved to be without foundation, but it led the European commanders to decide to defer the departure of the garrison until the next morning.[44]

Early in the morning of 10 August numerous Amerindians, most armed only with axes, some "even unarmed," returned to the entrenchment.[45] Brushing past the French guards, they entered the camp and began

Iroquois Warrior, by Jacques Grasset de Saint-Sauveur, engraver J. Laroque, c. 1795. When the garrison of Fort William Henry came into contact with Amerindians after the capitulation, most of the regulars and provincials very likely perceived them as resembling this caricature. Note the contrast between this unflattering image and the graciously benign portrait of Louis-Antoine de Bougainville earlier in the chapter. NAC C-003163

to harass the garrison just as the British regiments were forming up and preparing to march. Although outnumbered by armed enemies, the warriors appropriated weapons, clothing, and personal effects from the soldiers and civilians inside the camp. Once again, their seizures of matériel encountered no resistance.

Colonel Monro complained to French officers at the camp, who suggested that the British surrender their baggage in hopes that this would satisfy the Amerindians. Monro consented and the British proceeded to abandon their chests and other heavy baggage, which they could not in any event have taken with them in the absence of adequate numbers of horses and wagons. Frightened soldiers went further, and "immediately delivered every thing up to them, except their arms and the clothes on our backs, which we hoped they would suffer us to carry off. Instead of which they took our hats, and swords from us, and began to strip us ... [taking] the drums, halberds, and even the firelocks from the soldiers."[46]

Not all of those present in the camp were formed up with the regiments. When the column assembled, neither the British nor the French made any provision for the transportation or protection of the sick and wounded. Those who were not "able to crawl into the ranks" were left to their own devices.[47] While the collection of matériel from the garrison was still in progress, Amerindians inside the camp began to kill these invalids, whose afflictions made them unsuitable as prisoners. They next entered the ranks of regiments which were waiting to march and made prisoner both the small number of African-American slaves and Amerindians who accompanied the British force. The regular and provincial regiments made no attempt to protect their fellow soldiers, their human property, or their Amerindian allies.

However, these killings were enough to propel the British column into movement. It had been agreed that the British would assemble and march out at 9:00 a.m., escorted by a detachment of French regulars. Instead, so alarmed were the British soldiers that they left before the appointed time and before the French escort was entirely assembled and deployed.[48] In so doing, they rejected the advice of French officers who strongly recommended waiting until the remainder of the escort arrived.

The premature departure of the British wrecked Montcalm's carefully laid plan for ensuring their safety. The French general had arranged for the chiefs, interpreters, and colonial officers who had served with the Amerindians throughout the campaign to accompany the British column, so that they would be present to head off trouble before it could begin. Their efforts were to be supported by a detachment of regulars. The greater part of the escort, however, was a long way off and the chiefs, interpreters, and colonial officers nowhere in sight when the march commenced.

The British began their march through the gates in reasonably good order, assisted by that part of the escort that had arrived at the entrenchment, which marched at the head of the column. The captain of grenadiers who commanded the escort "himself stood at the gate of the camp to facilitate the passage of the garrison."[49] Nonetheless, the British had to push their way through a crowd of Amerindians and it was only "with great difficulty, [that] the troops got from the retrenchment."[50] The Amerindians did not interfere with the French soldiers who preceded the column and allowed the regular and provincial regiments to depart more or less intact. But as the last regiment cleared the gates, the Amerindians fell upon the tail of the column and began to seize prisoners.

At this point, British officers finally began to organize resistance. The regiments of the column were ordered to halt, "which was at last done in great confusion."[51] Unfortunately for the British, the seizures of prisoners at the rear led the hindmost troops to flee towards the front instead of turning about and holding off the Amerindians. This left a gap between the armed regiments and the non-combatants still in the camp, who were thus abandoned to their fate. Worse, as they ran, the soldiers from the rear crashed into those who were forming up, and the ensuing impact threw the entire column into confusion. At the same time, as soon as those in front heard of what was happening in the rear, they broke and fled forward. According to one participant, the Amerindians "fell upon the rear of our men, who running in upon the front put the whole to a most precipitate flight."[52]

Chaos ensued. Instead of forming up in ranks with fixed bayonets, soldiers took fright and scurried for safety, throwing away what remained of their arms, baggage, and even their clothing. The Amerindians, said one British officer, "struck so great a panic into the troops, who knew not where it would end, that all efforts proved ineffectual to prevent their running away in a very confused and irregular manner." From an organized body of armed soldiers, the garrison of Fort William Henry became "a crowd of unfortunates who ran at random, some towards the woods, others towards the French tents, these towards the fort, those to all the places that seemed to promise refuge."[53]

The Amerindians pursued. Individual warriors and a number of Amerindian women began to push their way into the column and drag out passive and unresisting captives. French observers watched with incredulous contempt as armed British soldiers "allowed themselves to be taken like sheep, in the midst of their battalions, armed, and taken away without making the least resistance ... If they had presented themselves with fixed bayonets and kept in order, not a Native would have dared to approach."[54] The pursuit continued for about seven kilometres along the road to Fort Edward. Before they abandoned the chase, the Amerindians rounded up seven hundred prisoners, mostly from the rear of the column, and killed perhaps thirty to fifty persons who were either sick or wounded or resisted capture.[55]

The French escort did what it could to defend the British. "Our escort," wrote one metropolitan officer, "although much too small, protected as many as they could, principally the officers. But, forced to keep in formation, to make themselves respected, it was possible to shelter only those who found themselves nearby."[56] Their efforts were supported by numerous French officers, including Montcalm and his senior subordinates who hurried to the road where they attempted to restore order.

In the ensuing scramble, two French grenadiers from the escort were wounded when they placed themselves between Amerindians and potential prisoners. Some of the British found refuge in an outpost held by French soldiers about a kilometre and a half from the fort. Others were released when Amerindians were intercepted by French regulars and compelled to hand over their prisoners. Priests, interpreters, and colonial officers obtained the release of several captives. Yet all of this effort produced only a relatively small number of liberated prisoners.[57]

More effective if less dramatic was the intervention of several Amerindian chiefs. As a degree of calm returned to the road to Fort Edward, they spoke to those warriors who had acquired prisoners and persuaded them to release their trophies. The chiefs then approached the French and "made a present to Montcalm of 400 of these prisoners."[58] The numbers released by French efforts were by comparison insignificant. After the intervention of the chiefs, a further three hundred prisoners remained in Amerindian hands. Other casualties of the siege included forty-one members of the garrison killed during the siege, and sixty-one wounded. The allies lost seventeen killed and forty wounded.[59]

With prisoners, scalps, and matériel now safely in hand, the greater part of the Amerindian contingent left later that afternoon for Montreal. A day later, only a few warriors from the Seven Nations remained with the French.

The fifteen hundred Britons who had escaped captivity marched on to Fort Edward with a French escort. Their officers, however, elected to remain behind with the French. The most senior, including Monro, became Montcalm's honoured guests. Other French officers looked after their British counterparts, with whom they shared their tents, provisions, and clothing. The enlisted prisoners who had been rescued by the French or returned by the Amerindians were escorted to the entrenched camp. Stripped naked by their captors, they were supplied with clothing that had been purchased from the Amerindians by French soldiers. This time, they were guarded by the La Reine Brigade and four brigades of militia who camped nearby, ready to intervene. On 15 August the four hundred returned prisoners, this time escorted by 250 French regulars, set out once more for Fort Edward, where they arrived without incident.[60]

Of the three hundred prisoners who were taken to Montreal, a few were killed en route by the western allies. Most of the remainder were ransomed by the governor general, along with the 161 prisoners taken by the Great Lakes nations on 24 August for whom receipts had been issued and a number of others taken in operations in the Lake Champlain area. Once redeemed, the prisoners were taken to Quebec and from there sent to Halifax by sea.[61]

For Amerindian participants, the campaign of 1757 ended on a high note with a hugely successful seizure of prisoners and matériel. In achieving this triumph they overcame both the resistance of their enemies and the interference of their friends. Of the two, the British proved the lesser obstacle. Indeed, the actions of the British proved to be as significant as those of the Amerindians in determining the course of events on 10 and 11 August. Most of the human trophies collected by Amerindians were soldiers from metropolitan and colonial regiments who retained their weapons and freedom of action after the capitulation and might have been expected to defend themselves. Instead, they surrendered their possessions, abandoned civilians and wounded comrades to their fate, and finally fled in disorder.

The alternatives open to the garrison are suggested by the actions of a French garrison under similar conditions. Following the capitulation of Fort Niagara in 1759, Amerindians attached to the British began to harass the garrison, and attempted to appropriate their weapons. The French held together, stood to arms, and prepared to defend themselves. The Amerindians backed off and a potentially serious situation ended before it began.[62] Compared to the performance of the disciplined, bellicose French regulars and militiamen, that of the garrison of Fort William Henry was abjectly inept. Amerindian imperatives may have demanded that prisoners be taken, but it was the passivity, disorganization, and irresolution of the garrison that made it possible for the Amerindians to do so with such ease.

During the campaign of 1757 the surrender of a fort once again represented a success for the French and failure for the Amerindians. The expulsion of the British from a strategic location on a major invasion route was a signal victory for France.[63] To do so without the opportunity to collect prisoners, scalps, and matériel represented absolute failure for the Amerindians. The warriors naturally refused to accept this failure, and prolonged hostilities until they too had achieved success. This difficulty might have been avoided if both groups had understood and respected the military aspirations of the other. Instead, each party refused to recognize the other's definition of victory as legitimate. Amerindians did not respect the French acceptance of the British surrender; Frenchmen did not consider the subsequent seizure of prisoners and property to be a legitimate act of war.

This lack of mutual understanding and respect appeared in every allied campaign of the war. However, under most circumstances, Amerindians could resolve this conflict by simply ignoring the French and going their own way. At Fort Bull in 1756, Canadian Iroquois politely refused to continue to accompany the French once they had fulfilled their own goals. If the French chose to continue an expedition after prisoners had been secured, that was their right, but Amerindians felt no obligation to participate. This pattern was repeated endlessly in raids and minor campaigns, to the extent that even recently arrived metropolitan officers were aware that once Amerindians had taken a prisoner, the campaign was over for them. Alternatively, at Monongahela and the ambush on the road to Lake George, engagements fought in the open forest rather than centred on a fort, Amerindians were able to wage their parallel war without interference from their allies. With combatants scattered here and there in the midst of a forest, warriors could round up prisoners and obtain scalps and matériel whenever and wherever they found them, regardless of the decisions or actions of the French.

Sieges, however, posed unique problems for Amerindians in pursuit of victory. At Fort William Henry in 1757, as at Fort Necessity in 1754 and Oswego in 1756, Amerindians found that their ability to engage freely in parallel war was constrained by the presence of a fort. A battlefield after a battle belonged to whoever occupied a given part of it, European or Amerindian. A fort, on the other hand, gave Europeans control over the post-siege field and allowed them to strike private deals among themselves regarding access to prisoners and property. These negotiations and agreements invariably excluded Amerindians, and took no account of their goals and sensibilities. Neither walls and entrenchments nor intra-European agreements, however, were strong enough to prevent Amerindians from continuing to fight until their criteria for victory had been met.

This prolongation of hostilities appalled the French but did not detract from the success of the campaign. The ultimate result of the siege of Fort William Henry was a double victory, one for the Amerindians and one for the French. The confusion and misunderstanding that accompanied the achievement of these victories should not obscure the fact that in the course of the siege Amerindians and Frenchmen succeeded in working together, each using their own particular abilities to contribute to the overall success of the allied army.

CHAPTER 7

FORT CARILLON, 1758

A fter the siege warfare of 1756 and 1757, the campaign of 1758 was notable for the return to a more comfortable and conventional style of war for the Canadian Iroquois. For Amerindians, the predominant actions of this campaign were large-scale raids conducted without conflict with the French over military customs and objectives. Nonetheless, the campaign of 1758 was also notable for the absence of the Great Lakes nations from the frontiers of Canada, the first battle won by the French without significant Amerindian assistance, and momentary discord with the French provoked by Montcalm. Yet before any of these developments came to pass, the year was marked by the single most spectacular feat of arms by an individual Canadian Iroquois that appears in the records of the Seven Years' War. This occurred in the course of an Oswegatchie raid on German Flats.

The growth of a flourishing trade between Oswegatchie and New York traders based in German Flats had not prevented the Oswegatchies from organizing a series of expeditions against British settlements along the Mohawk River in the late winter and spring of 1758.[1] In April of that year one of these expeditions nearly collapsed when the greater part of the participants chose to return home shortly after leaving Oswegatchie. One war chief, however, persisted, and persuaded two other fighters to join him.

This chief was Ohquandageghte, Vaudreuil's former candidate for a seat on the Oswegatchie council. Accompanied by his two followers, he continued southward until the night that they reached the first building on the outskirts of German Flats. There Ohquandageghte stripped off his clothing and, using a supply of black paint that he had brought from Oswegatchie, proceeded to cover his body with a series of elaborate designs. Thus ornamented, Ohquandageghte led his party to a low window in the wall of the house. Looking inside, the Amerindians saw eleven men, a detachment of

New York provincials, responsible for the security of the approaches to German Flats. Instead of keeping a lookout, however, the New Yorkers were peacefully gambling the night away. Their muskets had been left to one side, leaning against the same wall that contained the window.

Confronted with eleven enemy fighters, Ohquandageghte proposed an immediate attack. His companions, however, demurred, on the not unreasonable grounds that they were heavily outnumbered. After a few moments of unsuccessful exhortation, Ohquandageghte declared that "when I left [Oswegatchie], I staked my life; so I am going to attack, you can follow me, if you like."[2] As good as his word, he immediately flung himself through the window alone.

Ohquandageghte's motive for this single-handed attack is not recorded, but it is possible to speculate. His decision to paint himself in black, a colour associated with mourning and death, in place of the customary red, and his statement that he had "staked his life" instead of making probable survival a prerequisite for attack, both suggest that this venture held a special meaning for the young and ambitious war chief.[3] Less than a year before, Ohquandageghte's aspirations to higher status and leadership had been publicly rejected by the entire community. He had been described in open council as "this Onondaga who is not of the faith and who claims to be our chief."[4] His solitary assault may have represented an attempt to retrieve his standing among the Oswegatchies with a single dramatic exploit or die in the attempt.

In any event, Ohquandageghte's considerable panache did not impair his tactical judgment. By entering through the window, he placed himself between his enemies and their weapons. "Almost five feet nine inches tall, young and energetic," Ohquandageghte was a formidable opponent at any time.[5] Materializing out of the darkness, completely naked and shouting war cries, he was a thoroughly disconcerting adversary. As Ohquandageghte snatched up their muskets and flung them out the window, the gamblers abandoned their cards or dice, leaped to their feet, and fled to the farthest corner of the room where they cowered fearfully. Seconds after entering the guard house, the lone warrior had his enemies surrounded.

Once muskets ceased to fly out the window, his two comrades followed Ohquandageghte into the guard house. They found their war chief brandishing his knife at the thoroughly intimidated New Yorkers. Shaken but otherwise unharmed, the provincials quietly allowed themselves to be taken prisoner. The three Oswegatchies bound the captives and led them away to Oswegatchie and Montreal.

The French officer who recorded the raid in his memoirs considered this feat so incredible as to be unbelievable, but eleven prisoners paraded through the streets of Oswegatchie and Montreal represented uncontrovertible proof of Ohquandageghte's valour. If this attack did indeed represent an attempt to restore his position at Oswegatchie, it was entirely successful. When Ohquandageghte next appears in the documentation of the war, he is "that famous Native who took the English guard post by leaping through the window."[6]

Ohquandageghte's adventure might have been considered to be a good omen for the coming allied campaign. Yet even as he marched his prisoners back from German Flats, an important component of the Amerindian-French alliance system was shaken to its foundations as the western allies withdrew from the war.

In 1757 the Seven Nations had gone to war alongside a large contingent of warriors from the Great Lakes region. Travelling to Montreal and Fort William Henry, however, brought the westerners into contact with thousands of British and French regulars and provincials, some of whom were afflicted with smallpox. The Seven Nations were survivors of the 1755 epidemic, and thus largely immune to the smallpox virus. Those from the west were not: "All of these peoples, having descended for the siege of the fort [William Henry] ... carried smallpox back with them to their country where it made astonishing ravages."[7] A century later, this epidemic was remembered among the Odawas of Michilimakinac as an appalling catastrophe that virtually destroyed their community.

Although they knew as little as the French of the existence of microscopic viruses, the Great Lakes Amerindians were well aware that they had been infected during the campaign of 1757. Since the French had invited the westerners to the area where they had contracted smallpox, and Amerindian "custom in this situation is to say that the nation that invited them has given them an evil medicine," they held the French responsible for this catastrophe.[8] As a result, the Great Lakes nations temporarily withdrew from active participation in the war and did not send a contingent to serve with the Seven Nations and the French in the Lake Champlain area. The warriors of the Great Lakes would return in force to the St. Lawrence valley in 1759, but in the meantime, fighting on the frontiers of Canada was left to the Seven Nations and the French.

The campaign of 1758 began for the Seven Nations with an invitation to take part in a massive raid down the Mohawk River into western New York. This raid was to be conducted by about one thousand warriors of the

François Gaston, duc de Lévis, engraved by J. Porreau. Respected by Amerindians and Europeans, metropolitans and colonials, François de Lévis was the outstanding European general on either side during the Seven Years' War in North America. NAC C-009141

Seven Nations and sixteen hundred French regulars and militiamen. François de Lévis, second-in-command of the troupes de terre in Canada and the outstanding metropolitan officer of the war, had been selected by Vaudreuil to command the French component of this expedition.

After travelling to the site of Oswego and ascending the Oswego River, the allied army would portage at the Oneida Carrying Place and proceed down the Mohawk River, raiding British settlements and living off the country. Vaudreuil hoped that this venture would forestall any British movements on Lake Champlain by diverting British attention to the upper Mohawk settlements, provide a show of force that would favourably influence the League Iroquois, and prevent the British from rebuilding Oswego.

In June of 1758 the Seven Nations proceeded to the outlet of Lake Ontario, where they paused and awaited their French allies.[9]

These allies never reached Lake Ontario. On 29 June word reached the governor general in Montreal that a British army was en route to Fort Carillon. After two years on the offensive, the French were back to responding to British movements rather than taking the initiative themselves. The Mohawk valley operation was abruptly cancelled and the allied strike force recalled and diverted to Carillon.

But only the metropolitan regulars arrived in time to be present as two European armies met at Carillon on 8 July. The British force, commanded by James Abercromby, consisted of fifteen thousand regulars and provincials. They confronted Montcalm and three thousand metropolitan regulars, four hundred colonial regulars and militiamen, and fifteen Amerindians.[10]

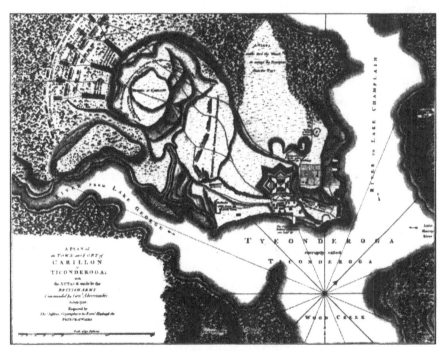

MAP 10. The Battle of Carillon, 1758.
The wide gap between the French entrenchment and Lake Champlain that offered the British an unobstructed passage to the French rear is clearly visible on this map. "A Plan of the Town and Fort of Carillon or Ticonderoga with the Attack made by the British army commanded by Gen Abercrombie, 8 July, 1758," anon., engraver Thomas Jeffreys. NMC 7744

The ensuing battle was a stunning display of mutual incompetence. Montcalm abandoned a strong position on the shore of Lake George to occupy an improvised fortification that could only be defended from an attack from the front. Abercromby, faced with a position open to attack on the flanks and vulnerable to artillery, launched a frontal assault with unsupported infantry on Montcalm's entrenchment. Firing from cover behind a barricade of tree trunks, the French easily beat off a series of increasingly desperate attacks, systematically shooting down wave after wave of British soldiers. They were unexpectedly assisted in this process by the British provincials who, in the words of one British regular officer, "came up to sustain us, but they began to fire at such a distance they killed several of our men."[11] Abercromby, for his part, succeeded brilliantly in demonstrating why Amerindians believed that frontal assaults on fortifications were not a good idea. After suffering heavy casualties, the British withdrew and returned to New York.[12]

All of this was neither here nor there as far as the Seven Nations were concerned. Too far west to make it to Carillon in time for the battle, they were in transit during the major engagement of the campaign. Not until 11 July did the first group of three hundred Canadian Iroquois, Abenakis, Hurons, and Odawas reach Carillon.[13] Following their arrival, the chiefs met in council with Montcalm on 12 July and formally congratulated the French general for his victory. This courtesy was not appreciated by the metropolitan officers. Montcalm's aide-de-camp wrote: "Councils upon councils with the Natives; mosquitos one thousand times more troublesome than the real ones."[14]

One of these "mosquitos" may have been Atiatonharongwen. Now eighteen, he was "tall and athletic, broad shouldered and strongly built, with a very dark complexion, and somewhat curly hair." After serving his apprenticeship on the Ohio, Lake Ontario, and Lake Champlain frontiers, Atiatonharongwen's growing reputation as a fighter and his ability to speak French had won him his first position of responsibility, as the leader of a small Kahnawake war party that joined the allied force at Carillon at some point in July.[15]

Whether Atiatonharongwen was among them is unknown, but on the sixteenth, the three warriors then present on the frontier, together with two hundred Canadians, left Carillon and travelled to Fort Halfway Brook, a minor outpost between Fort Edward and Lake George. Here, on 20 July, they became involved in skirmish with a convoy escort, reinforced from the garrison. The war party returned on 21 July with twenty scalps and eight prisoners, but had lost one Canadian Iroquois killed and two wounded.[16]

Prior to their departure, a number of warriors, mostly Abenakis, began to display that whimsical indifference to western concepts of property that so impressed the philosophes of the Enlightenment. The uninspiring rations of salt pork and biscuit that Amerindians drew from the French commissary could not begin to compete with venison dipped in maple sugar, and these fighters began to consider alternative sources of food. They did not have to look far, since French officers, more willing to risk death than endure inconvenience, demanded high standards of comfort in the field and went to war accompanied by private supplies of alcohol and food, including herds of livestock. Under these conditions, it is perhaps not surprising that numerous warriors began to supplement their military rations with various items from the personal stores of metropolitan officers. This naturally created a certain tension among their allies, who accused them of "making war on our sheep, on our chickens, on our brandy, and on all of our provisions."[17]

None of this encouraged Montcalm to think kindly of his allies. Furthermore, the general and his staff considered the presence of the Amerindians to be part of a sinister plot by Vaudreuil to discredit the victor of Carillon. After the battle, Montcalm and many of his officers began to display a distinct tinge of paranoia. Judging from their correspondance, they believed that the metropolitan regulars had been deliberately abandoned by Vaudreuil to face a massive enemy force alone. Montcalm himself went so far as to write that the soldiers and officers of the troupes de terre at Carillon "say loudly that M. de Vaudreuil wanted to have us slaughtered by giving me so few men to face a real danger, while he uselessly retained a corps of two to three thousand men sent to attempt to accomplish something in the country of the Five Nations where five hundred men would be sufficient."[18]

Vaudreuil, whose post as governor general of New France made him commander-in-chief of the French armed forces in North America, had spectacular bad luck with his metropolitan generals during most of the Seven Years' War. Not until Dieskau and Montcalm were succeeded in September 1759 by Lévis did he find a competent field commander, respected by Amerindians and Frenchmen alike, to whom he could safely entrust the direction of the war. In the meantime, by 1758 Vaudreuil had just about lost patience with Montcalm, who had only undertaken the siege of Oswego as the result of considerable pressure from colonial officers, had

Montcalm and Languedoc Regiment, Fort Carillon, July 1758, by James C. Tilly, 1961. NAC C-020695

failed to follow up his victories at Fort William Henry and Carillon, and was actively conspiring to replace Vaudreuil as governor general.[19]

The metropolitans believed that the dispatch of Amerindians to Carillon, along with orders to use them to disrupt British communications, was intended to saddle them with "a crowd of passers-by, who serve only to occasion a frightful consumption of supplies." Vaudreuil could then claim that Montcalm had been reinforced, but had failed to use these forces effectively. "This," wrote one close associate of the metropolitan general, "is the secret thrust ['botte,' a fencing term, in this case implying a stab in the back] of the year."[20]

The metropolitan regulars further considered the battle of Carillon a turning point in the conduct of the war. For the first time they had won a victory on their own, without the support of Amerindians or colonials. In their opinion, "what must excite the greatest admiration and public joy is that not a single Native contributed to this great event, something that has never happened in this country."[21] This led to a new perspective among metropolitan officers regarding warfare in North America. In the wake of the battle, Montcalm's aide-de-camp exulted in a much-cited passage "Now war is established on a European footing. Plans of campaign, armies, artillery, sieges, and battles. It is no longer a case of striking a blow, but of conquering or being conquered. What a revolution! What a change!"[22] Another staff officer declared, with less exuberance but more precision, that "War is now conducted here as in Europe."[23]

After Carillon, the metropolitans discarded the assumption that a European army needed Amerindian assistance to win a battle in North America. From this point on, a new theme enters the Amerindian-French discourse - the assertion by metropolitan officers that the alliance was more a nuisance than a necessity. This became manifestly apparent on 16 July, when a second Seven Nations contingent appeared on the scene. This time, the reinforcements were two hundred Kanesetakes, Nipissings, and Algonquins.[24]

Like the first group, they followed the dictates of protocol and met with Montcalm soon after their arrival. Their reception, however, was rather more exciting than the usual ceremonial exchange of compliments. After congratulating Montcalm for his victory, they received the following reply: "You have come at a time when I have no more need of you. Have you only come to see dead bodies? Go behind the fort and you will find them. I do not need you to defeat the English."[25] This sort of language in a formal meeting between leaders of nations who had been close allies since the previous century was as unprecedented as it was impolitic. Even the colonial officers who threatened the Ohio nations with annihilation in 1753 had been more polite. The nonplussed Amerindians, accustomed to dignity and courtesy in council, were shocked but restrained. They quietly took their leave and met to discuss the matter among themselves.

When they again met with Montcalm on the following day the chiefs raised the possibility that they might form a raiding party to strike at British lines of communications above Fort Edward, a measure wholly in accord with Vaudreuil's policy. Montcalm's response, however, was even less diplomatic than before: "He struck his table with his fist, and said to us you will not go, go to the devil if you are not content." Moreover, the general's tone and gestures were such that the Amerindians later noted that "we did not need interpreters to immediately understand his words." The chiefs replied that they were a little surprised at his anger, as they had given no provocation, then left to meet and once more discuss this remarkable behaviour.[26]

With friends like this, the Seven Nations didn't particularly need enemies. A metropolitan officer recorded their opinions after these meet-

The Indians giving a talk to Col. Bouquet in a conference at a council fire, ... 1764, by Benjamin West, engraved by Grignion, 1868. Councils were much more formal this engraving suggests, with participants seated in a circle and following rigid protocol. NAC C-000299

ings, reporting that "they complained that they were not received as usual; that it seems that the victory won without them had made the French overproud, that they thought they could do without them."[27] One young chief, probably Ganetagon, "drunk with rage" after being forcibly ejected from Montcalm's headquarters, wanted to leave for Montreal immediately. He was restrained by his colleagues, for simply abandoning the army without taking formal leave would have represented a serious breach of protocol.[28]

Confronted with grotesquely insulting behaviour on the part of a senior allied leader, the chiefs responded calmly and rationally. Judging from their actions, their goal was to contain the situation and not allow Montcalm's disturbing speeches to escalate into a diplomatic incident that would undermine their relationship with the French. They might have a problem with Montcalm, but their primary relationship was with Onontio in Montreal, not his general in the field. Consequently, they resolved to return to Montreal, meet with Vaudreuil, and allow him to resolve the situation.

Montcalm, after learning of this decision and perhaps realizing that he had not been having an altogether positive influence on inter-allied relations, called another council on 22 July. There he presented a string of wampum symbolizing his request that they remain at Carillon. "He has," wrote one of his officers, "blocked the road to Montreal with a collar and has assured them that he has nothing in his heart against them, that he will be very pleased to retain them." The Seven Nations agreed to respond the next day.[29]

The chiefs consulted their warriors regarding a reply, then met in council. Ganetagon argued that "one would have to be insensible to accept this proposal" and demanded that they all go to Montreal. The Kanesetakes and others agreed, but the question arose as to who was going to tell Montcalm. Apparently no one was particularly enthusiastic about this part of the process. Protocol nevertheless made a meeting with Montcalm essential, and "the most resolute" agreed to speak with the general once again.[30]

While the chiefs deliberated, the warriors remained in camp. A large war party had been scheduled to set out that day for the road between Fort Edward and Lake George. Canadian Iroquois and Abenaki warriors, however, declined to leave, ostensibly to compete for belts and strings of wampum worth 6,600 livres in a lacrosse tournament.[31] Their motives were likely more political than athletic. For the Seven Nations at Carillon, the war came to a brief halt as their chiefs sought to restore harmony to their relations with the French.

These chiefs met once more with Montcalm on 23 July. The reluctant emissaries "were obliged to tell him that his head had been turned since he had beaten the English without us, and that [in the future] he might have need of us, but he would not find us."[32] Upon hearing this declaration, Montcalm asked that they at least leave some warriors behind. The chiefs replied that the fighters were unwilling to remain.

The council then recessed, and Montcalm arranged for Lévis, whom Ganetagon personally respected, to speak privately with the young chief. This intervention proved effective, and when the council reconvened the Seven Nations agreed to maintain a presence on the Lake Champlain frontier. A French officer recorded that "the Iroquois replied to the general that they thought he was angry because he had reproached them, that since he had opened his heart to them, they would leave a party of their warriors."[33]

On 24 July the Amerindians at Carillon divided. About four hundred, along with two hundred Canadians, headed south and attacked a British convoy south of Halfway Brook. For a loss of one Kahnawake killed and ten wounded the allied force took eighty-four prisoners, including Abercromby's entire military band. They also obtained 110 scalps and carried off a good deal of matériel. Upon their return to Carillon, the Seven Nations profitably disposed of much of this matériel by selling it to French soldiers.[34]

The remaining Canadian Iroquois, Algonquin, and Abenaki fighters of the Seven Nations, along with some Ojibwas, went north with Ganetagon and his colleagues to meet with Onontio in Montreal. On 30 July they spoke at length with the governor general regarding recent events at Carillon. Vaudreuil, perceiving that the Seven Nations were deeply and justifiably offended but hoping to avoid a breach, found a face-saving formula to excuse Montcalm. He suggested to the Amerindians that Montcalm's interpreters had been at fault and secured their agreement to return to Carillon. The chiefs, who were seeking the restoration of amicability and good relations, agreed.[35]

With Amerindian concerns thus allayed, Vaudreuil turned to the person who had provoked the crisis. He sent Montcalm a blistering reprimand, reminding his general that the Seven Nations "have contributed for a long time to the honour of the arms and the defence of the colony" and ordered his general "to have for these nations all of the consideration that they merit."[36]

With harmony between the allies restored and disharmony among the French inflamed, the war against the British continued. In August a third detachment of about four hundred Seven Nations fighters and French militiamen and colonial regulars set out towards Fort Edward. On the 8th, they fell in with a force of seven hundred British rangers, light infantry, and provincials. In the subsequent engagement, the allies lost eight killed and twelve wounded. They retired from the field after killing forty-nine of the enemy and taking six prisoners.[37]

With this encounter, the campaign of 1758 came to an end for the Canadian Iroquois. For their allies, fighting to advance the interests of the French empire, victory at Carillon was balanced by defeats at Louisbourg in Acadia, Fort Frontenac on Lake Ontario, and Fort Duquesne in the Ohio valley. For the Canadian Iroquois, fighting for prisoners, no such reservations applied. From a military perspective, their operations in 1758 had been reasonably satisfactory. Although the campaign had not produced a massive collection of prisoners and matériel comparable to the results of the siege of Fort William Henry, the raids against the British below Lake George had all been at least moderately successful.

Unlike the siege of Fort William Henry, these operations had been conducted in the open forest, unobstructed by the presence of a fort. Under these circumstances, there had been no opportunities for Europeans to strike private deals among themselves and attempt to bring an engagement to a premature end. The Canadian Iroquois in 1758 were thus free to harvest prisoners and matériel undisturbed by French attempts to deprive them of their victory for the sake of European conventions.

Weighed against these tangible military victories, the confrontation with Montcalm was irritating, but its practical importance was quite limited. Since Vaudreuil rather than Montcalm commanded the French armed forces in North America, his opinions and actions were infinitely more important to the Canadian Iroquois than those of an increasingly dysfunctional metropolitan general.

Indeed, the diplomatic crisis of 1758 ultimately said more about the inherent strengths of their alliance to the French than Montcalm's weakness as a diplomat. It revealed the alliance to be sufficiently strong that even very irregular behaviour on the part of a senior French officer could be smoothed over without serious consequences. The Canadian Iroquois had not chosen the French as allies on account of their good manners, but because alliance with the French crown suited their needs. Resolving the disharmony created by Montcalm's outbursts had only momentarily disrupted Canadian Iroquois military operations. Even as the chiefs met in Montreal with Vaudreuil, a major war party was out in the field carrying the war to the enemy. Many cultural differences divided the Canadian Iroquois and the French, but they remained close allies, "linked together in each others Arms" and serving together in a war against a common adversary.[38]

CHAPTER 8

LAKE CHAMPLAIN, LAKE ONTARIO, AND QUEBEC, 1759

In 1755 four outposts on the margins of the French empire in North America had been threatened with attack; in 1759 the heart of that empire was under siege and British forces reappeared in areas that had been the scene of major allied victories. At Oswego the site of Fort Ontario was reoccupied, fortified, and used as a staging area for a British siege of Fort Niagara. At the southern tip of Lake George, Fort George rose on the site of the entrenched camp to the east of Fort William Henry. It too became a base of operations for a British offensive, in this case directed against forts Carillon and St. Frédéric and the St. Lawrence valley. To the east a new area of operations opened up when a British amphibious expedition sailed up the St. Lawrence River to besiege the fortified port of Quebec.

The straitened circumstances of their allies did not, however, affect Amerindian military support for the French in 1759. In that year, with New France facing threats from all directions, the total numbers of Amerindians serving alongside the French in Canada equalled the numbers engaged in 1757, when French fortunes were at their height. For the second time in the war, warriors from both the Seven Nations and the Great Lakes appeared in force on the frontiers of Canada. With their French allies under pressure on three fronts, Amerindians served in the Lake Ontario, Lake Champlain, and Quebec regions. There were about three hundred warriors active on the upper St. Lawrence and Lake Ontario, three to four hundred on Lake

Champlain, and one thousand to twelve hundred present at the siege of Quebec.[1]

In the Seven Years' War in North America, Quebec was the key to victory for both sides. The French had to hold it if they were to continue to receive supplies and reinforcements from France; the British had to take it if they were to sever this link entirely. The British could achieve this goal by blockade in North American or European waters, but the fall of Quebec would make the fall of New France within a year a virtual certainty.

Quebec was defended less by fortifications than by the immensely strong natural defences provided by its location on a rocky promontory, flanked by high ground to the east and steep cliffs to the west. These natural defences were artificially strengthened by the French, who sealed off the high ground with a line of fortifications between Quebec and the Montmorency River and a chain of outposts extending from Quebec to Cap Rouge guarding avenues leading up the cliffs.

Following their arrival, the British, led by Vice-Admiral Charles Saunders and Major-General James Wolfe, established fortified enclaves at the Ile d'Orléans, Pointe Lévis, and just east of the mouth of the Montmorency River. Throughout June, July, and August, soldiers based in these camps attempted to crack the allied outer perimeter and failed utterly.

A general view of Quebec from Point Levy, September 1st, 1761, by Richard Short, engraver P. Canot. NAC C-000355

The Canadian Iroquois did not play a major role in the defence of Quebec, where the Amerindian contingent was composed for the most part of "Abenakis and different nations of the *Pays d'en Haut*."[2] Some of the westerners were serving at Quebec because they refused to serve in other areas. When three hundred fighters from the Great Lakes arrived in Montreal in June, they were invited to take part in the defence of the Lake Champlain frontier. The westerners, however, refused: "They did not want to go to Carillon saying that their father Onontio was on the shore of the great lake, and that they wanted to join him to make the great war."[3]

Fighting in the great war on the shore of the great lake exposed Amerindians to a new style of war in a new setting. Previous battles had taken place in the forest itself or in clearings surrounded by forest. This time Amerindians went to war amidst the fields and farmsteads of rural Canada, in an area of operations described by one British participant as dominated by "vast tracts of ground covered with grain, for thirty leagues [about 150 kilometres] on both sides [of] the river."[4] Within this neo-European landscape Amerindians were privileged once again to observe new and interesting ways of making war. There were massive warships, fleets of transports, amphibious assaults, fireships, kilometres-long fortified positions, burning homes and farm buildings by the thousand, and the bombardment of a town.

Yet in the midst of novelty, Amerindians found an outlet for their traditional military skills. Operating from a secure base within the allied perimeter and moving under cover of the forests that still flourished in the region, Amerindians repeatedly lashed out at the British. While the regulars remained in safety within the lines ready to take to the field should the British break through, Amerindians and militiamen roamed the region, relentlessly harassing the invaders.[5] British landings were opposed by parties that vanished into the forest; patrols and woodcutting parties were ambushed; sentries vanished in the night; British raiding parties that devastated whole parishes became targets themselves. Although they had come to besiege Quebec, the British felt themselves to be in a state of siege, huddled within their fortified enclaves, constantly under threat from "the skulking parties of Canadians and Indians ... who continually kept hovering, night and day, about the flanks and rear of our camp[s]."[6]

Amerindians were particularly impressed by their role in harassing the British at Montmorency. Here, at the one point where the British and the allies were not separated by the width of the St. Lawrence, there was always the risk of a sudden attack on the allied left. Immediately following

A view of the church of Notre-Dame-de-la-Victoire, Dominic Serres, 1760. Service in the Quebec theatre in 1759 exposed Amerindians to a variety of new and terrible ways of making war, including the bombardment of a city. NAC C-025662

the British landing east of the river on 9 July, about 350 Abenakis and Odawas crossed the Montmorency to reconnoitre. Approaching the British encampment, they ambushed a party engaged in cutting wood to make fascines. The woodcutters were driven back, but this encounter turned into a major firefight when British reinforcements arrived. Obliged to retire in their turn, the Amerindians were covered by a force of militiamen as they withdrew over the river into the allied perimeter with five prisoners. This was only the first of a series of skirmishes and raids that continued until the evacuation of the Montmorency camp on 3 September.[7]

Even the Royal Navy was not immune from attack. Before they could assault the allied lines, the amphibious invaders needed to sound and chart the St. Lawrence in small boats, an activity that exposed them to attack from Amerindians in canoes. In one instance, when the cutter from HMS *Lowestoft* appeared off the mouth of the Montmorency on 7 June, a party of Amerindians flung themselves into five canoes and gave chase. They pursued the cutter to the shore of Ile d'Orléans, where its crew fled inland.

Continuing the chase ashore, the warriors captured one sailor, then killed him with a spear when he refused to come away with them. When a column from the British camp on the island marched up to rescue the seamen the Amerindians engaged them for about half an hour before retiring in good order.[8]

When the British launched their first major assault on the allied perimeter, Amerindians played a role in their defeat. On 31 July two British forces, one landing from boats, the other marching along the tidal flats from the camp east of Montmorency, attempted to storm the allied lines. The British captured an advanced redoubt, then made a frontal assault on the main allied position. This charge was shattered by a combination of devastating fire from the Montreal militia battalion that held the lines above the redoubt and a torrential thunderstorm.

Holding the lines to the west of the Montreal battalion were an another militia detachment and the entire Amerindian contingent. As the Montreal battalion engaged the front of the British attack, the Amerindians fired into their flanks.[9] Although it was the Montreal battalion that won the engagement for the allies, one French source said of the Amerindians at Montmorency that "their cries and their challenges intimidated our enemies who ... returned rapidly to their vessels and left us masters of the field of battle."[10] As the British withdrew, Amerindian warriors left the lines and pursued until the enemy had been driven from the field.[11]

For Amerindian participants, the Quebec campaign up to mid-September was characterized by a series of "raids on the enemy in which we always had the advantage."[12] When warriors of the Canadian Iroquois described the Quebec campaign in July, they said that "the English had not passed the Montmorency falls and that one harassed them with success; that the Canadians, the Natives, and other volunteers killed many of them, and that they could not take a step without being fired upon."[13] The conditions of the siege allowed warriors to gather prisoners, scalps, and matériel, while supporting their allies by keeping the British under observation and off-balance. Both parties thus had good reason to be satisfied with the siege as August of 1759 drew to a close.

By the beginning of September, an allied victory was in sight. The allied lines remained intact and the British would soon be forced to retire or risk entrapment in the ice of the St. Lawrence. On 9 September the westerners left to return to their homes.[14] Yet if victory loomed at Quebec, allied campaigns on the Lake Ontario and Lake Champlain frontiers had been much less successful.

Major-General James Wolfe, by J.S.C. Shaak, engraver R. Houston. The landing at the Anse au Foulon and subsequent engagement are portrayed in the background. NAC C-005561

In the Lake Ontario area the campaign of 1759 brought the Canadian Iroquois back to Oswego. With a British army known to be on the march towards Lake Ontario and an attack on Niagara or Montreal apparently imminent, Vaudreuil sent Luc de la Corne and a small allied force to shore up the French position in the region. Seventy-one Canadian Iroquois accepted an invitation to join this expedition, which also included thirty-one other Amerindians and 1,081 colonial regulars and militiamen. This army was intended "to harass the enemy in their march or communication" along the Oswego River. If this proved impossible, they were to withdraw to the upper St. Lawrence and await the enemy at the head of the rapids.[15]

A failure before it properly began, the expedition did not get under way until 29 July, just three days before a British army of twenty-five hundred which had already reached Oswego departed unmolested for Niagara. They left behind a detachment of thirteen hundred regulars, provincials, and Amerindians under Lieutenant-Colonel Frederick Haldimand with orders to build a new fort on the site of Fort Ontario.[16]

On 4 July the allies reached La Petite Anse, disembarked, and sent out scouts towards the Oswego River. Upon their return, the scouts reported sighting British troops camped on the east side of the river. After a council, the allies decided to launch simultaneous attacks from several directions and overwhelm the British.

As dawn broke the next morning, the allies marched on the British position with the Amerindians in the lead. Part way towards the river, however, the warriors caught sight of a party of British soldiers who appeared to be cutting wood. Left to their own devices, these "woodcutters" could raise the alarm while the allies were still some distance from the camp. The warriors consequently paused and informed the French. After a hasty consultation, a party of sixty Amerindians and Frenchmen was formed to capture the inconvenient Britons. They were about to attack when the British opened fire.

In 1756 an allied army of thousands had reached Oswego undetected. This time the Seven Nations and the French had been observed by Amerindians allied to the British soon after they landed. Forewarned, the regulars and provincials set to work building an entrenchment. Once his troops were safely dug in behind this barrier, Haldimand sent out the patrol that was mistaken for a party of woodcutters by the Seven Nations and inadvertently interposed itself between the British camp and the allied attack.

Although surprised, the allies quickly gained the upper hand in the ensuing engagement and drove the British back to the shelter of Haldimand's camp. There, however, the allies faced an enemy that had been warned of their presence and was now fully alert and standing to behind entrenchments mounting three cannon. The allies, who had planned to limit their activities to harassing British lines of communication, had no artillery and no serious chance of making a successful attack on a fortified position. The French officers held a private meeting and decided to withdraw, on the grounds that they had lost the advantage of surprise and were unsure of the morale of the militia. The Amerindians, however, refused to abandon the enterprise. When their allies retreated, they remained behind, along with a few soldiers. Concealed among trees felled by Haldimand's troops at the edge of the forest, the warriors continued to fire at the British throughout the remainder of the day and well into the night.

That night the Amerindians proposed a renewal of the attack on the next day. La Corne consented, but the assault was disrupted when militiamen prematurely opened fire before the entire allied force was in position. The ensuing exchange of fire lasted for about three hours, after which the allies withdrew, following the same road that Montcalm's engineers had built for the artillery in 1756.[17]

The attack on Haldimand's encampment was the most thoroughly unsatisfactory allied venture since Dieskau's débâcle at Lake George. The French failed to have the slightest influence upon British movements in the region in a campaign that left the British in control of two key points on Lake Ontario. The Amerindians had only casualties to show for their efforts alongside the French. Moreover, the success of the British campaign exposed Oswegatchie and northeastern Kanienkeh to attack from the west.

The defeated allies returned together to Oswegatchie, where they learned of the fall of Fort Niagara, which had surrendered on 26 July. Within Canada, there were fears that the British would follow up this victory with an advance down the upper St. Lawrence. La Corne, believing that he could not resist invasion with the forces at hand, prepared to withdraw towards Montreal if necessary.

With the situation on the upper St. Lawrence apparently desperate, Vaudreuil sent Lévis from Quebec to take command of the French forces in the region. Once on the scene, Lévis soon came to the conclusion that the British would limit themselves to holding Oswego and Niagara and set about organizing defences for the next campaign. Most important, he ordered the construction of a fort on an island about five kilometres downriver from Oswegatchie, which became known as Fort Lévis. This outpost had a dual purpose for the French. As well as holding off the British, Fort Lévis was expected "to control the Natives of the region."[18] But if Fort Lévis was seriously intended to intimidate the Oswegatchies, it failed miserably. The Oswegatchies cooperated with the French to the extent of selling them the right to build their new fort upon land used for planting crops. Yet there is no evidence whatever that the presence of the new French outpost and garrison exercised any control whatever over their subsequent actions.

Canadian Iroquois fighters were also active participants in the defence of the Lake Champlain frontier, serving alongside fighters from the Great Lakes as part of an Amerindian contingent numbering between three and four hundred. The Amerindians were joined by three thousand French regulars and militiamen under the command of François-Charles de Bourlamaque.[19] Bourlamaque, who had directed siege operations at Oswego and William Henry and played an important role in the Battle of Carillon, was a competent soldier but would prove to be a most difficult ally for the Canadian Iroquois.

French expectations for the Lake Champlain frontier in 1759 were not high. British forces in the region were too powerful to be engaged directly, and of the existing French forts on Lake Champlain, St. Frédéric was considered to be indefensible and Carillon capable of resisting for only a week. Instead of attempting to hold these outposts, Bourlamaque had been ordered to make a token defence of Carillon, abandon St. Frédéric, then withdraw to the outlet of Lake Champlain, where a new French fort was under construction at Ile aux Noix.[20] No one, however, bothered to inform the Amerindian element of the Lake Champlain army of this strategy. Impressed by the French victory at Carillon in 1758, they entered the campaign of 1759 in the expectation that their allies would be making a serious attempt to defend Fort Carillon.

Beginning in May, Canadian Iroquois, Abenaki, Nipissing, Menominee, Odawa, and Ojibwa fighters based in Carillon took part in a series of raids on the British. These raids were directed against both the growing British presence between Fort Edward and Lake George and the British partisans who appeared with increasing frequency on that lake.[21] On 8 July, in a typical encounter, a party of about seventy-five Kahnawakes on Lake George encountered three whaleboats carrying four British colonials and twenty-two Amerindians, mostly Mohicans, all serving in Rogers' Rangers. Immediately they caught sight of the rangers, the Kahnawakes flung their canoes in the water and set off in pursuit. The rangers first attempted to land, then fled precipitately, closely followed by the Kahnawakes. There ensued a chase that could easily have taken its place in the lurid frontier melodramas of James Fenimore Cooper or Francis Parkman.

As the swift, sleek birchbark canoes began to overtake the slower, less agile whaleboats, the rangers opened fire on the Kahnawakes, who refrained from responding since this would have slowed them down and perhaps allowed the enemy to slip away. Unable to escape on the lake, the fugitives finally managed to land on the western shore, then scattered in the forest with the Kahnawakes right behind them. After a relentless pursuit through the forest that lasted between three and four hours, the Kahnawakes took four prisoners and four scalps. The remaining rangers escaped.[22]

Colonial officers considered this minor collision between parties of scouts to be a significant demonstration of the commitment of the Kahnawakes to their alliance with the French, since they had proved willing to press home attacks in spite of the presence of Amerindians among the rangers. One officer wrote that as a result of this engagement "one must have great confidence in the Iroquois of the Rapids [Kahnawakes] who could have thought that they [the Amerindian rangers] were their Brothers the Mohawks." Moreover, in conference with Amerindians from the Great Lakes region shortly after this incident, Kahnawake speakers reiterated their commitment to "contribute with their western brothers to the defence of this frontier."[23]

Yet if this engagement demonstrated the Kahnawake commitment to the French alliance, it also revealed something of the divisions among the Kahnawakes produced by the Anglo-French war. Most of the Amerindians in the British party were Stockbridge Mohicans. One, however, was a Kahnawake named Joseph, who had been living with the League Mohawks for some time. Joseph came from a family that had come apart over the question of participation in the Seven Years' War. While Joseph left home and eventually enlisted in Rogers' Rangers, his brother remained at Kahnawake, fought alongside the French, and was among those who had pursued the British detachment down the lake. After the action, this brother was heard to assert "that he would have taken the scalp [of Joseph] if he had caught him."[24]

Nevertheless, the respect accorded Amerindians by colonial officers as a result of the actions of warriors like Joseph's brother was not shared by their metropolitan colleagues, whose disdain for Amerindians became more and more overt after the Battle of Carillon. Shortly after the interception of the rangers, these attitudes were once again publicly paraded by a senior metropolitan officer, following an unfortunate display of exuberance on the part of the western allies.

If the western allies had recovered their willingness to stand by the French, they had lost none of their inclination to supplement military rations with whatever live animals were available. In the past, this had led to the rounding up of "prey" defined by the French as livestock belonging to individual officers or the crown. In July 1759 a group of Menominee, Odawa, and Ojibwa warriors went further. One afternoon, in an excessively lighthearted moment, they opened fire upon the dogs and chickens of the French camp. This provoked an understandably negative reaction from the French, who objected both to the loss of their animals and apparently random gunfire in their direction. Yet the incident remained a relatively minor annoyance until Bourlamaque called the Amerindians to council and did his best to put them in their place. In the course of an angry tirade, Bourlamaque sternly reprimanded the westerners, and reminded his allies that "We know how to make war without you, what have you been good for up to now? We beat the English last year [at Carillon] without any of you; we will do so again this year. If there arrives the smallest accident to any of our officers, I will open fire on all of your chiefs, and I will have ten of your young men killed for each wounded soldier."[25]

French interpreters attached to the various nations also suggested strongly, if rather more tactfully, that the Amerindians had gone a little too far this time. The westerners, however, considered Bourlamaque's words a major affront and reacted accordingly. Faced with a similar situation in 1758, chiefs of Seven Nations had practised quiet diplomacy and sought redress from Vaudreuil. In 1759 infuriated western leaders removed the medals that symbolized their relationship with the French and threw them at Bourlamaque's feet.

The incident was eventually resolved and a degree of amicability restored. Having made their point, many of the chiefs took up their medals once again. Others, however, remained deeply offended by Bourlamaque's

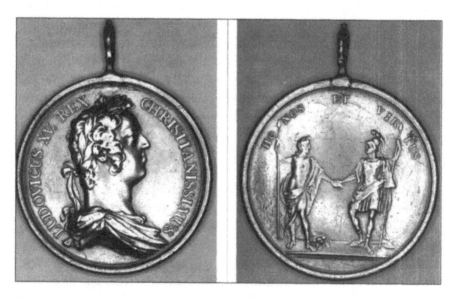

French medal, cast by Jean Duvivier. NAC C-062181 (obverse), NAC-062182 (reverse)

tirade. One Odawa chief who did not seek to recover his medal "said that the French were dogs."[26]

Even as this exercise in inter-allied harmony was in progress, the war continued and French preparations to abandon the region proceeded apace. On 26 June engineers set to work readying Fort Carillon for demolition. Four days later the invalids of the garrison and field army were quietly evacuated and on 5 July the heavy baggage of the army was embarked in the vessel *La Facile* and whisked away to safety.[27] A little over two weeks after the departure of *La Facile*, the British finally arrived. On the morning of Sunday, 22 July, scouts from Carillon setting out on a routine patrol emerged from the forest on the shore of Lake George and found the lake covered with an armada of whaleboats carrying a British army.

When the scouts raised the alarm, most of the regulars and militiamen of the field army occupied the entrenchments in front of the fort. A force of Amerindians, grenadiers, light infantry, and militiamen marched out and engaged the British at the head of the portage leading to the fort. After skirmishing with the British advance guard throughout the day, the allies were pushed back to the fort.

Some Amerindians refused to join this detachment. Those who accompanied the French, however, played a prominent role in resisting the British advance. One British officer wrote that after the landing, "the rangers met with a party of French and Indians, attacked them and drove them [back]" and then later "some Indians came up to the front of Gage's, fired and made off, and others fell in at night with some of our sentries upon the road."[28]

Behind the advance guard, an army of eleven thousand regulars and provincials under Major-General Jeffrey Amherst landed and began to make preparations for a siege.[29] As Amherst prepared to attack, Bourlamaque prepared to retreat. That afternoon a French advance party left Carillon for the Rivière à la Barbue, midway between Carillon and St. Frédéric, which had been chosen to serve as a temporary camp during the withdrawal.[30]

With the retreat already under way, the Amerindians, who had been expecting a major engagement to defend the fort, were finally informed by the French of the plan to abandon Carillon. The chiefs and warriors exhibited "astonished surprise to see us abandon the entrenchments [made] so famous by our victory in the preceding year, and for our work to perfect it. They did not want to believe any of this, when they were told that they might make their retreat, and said: What? the French abandon the house, the cabin where they worked so much? No, that cannot be."[31]

Sir Jeffery Amherst, K.B., by Sir Joshua Reynolds, engraver James Watson. In the background, Amherst's army is running the rapids of the upper St. Lawrence in 1760. NAC C-000561

Nonetheless, the entire allied field army, including the Amerindians, embarked at midnight under cover of darkness and heavy fog. They followed the advance party along the west shore of Lake Champlain to the Rivière à la Barbue, where they arrived safely the next morning.[32] Behind at Carillon, the allies left a garrison of about four hundred.[33] With the field army gone, this garrison watched on 23 July as the British advanced, occupied the entrenchments abandoned by the French, and began digging trenches in anticipation of conducting a regular siege.

That evening the Canadian Iroquois, who formed the largest Amerindian group, began a council that would last until 9:00 a.m. the next day. The western allies attended for a while then withdrew and left the

Iroquois to their deliberations. In the course of this meeting, the Canadian Iroquois made a thorough review of Bourlamaque's performance as an ally. Speaker after speaker commented extensively on his failure to observe the ceremonies appropriate to alliance through the formal presentation of a belt of wampum and his exceedingly tactless remarks earlier in the month. At 10:00 a.m. on 24 July the Canadian Iroquois met with Bourlamaque to explain their concerns. Presented with a final opportunity to repair relations with allies who were on the verge of abandoning the campaign, Bourlamaque replied that they could go or stay as they wished, and that he would use militiamen as scouts. The Canadian Iroquois took him at his word and departed, along with the westerners.[34]

This departure did not represent a final breach between the Canadian Iroquois and the French. The warriors who had returned home were replaced on 26 July, when seventy Canadian Iroquois arrived at the Rivière à la Barbue.[35] In spite of the allied defeat and Bourlamaque's less than endearing personality, the Canadian Iroquois would maintain a presence in the region until the end of the campaign.

Back at Fort Carillon, the garrison continued to resist until British batteries were in place and ready to open fire. On 27 July the French evacuated the fort and joined the field army at the Rivière à la Barbue. Behind them, explosive charges detonated at midnight, reducing the southernmost French outpost on Lake Champlain to shattered ruins. On 29 July the allied army withdrew to Fort St. Frédéric, which was itself mined and abandoned two days later when the allies sailed for Ile aux Noix.[36]

French strategy on Lake Champlain may not have been very heroic, but it worked. The allied army was not pursued by Amherst, who converted his soldiers into labourers and employed them in building Fort Ticonderoga on the site of Fort Carillon and Fort Crown Point near the site of Fort St. Frédéric. Apparently fearing a French counterattack, he ordered that each fort be sufficiently strong that "it may not be in the power of the enemy ever to take possession again of this post." With only a much smaller allied army between his force and Montreal, this decision represented an extremely conservative estimate of British prospects in the coming campaign.[37] Amherst lurched into motion again in October and sailed north on Lake Champlain to attack Fort Ile aux Noix, only to turn back when his flotilla encountered adverse winds.[38] This brought the campaign to a reasonably satisfactory end for the French.

This satisfaction was perhaps not shared by the Canadian Iroquois. If the campaign of 1759 in the Lake Ontario region had ended with

A South West View of the Lines and Fort of Ticonderoga, by Thomas Davies, 1760. NAC C-010653

Oswegatchie exposed to attack by the British, on the Lake Champlain frontier the British had actually invaded and occupied a part of Kanienkeh. The territory so lightly abandoned by the French had not, in Canadian Iroquois eyes, been theirs to give. Referring to the Lake Champlain region in 1766, Canadian Iroquois speakers declared that:

> As to the Original owners thereof any one that knows the history of this country before that period [the arrival of Europeans] will testify it to have been then the undisputed Right of the 6 nations & their allies & was chiefly occupied in the hunting seasons by the ancient Mohawks whose descendants we are."[39]

Although the campaign of 1759 on the Lake Champlain frontier produced a whole series of minor victories in ambushes and skirmishes, it proved to be a most unsatisfactory experience for the Canadian Iroquois. For the second year in a row a senior French officer had displayed a spectacular disregard for the ceremonies and courtesies of alliance. Worse, in the course of the campaign, the French had demonstrated their willingness to abandon both French forts and Canadian Iroquois land without a fight.

For the Canadian Iroquois, the turning point of the Seven Years' War came with the nearly simultaneous fall of Fort Carillon on Lake Champlain and Fort Niagara on Lake Ontario in late July of 1759. Two months before the capitulation of Quebec on 18 September, these defeats had "produced a considerable sensation within the colony; one expected the enemy to appear at the head of the rapids [of the upper St. Lawrence]."[40] The Canadian Iroquois evidently shared these perceptions, for within days of the arrival of news of the fall of Carillon and Niagara they were considering neutrality. In August 1759 Luc de la Corne reported that although "our Natives are most favourably disposed, and say that they will never abandon the French," many "good Natives [bons sauvages]" had informed him that "if the English invade our land, the people of the rapid [Kahnawakes] will remain neutral." It was under these circumstances that the Oswegatchies were approached by an embassy representing Sir William Johnson.[41]

For the British, the Canadian Iroquois represented a formidable obstacle to an invasion of Canada from the west. These nations had mobilized 355 fighters in 1757 and could do so again.[42] Although their numbers were

Cedar Rapids in the St. Lawrence River, by William Roebuck, c. 1820. Any invasion of Canada from Lake Ontario would have to overcome this natural barrier. NAC C-040371

relatively small in a war that by 1759 was dominated by thousands of European soldiers, their effectiveness in action would be multiplied by the rapids of the upper St. Lawrence. Among the "broken rocks and inaccessible islands, interspersed in the current of a rapid river, and the foaming surges rebounding from them,"[43] local knowledge and skill in partisan warfare could be employed to devastating effect upon an invading army that attempted to make use of this waterway. To secure the neutrality of the Canadian Iroquois thus became a major preoccupation for Johnson and his subordinates in the closing years of the war.

The Canadian Iroquois first learned of Johnson's intentions in the first weeks of September, when a party of eleven League Onondagas and Senecas bearing a message from Johnson arrived at Oswegatchie. Speaking in council, they informed the Oswegatchies that a British army was about to advance down the St. Lawrence and presented their hosts with a stark choice between neutrality and destruction: "if they would quit the French interest, and leave the settlement, they had an opportunity of saving themselves and their families. If not, this would be the last warning they were to expect."[44]

Four years before a similar, if less threatening, overture to a Canadian Iroquois community had been politely but unequivocally rejected by the Kahnawakes. In September 1759, on the other hand, the British request was received by communities that were already contemplating neutrality. The Oswegatchies themselves asked the messengers to inform Johnson that "they would not only quit the French interest, but on our approach meet and join us and show us the best way to attack the enemy on the island [Fort Lévis], who were not above six hundred." Later that fall, when word of these transactions reached Kahnawake and Kanesetake, these communities sent two Kanesetakes to Oswego. Upon their arrival on 30 September the emissaries met with Johnson to pass on their own assurances that the Kahnawakes and Kanesetakes would "never more assist the French."[45]

On 11 October the two Kanesetakes, together with an Oswegatchie took part in a general meeting with League Onondagas, Senecas, Cayugas, Oneidas, and Mohawks, and the British. There, the Canadian Iroquois delegates were told that the projected offensive down the St. Lawrence had been postponed and warned that if they were to act against the British, Johnson "would never speak a word in their favor, but advise the general to cut them to pieces." The two Kanesetakes returned to northeastern Kanienkeh bearing a chilling warning. "They have it in their power now," Johnson had declared,

> by quitting the French, to become once more a happy
> people, but if, contrary to the many and solemn profes-
> sions made to me and the Six Nations, and the assurances
> they lately, by belts and strings of wampum, gave me of
> their fixed resolutions to abandon the French, they should
> act a different part, they must expect no quarter from us.[46]

Following these diplomatic exchanges, the Canadian Iroquois withdrew
from active participation in the war in the Lake Ontario area. Only the
Mississaugas continued to make an occasional foray against the British at
Oswego.[47]

A second British diplomatic initiative was directed at the Abenakis of
Odanak. On 22 August a party of Abenakis from that community encountered Captain Jacob Cheeksaunkun and six other Stockbridge Mohicans
escorting two British officers. These officers, dispatched to establish communications between Amherst and Wolfe, carried both an official letter from
Amherst to Wolfe and a number of private letters from officers in Amherst's
army to friends in Wolfe's army. En route, they were to make contact with
the Abenakis of Odanak, inform them in Amherst's name that the general
was about to invade Canada, and

> offer them my friendship upon condition that they do
> remain neutral, and do not join with any of His Majesty's
> enemies in any act of hostilities against his army, or any
> one of his subjects, in which case I am not come with an
> intention of dispossessing or annoying them. I will protect
> and defend their persons & properties and secure unto
> them the peaceable and quiet possession thereof.

Otherwise, the Abenakis would be "reduce[d]" along with the French. The
Abenaki response would be taken to Wolfe. If positive, he was to "treat
these Eastern Indians as our friends & allies."[48]

The Abenakis, however, proved less receptive than the Oswegatchies.
Upon sighting the British party, they pursued immediately. The Mohicans
and British first attempted to flee, then destroyed their official dispatches.
The officers next offered money and attempted to convey Amherst's offer of
neutrality. Spurning both bribes and blandishments, the Abenakis took the
entire party prisoner. From Odanak, the captives were taken to Trois
Rivières, where they ended up in irons on the French frigate *Atalante*.

The European officers remained in irons only until their identities and officer status were established. At this point, professional, racial, and class solidarity asserted itself and the two European regulars were treated as prisoners of war. On 15 November they were returned to Amherst's army in a prisoner exchange. Captain Cheeksaunkun was exchanged in August of 1760. The other Stockbridge Mohicans were freed either in prisoner exchanges or at the end of the war.[49]

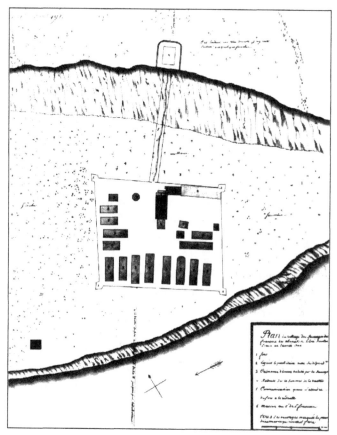

MAP 11. Odanak in 1704
The buildings numbered 2 are the church and presbytery, those marked 3 are Abenaki homes. The St. Francis River is at the bottom of the map. The council house in which the Abenakis gathered on the evening before the raid had not been constructed when this map was made and the town was no longer surrounded by a stockade.
Plan du village des sauvages des francoix des Abenakis... en l'année 1704. NMC 4901

The capture of the British messengers by the Abenakis was not without consequences. Amherst considered the Abenaki attack upon enemy soldiers carrying official dispatches in time of war to be an outrageous war crime and took time away from his construction program to plot revenge on the people of Odanak.

On the evening of 5 October the greater part of the adults of Odanak were having a party in the council house, which stood next to the parish church. According to their oral traditions, the Abenakis: "danced and sometimes celebrated late, dancing and sometimes going out because it was a nice cool night. They rested, some went out to smoke and rest ...[then] they went into the council house to dance again."[50] One young woman remained outside for a little longer. She was about to go in as the dancing resumed, when she was approached by a stranger. This stranger informed her that he was a Mohican from a war party that was going to raid the village the next morning, then vanished into the night.[51]

The young woman went inside with this warning. Many believed her. Parents left the dance and returned to their homes to collect their children, then slipped away in the dark and went to hide in a ravine outside Odanak. Once their families were safe, the warriors returned to defend their homes. They fortified the council house and awaited the enemy. Others did not believe the warning and remained asleep in their homes with their children.[52]

Those who failed to heed the warning were sadly mistaken. The next morning Amherst took his revenge when 140 rangers led by Robert Rogers fell upon the Abenaki community. The warriors in the council house fought back tenaciously in defence of their homes. After an engagement lasting several hours, the defenders were forced to withdraw. The rangers looted the church and houses of Odanak, then burned them to the ground. About thirty Abenakis were killed, many of whom were women and children. Two boys and three girls or women were taken prisoner.

Two of these prisoners, a small boy and a young woman, endured a truly horrifying experience. Following the attack, the rangers broke up into small groups and began to make their way southward to the haven of the British colonies. The two Abenakis were taken by five men towards Missisquoi Bay, where Rogers had concealed several whaleboats en route to Odanak. At some point between Odanak and Missisquoi, the rangers ran out of food. They murdered the young boy and ate part of his body. The remainder was packed up and carried by two of the rangers for later consumption.[53]

As Abenaki non-combatants cautiously returned to the smoking ruins of their homes looking for friends and relatives, allied fighters were after the rangers like a whirlwind. Abenakis from Odanak, joined by militiamen from Trois Rivières, pursued the raiders south and caught up with one party of "upwards of twenty in number" who were all killed or taken prisoner.[54] Ten captives were taken back to Odanak, where some "became victims of the fury of the Native women."[55]

Other rangers were intercepted by allied parties from the Lake Champlain army. Even before the attack, scouts from Ile aux Noix had located the whaleboats at Missisquoi Bay. While one party waited in ambush at the bay, a second group unsuccessfully pursued the raiders. On 2 November reports of sightings at Missisquoi caused Bourlamaque to send out twenty Amerindians, followed by forty-seven regulars and militiamen. Three Abenakis with this party captured five rangers, who reported that more of Rogers' men were in the vicinity. Five days later a second group of Abenakis and other Amerindians captured the rangers who had killed and eaten the Abenaki child. The two rangers found to be carrying pieces of the young boy's body were both killed on the spot. Showing considerable restraint, the Abenakis brought the remaining three rangers back to Ile aux Noix unharmed, along with the rescued Abenaki woman. Revenge was small consolation. With Odanak in ruins, the survivors first considered wintering east of Montreal Island, then accepted an invitation to temporarily relocate to Akwesasne.[56]

The attack on Odanak provided the Canadian Iroquois with unmistakable evidence that the British might have meant exactly what they said when they offered a choice between neutrality and destruction. Henceforth, the presence of Abenaki refugees at Akwesasne would serve as living reminders of the real and apprehended dangers facing the Canadian Iroquois in the last year of the war.

While these events were in progress on the Lake Ontario and Lake Champlain frontiers, the siege of Quebec was drawing to a close. There, following a summer of successful resistance, the defenders found themselves confronted with a final British assault.

After failing to breach the allied perimeter east of Quebec, Wolfe unleashed his troops on the surrounding countryside. So effective were the British forces at burning homes, farm buildings, and crops that by the end of August many of the parishes in the Quebec area had been devastated. At the same time British batteries at Pointe Lévis bombarded Quebec, reducing much of the town to rubble. The walls of Quebec, however, remained very much intact, along with the allied outer perimeter and the allied army. Three months after their arrival, Wolfe and his troops were no closer to taking Quebec than on the day the siege began.

Left to himself, Wolfe would have launched another frontal attack on the entrenchments east of Quebec and very probably handed the allies another easy victory. His brigadiers, however, suggested an alternative. Landing above Quebec would allow the British to cut allied supply lines to a major provision depot at Batiscan and thereby force the allies to come out from behind their entrenchments and give battle. Wolfe accepted this advice, assembled his army above Quebec, then changed his mind and decided to land about two kilometres west of the town at the Anse au Foulon. On the night of 12-13 September the British force embarked in a flotilla of flatboats and small ships and headed downstream for Quebec.

The garrisons of allied outposts between Cap Rouge and Quebec had been warned to expect a convoy of provisions which was subsequently cancelled. French lookouts, who had not been informed of this change in plans, allowed Wolfe's flotilla to pass unmolested and did not raise the alarm until British troops had actually landed. Once ashore, Wolfe marched his battalions to the Plains of Abraham, an area of open farmland just west of Quebec, and awaited the French.

Some of the first shots of the Battle of the Plains of Abraham were fired by Amerindians. While French regiments were crossing the St. Charles River from their camp east of Quebec, filing onto the field and taking up position along the crest of the ridge in front of the town, Amerindians were already engaging the enemy. They formed part of the seven to eight hundred warriors, militiamen, and colonial regulars who took up positions "upon our [the British] left flank and rear, and along the face of the hill below our right, where the bushes afforded them all the advantages they could hope for."[57] In the hours before the battle, as both armies assembled, the Amerindians joined the colonials in inflicting a steady, accurate fire upon the British. "The enemy," wrote one British participant "lined the bushes in their front with 1500 [*sic*] Indians & Canadians, & I dare say had placed most of their best marksmen there, who kept up a very galling, though irregular fire upon our whole line."[58]

This galling, irregular fire had a significant influence on British deployment. At 8:00 a.m. Wolfe had eleven battalions ready to engage Montcalm's regulars and one screening the British rear. However, such was the strength of the pressure from the Amerindians and militiamen to the

Battle of the Plains of Abraham, by J. Walker, 1877. This fanciful reconstruction of the battle is most notable for its portrayal of Amerindians firing into the British ranks. NAC C-06491

right and left that Wolfe found himself compelled to detach several units to protect his flanks. By 10:00 a.m. four battalions were tied down holding off the allied skirmishers. With one more sent to guard the Foulon, only seven remained to confront the French regulars.[59]

Throughout the early morning, as Wolfe's battle line grew weaker, that of the allies grew stronger. The British landing had caught the allies by surprise, but as the morning wore on the allied position steadily improved. Regiment after regiment of metropolitan regulars assembled on a ridge in front of the walls of Quebec where they could only be reached by an uphill charge over broken terrain. A second allied force composed of elite regulars and militiamen was advancing from the west and closing in both on the British rear and their only avenue of retreat. Artillery that could smash the British army into fragments was on the way, along with the two Montreal militia battalions.

Then at 10:00 a.m. with victory within his grasp, Montcalm threw it away by ordering a precipitate downhill charge that ended in disaster. The metropolitan regiments lost their cohesion and were driven back in disor-

Death of General Wolfe at Quebec, by Benjamin West, engraver William Wollett. An artistic but wholly imaginary portrayal of the death of James Wolfe, which includes a romantic representation of an Amerindian. Canadian War Museum

der. Only the resolute resistance of a body of militiaman and Amerindians held off the British while the regulars escaped over the St. Charles River. Joseph Trahan, who was present at the battle as an eighteen-year-old Quebec militiaman, later recalled this incident: "I can remember the Scotch Highlanders flying wildly after us, with streaming plaids, bonnets and large swords - like so many infuriated demons - over the brow of the hill. In their course was a wood, in which we had some Indians and sharpshooters, who bowled over the *Sauvages d'Ecosse* in fine style."[60]

Following the battle, rather than attempting to hold out within the walls until colder weather forced the British to retire, the French army abandoned Quebec and retreated in some confusion towards the west. The Amerindians, for their part, gathered what supplies they could salvage from French storehouses and joined the retreat.[61] The Hurons of Lorette forsook their homes and travelled as refugees to Montreal.[62] Behind them in

Quebec, a garrison under Brigadier-General James Murray took possession of the town and prepared to spend the winter in what was now a British enclave, deep in the heart of New France.

If there was any single moment that marked the beginning of the end of the longstanding relationship between the Canadian Iroquois and the French, it was the afternoon of 22 July 1759, when incredulous chiefs and warriors learned that their allies were about to abandon Fort Carillon without a fight. It was after this incident, together with the surrender of Fort Niagara, that the Canadian Iroquois began seriously to consider neutrality.

During the greater part of the Seven Years' War, the Canadian Iroquois had been able to support their allies without endangering their communities, which were comfortably distant from the various theatres of operations. In the last years of the Seven Years' War, however, the Canadian Iroquois found themselves in a new and precarious situation. Canada had

The Death of Montcalm, by G. Chevillet. This even less accurate reconstruction of the death of Montcalm shows the fallen hero nobly expiring in the shade of one of Canada's numerous palm trees. Canadian War Museum

been invaded in the spring of 1759, and by late summer it was apparent that their French allies might suffer defeat. Under these conditions, the pursuit of personal achievement through fighting alongside the French and even the maintenance of the French alliance itself became secondary considerations. Instead, the priorities of the Canadian Iroquois shifted to securing the safety and integrity of their communities in an increasingly dangerous and rapidly changing geopolitical environment.

So when Johnson's emissaries appeared at Oswegatchie, the Canadian Iroquois had listened and responded positively. Yet at the same time, they avoided an overt break with the French, thus contriving to place themselves on reasonably amicable terms with both European powers. This represented a strategy which the Canadian Iroquois would follow throughout the remainder of the war, as they manoeuvred cautiously between continued support for the French outside the Lake Ontario region and continued diplomatic contacts with the British at Oswego.

CHAPTER 9

LAKE ONTARIO AND THE ST. LAWRENCE VALLEY, 1760

The relationship of the Canadian Iroquois with the French was much more than a simple military alliance. It was an institution that had evolved since the late seventeenth century in accordance with the needs and aspirations of both parties, and continued to fulfill the requirements of Amerindians. The British, on the other hand, were potentially much less satisfactory allies.

Canadian Iroquois opinions regarding the difference between the British and the French had been articulated in 1754 at a secret meeting with a delegation of Cayugas, Oneidas, and Tuscaroras of the Iroquois League. During this conference, the speakers of the Seven Nations had compared the British unfavourably with the French:

> Are you not aware, our Brothers, what difference there is between our Father [the French] and the English. Come and see the forts that our Father has built, and you will see there that the land under the walls is still good for hunting, [and that French forts are] only placed in the places that we frequent to supply our needs. When the English on the contrary are no sooner in possession of land than the game is forced to flee, [and] the woods fall before them.[1]

Kisensik, speaking on behalf of the Seven Nations in 1757, made an implicit comparison between the behaviour of the French as neighbours and allies and that of the British as potential conquerors when he declared that a British occupation of Canada would be followed by the displacement of the Seven Nations. "The English," he said, "wish to make themselves master of them [our lands] in order to chase us away."[2] The French alliance was thus not a relationship that the Canadian Iroquois would willingly set aside until this became absolutely necessary.

Faced with an apprehended British intrusion into northeastern Kanienkeh in the fall of 1759, the Canadian Iroquois had gone a long way towards aligning themselves with the British. Yet after this invasion failed to materialize, they drew back a step. While remaining in contact with the British, in the course of the following winter and spring the Canadian Iroquois gave both verbal and material evidence of their willingness to continue to stand by the French.

In February 1760 a delegation from the League Onondagas arrived at Oswegatchie, a community founded in 1749 by Catholic Onondagas. There, they extended an invitation to rejoin the Onondagas living south of Lake Ontario. The Oswegatchies first refused to hold a council without a French officer present, then listened to the Onondaga request but "said they would not come home at all."[3] Later that month the Canadian Iroquois reaffirmed their strong commitment to the French alliance in a meeting with the League Iroquois at Onondaga. The Canadian Iroquois had sent a delegation there as part of an effort to re-establish harmonious relations between themselves and the League Iroquois and heal the breach that had been caused by fighting on different sides in the Anglo-French war. When Canadian Iroquois delegates were formally asked by the League Iroquois "to keep out of the way, when the English army approaches" they refused, and, like the Kahnawakes in 1755, employed religious imagery to illustrate the strength of their relationship with the French. An orator, speaking on behalf of "22 Nations in the French Interest," declared that "as the French have persuaded us to stay, and embrace their religion, by which we are to be saved, it would be hard brothers for you to expect we should leave them altogether."[4] Both diplomatic encounters thus closed with a strong reaffirmation of Canadian Iroquois commitment to the French alliance.

More tangibly, the Canadian Iroquois continued to fight alongside the French outside the Lake Ontario region. On 15 February twenty-five Oswegatchie fighters arrived at Montreal to take part in an allied offensive against the British garrison of Quebec. The Oswegatchies joined a force numbering 270 Amerindians, including the African-Abenaki Kahnawake war chief Atiatonharongwen, and 6,990 regulars and militiamen that sailed for Quebec on 20 April with Lévis in command of the French contingent.[5]

The allies sailed unaware that their plans had been betrayed by a British agent working at the very highest levels of the French command. This represented a new development in the Seven Years' War. When Wolfe and Saunders ascended the St. Lawrence, their best intelligence came from British prisoners who had been exchanged and from Pierre Charlevoix's *History and General Description of New France*. The occupation of Quebec, however, placed the British in contact with local merchants, some of whom were willing to collaborate. In exchange for access to matériel seized from French government stocks and permission to leave Quebec to travel to Montreal, where there was a ready market for this merchandise, these merchants agreed to provide James Murray with intelligence.

Murray's prize agent was a leading Quebec merchant, Barthélemy Martin, who travelled to Montreal in December 1759. There he contacted François Bigot, the intendant of New France. He informed the colony's senior administrator that he was in a position to procure merchandise from "English merchants" at Quebec. Later that winter, when the French found themselves in need of commodities that were not available in Montreal and sought to obtain them covertly from Quebec, Bigot turned to Martin.

Battle of St. Foye, (sic) anon. NAC C-002069

Murray's agent thus became involved in logistical preparations for the allied offensive, dealing personally with Bigot, Lévis, and Vaudreuil. He was consequently able to provide Murray with a series of detailed reports regarding allied intentions and movements. Lévis had hoped to take the British by surprise. Instead, thanks to Martin, by 24 April Murray was aware that the allies would reach Quebec within days and took appropriate precautions.[6]

Nonetheless, the last allied army to take the offensive arrived without incident on the Plains of Abraham on 28 April 1760. They found the British force of 3,647 regulars under James Murray drawn up on the ridge occupied by Montcalm in 1759. Like Montcalm, Murray occupied a strong defensive position, and like Montcalm, he threw this advantage away. Catching sight of the leading elements of the allied army, Murray ordered a downhill charge in hopes of catching the French before their main body could form on the field. Instead, the French regulars and militiamen wavered, but quickly recovered and counterattacked. In the subsequent Battle of Ste. Foy, the British were defeated and forced to retire within the walls of Quebec.[7]

Circumstances did not permit the Seven Nations to play a major part in the second Quebec campaign. The Amerindian contingent was in the van as the allies came in sight of Ste. Foy, just west of Quebec, and took an active role in skirmishing with outlying detachments of the garrison. On 27 April the warriors were forced to halt and wait for the arrival of the French advance guard when they became entangled with a force of Highlanders and threatened with defeat. During the battle itself, however, the Amerindians found no scope for the exercise of their particular military skills and remained on the sidelines.[8]

In the battles of Montmorency and the Plains of Abraham, Amerindians had been able to take cover and fire on British regulars standing upright in the open over extended periods of time. This was not the case at Ste. Foy, a battle that consisted of a series of confused charges and counter-charges. An engagement of this nature was entirely unsuited to Amerindian military skills, and throughout the war they had stated very clearly that they would not take part in battles on open ground.

In the event, the French won the battle without their support and Amerindians did not appear on the field until the British had been driven back to Quebec. When they sought to take prisoners from among British survivors, however, the warriors who had led the advance to Ste. Foy found their French allies actively cooperating with their British enemies to thwart the achievement of this objective. Once again refusing to accept Amerindian military goals as valid, the French sent out parties to search for wounded officers with the specific intent of forestalling Amerindian efforts to secure captives and wherever possible surrounded their own British prisoners with a hedge of bayonets.[9]

The adjutant of one of the battalions of the Berry regiment played a particularly notable role in this activity. Almost immediately after accepting the surrender of Lieutenant Henry Hamilton of the 58th Regiment, the adjutant caught sight of a body of Amerindians. "Sir," he said to Hamilton, "your situation is very dangerous, ... exchange uniforms with me, I will furnish you with an escort." Hamilton quickly donned his fellow-European's greatcoat and the white cockade that marked him as a French officer. Then, as the Amerindians drew near, he "turned to my escort and with the authority of an officer wearing a French cockade cried [in French], 'Forward march!'" The French soldiers "relished the gasconade" that deceived their allies and escorted their British prisoner to the safety of the rear.[10]

With Murray defeated in the field and their British prisoners safely ensconced in the General Hospital, the French proceeded to besiege Quebec. This siege was a token effort directed more at keeping the allied army in place outside the town than seriously threatening the garrison. With most of the heavy artillery of New France mounted on the walls of forts that had fallen in 1759, effecting a practicable breach in the ramparts of Quebec was out of the question. Lévis' troops constructed a parallel and batteries along the crest of the ridge occupied by Montcalm in 1759, but the real hope of the allies lay in the arrival of matériel and reinforcements from France.

The garrison of Quebec was equally helpless. Too small and battered to threaten the allies, Murray's army relied more upon the arrival of outside assistance than its own resources to break the siege. With neither the allies nor the garrison in a position to seriously harm the other, the outcome of the siege thus depended upon whether a French or a British squadron reached Quebec first.

During the siege the fighters of the Seven Nations performed their accustomed scouting and patrolling role. Indeed, it was a prisoner taken by Amerindians that gave the first intimation that British rather than French ships were making their way up the St. Lawrence to Quebec.[11] When first HMS *Lowestoft* and then a British squadron appeared on the river below Quebec, the allies lifted the siege that had lasted from 29 April to 17 May and retired towards Montreal.

The siege ended on a sad, sour note for the allies. As the army prepared to depart on 16 May, a number of Amerindians began to gather matériel, not from the British, but from the French camp and provision stores. When French grenadiers attempted to restrain them, one Amerindian and one grenadier were killed and one grenadier wounded in the ensuring altercation.[12] On the same day numerous militiamen and regulars deserted, while other French soldiers broke into the stores of brandy located at the Anse au Foulon and proceeded to drink themselves into oblivion. Only the troops occupying the siegeworks and the grenadiers (who served as enforcers for the French army as a whole) remained under discipline.[13]

When the allies retreated, they left behind a force of eighteen hundred men in three outposts to the west of Quebec. Among these were a number of Amerindians who joined French soldiers and militiamen in observing the movements of the British garrison in the last months of the war.[14]

One anonymous party of Amerindians, however, chose this moment to make their peace with the British. Towards the end of May or the beginning of June they approached the garrison of Quebec and met in council with the British governor. Murray, reporting the incident, identified neither the Amerindians, who were probably Gens de Terre (Cree) or Montagnais, nor the terms of the agreement. Instead, he contented himself with noting that "a Nation of Indians has surrendered, and enter'd into an Alliance with us."[15]

For the French, the siege of Quebec had been a worthwhile gamble that failed to pay off. Rather than hoarding his resources for a defence of Montreal against an enemy possessed of overwhelming superiority in personnel and matériel, Vaudreuil had thrown everything into an all-or-nothing strike against his enemy's weakest point. This operation, if successful, could have changed the course of the Seven Years' War in North America. Once it failed, there was nothing left. Now desperately short of soldiers, munitions, provisions, and artillery, the French lost the ability to influence the course of the war. Unable to maintain an army in the field, Vaudreuil billeted his soldiers on the habitants and awaited developments.[16]

The implications of the withdrawal from Quebec were not lost on the Canadian Iroquois, who considered that the French had suffered crippling losses of irreplaceable matériel and personnel. Prior to the campaign, one Kanesetake had predicted that "if they [the French] do not succeed in their last effort against Quebec, it would be in vain to make any further opposi-

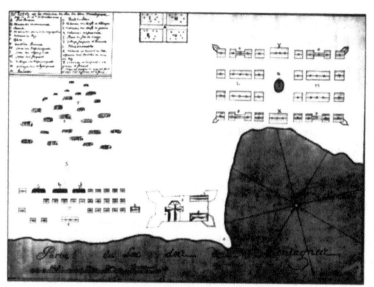

MAP 12. Kanesetake in 1743

Kanesetake's isolated location made it a safe haven for Amerindian refugees in 1760. Many of the buildings on this map were projected rather than actually built. The town of Kanesetake thus consisted of a row of houses extending along the shoreline east of the fort and a scattering of bark lodges to the north.

A. French fort
B. House of the missionaries
C. Stables (projected)
D. House of the Sisters of the Congregation
E. King's cabin (projected)
F. Church
G. French cemetery
H. Nipissing cemetery
I. Algonquin cemetery
K. Iroquois cemetery
L. Nipissing village (projected)
M. Algonquin village (projected)
N. fountain
O. Pointe du lac
P. Cabins of village chiefs
Q. Cabins of war chiefs (projected)
R. Cabins of the poor
S. Lacrosse field
T. Iroquois and Huron village
U. Place of assembly (not marked)
X. Council house (projected)
Y. Cabin where war parties form (projected)

Plan de la mission du Lac des deux Montagnes par M. le Ch'er de Beauharnois. Claude-Charles de Beauharnois, 1743. NMC 4915

tion against the English."[17] Subsequent events confirmed the accuracy of this assessment of the North American strategic situation.

In May 1760 an Amerindian delegation attempted to raise the question of the deteriorating allied position with Vaudreuil. They found the governor general's reaction more resolute than realistic. When the Amerindians "expressed themselves as though the English should get possession of the country," Vaudreuil, instead of addressing this concern, sought to assure them that everything was under control. Speaking through his interpreter, he firmly replied, "Never." An Amerindian orator, apparently more than a little sceptical, but remaining within the bounds of diplomatic decorum, responded "Oh forever never!"[18]

Notwithstanding Vaudreuil's disingenuous reassurances, the prospect of a British invasion produced considerable alarm among the Canadian Iroquois. As British armies converged on Montreal, they could reasonably perceive themselves to be in danger from an enemy that had already displayed considerable ruthlessness against the Acadians in 1755 and the civilian population of the Quebec area and the Abenakis of Odanak in 1759.

Fear of the British was particularly apparent at Oswegatchie, the most exposed Canadian Iroquois community and the only one for which a record of events in the summer of 1760 is available. By spring or early summer the town itself had been abandoned by many Oswegatchie families who relocated to nearby Ile Piquet, a little under five kilometres from Fort Lévis. On 14 June a Mississauga returning from Oswego passed on a message that a British army was on the way and that those Oswegatchies who did not want to die should go to Toniata, an island above Oswegatchie. Five families travelled there, raised a Union Jack, and remained until persuaded to return home on the nineteenth. On 22 July a woman from Oswegatchie informed a party of League Onondagas and Oneidas "that she and the other Native women planned to descend to Montreal soon, because they were afraid." Five days later sixty-seven women, children, and elders actually left Oswegatchie and travelled to the supposed safety of Montreal and Kanesetake. A French officer noted that "fear made them flee."[19] On the twenty-ninth, the appearance of a British warship off Cataraqui Bay was enough to send Oswegatchie fishermen hurrying for home.[20]

Caught between the growing probability of a British victory and growing fear of its consequences, the Canadian Iroquois waited and pondered their options. Their debates were summed up by two escaped British prisoners who passed through Kahnawake on 10 June and observed that "the Cocknawaga Indians are divided, one half proposes to go to Sir William

Johnson, the other into the woods."[21] In the end, the Canadian Iroquois continued until the last days of the war to give the appearance of being willing to fight for the French, while responding positively to overtures from the British. The implementation of this policy was facilitated by a hiatus in military operations during most of the summer, the desire of the British for the neutrality of the Canadian Iroquois, and the willingness of the League Iroquois to intervene on their behalf.

During most of the spring and summer of 1760, with the British preparing to attack and the French unable to resist, the war ground gently to a halt. As a result, the Canadian Iroquois were under no pressure to participate actively in the war between May and August of 1760.[22] This deferred the necessity of making a final commitment to either European power until the last month of hostilities, when the outcome of the war had become virtually certain. Throughout this interval, Canadian Iroquois diplomacy proceeded apace. This diplomacy centred on Oswegatchie, which

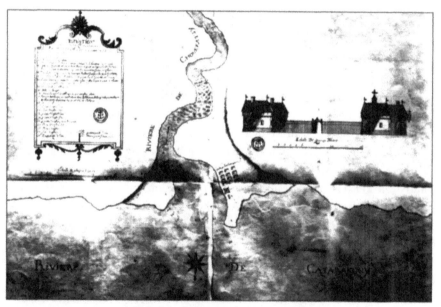

MAP 13. Oswegatchie in 1752
The Rivière de Catarakouy is the St. Lawrence and the Rivière de Choüekatsy is the Oswegatchie River. Oswegatchie itself is the "village des sauvages" located to the right of the river mouth on the south bank of the St. Lawrence.
Elevation du fort de la presentation par Paul La Brosse en l'anné 1752. Paul La Brosse. NMC 7760

became the primary point of contact between the Canadian Iroquois and the League Iroquois and the British.

The British did not fully trust the Canadian Iroquois. Following their contacts with the League Iroquois and the British in the fall of 1759, the winter of 1759-60, and the following spring, Akwesasnes, Kahnawakes, Kanesetakes, and Oswegatchies began to travel regularly to Oswego and Johnson Hall to reaffirm their pacific intentions and to trade. Some brought British prisoners as tokens of good faith. Speaking with British officers at Oswego, successive parties of Canadian Iroquois gave the impression that their communities would not just renounce the French, but begin to provide military support to the British. They made "repeated assurances that at that time [the spring of 1760] all their sachems will be here, When they will endeavour to make amends for their past folly, & give convincing proofs of their attachment [to the British]."[23] These assurances did not allay the scepticism of the British, who accepted declarations of neutrality but continued to consider the Canadian Iroquois as potential adversaries. Johnson himself was of the opinion that "this seeming good disposition of theirs proceeds not from any real regard for us, but from the low circumstances of the enemy, & their own distress."[24]

Nonetheless, the British continued to seek the neutrality of the Canadian Iroquois. Victorious on all fronts in 1759, they expected to continue their invasion in the following year. Rather than planning to defeat the Canadian Iroquois as well as the French, Amherst ordered Johnson "to exert yourself to the utmost in bringing over to his Majesty's Interest all such or as many as possible of the Enemy Indians as still remain attached to them."[25] Successfully neutralizing the Canadian Iroquois would both significantly weaken the French and remove a major obstacle to the invasion of Canada from the west.

With the British actively seeking Canadian Iroquois neutrality and the Canadian Iroquois seeking to open negotiations with the British, the League Iroquois performed a key role as intermediaries between the two parties. In the last years of the Seven Years' War, as British fortunes rose, significant factions among the League Iroquois had become steadily more disturbed by the implications of a French defeat. The League Iroquois, who strongly desired to keep their territory free from European domination, had joined with the British in the summer of 1759 to expel the French from Niagara. Yet after the 1759 campaign the British not only repaired and occupied Fort Niagara, but built a new stronghold at Oswego. A British conquest of New France, moreover, would upset the strategic equilibrium in northeastern

North America to the detriment of the League Iroquois. Saoten, an Oswegatchie who met with several League Onondaga leaders during the summer of 1760, reported that "the ... [Six] Nations were beginning to reflect, and feared that as soon as there were no more Frenchmen, the English would want to destroy them; that at present they were closed in by all of their forts."26

Lacking the strength to either end the intra-European war or expel the British from their territory, the League Iroquois could and did attempt to prevent the Canadian Iroquois from being caught in the crossfire of a final Anglo-French battle for Canada. This goal was articulated on 22 July by a party of Onondagas and Oneidas who assured a woman from Oswegatchie that the League Iroquois contingent that was going to accompany a British army invading Canada by way of the upper St. Lawrence "would be stronger and more numerous than the English, and that they were coming expressly to prevent anyone from harming the Natives."27

In the meantime, the League Iroquois worked to open lines of communication between the British at Oswego and the Canadian Iroquois at Oswegatchie. Their intervention began on 30 March 1760 when Teyohaqueande, a League Onondaga chief, arrived at Oswegatchie. He bore an invitation on behalf of the League Iroquois for the Canadian Iroquois to travel to Onondaga for a council to "decide on what would be best for them to do." Following the receipt of this message, the Oswegatchies held a grand council on 27 April, at which the assembled clan mothers and chiefs decided to send an embassy to the League Iroquois. Two envoys left for Oswego the next day, but the outcome of their mission was inconclusive.28

On 12 June a second delegation set out for Oswego. This time, Ohquandageghte led the delegates. Baptized on 27 April, he had won acceptance among the Oswegatchies based on his own merits, rather than Vaudreuil's clumsy recommendation. On 10 June, Ohquandageghte was described by Johnson as "the Head Man of the [O]Swegatchy Indians, originally an Onondaga."29 This would seem to indicate that he had achieved his ambition of a seat on the council. Now Ohquandageghte joined Oratori and four other chiefs as representatives of Oswegatchie.

Their reception at Oswego was not entirely encouraging. After they had "arrived at Oswego with their Ensigns of peace,"30 the delegates held a series of meetings with League Onondaga chiefs and Haldimand, now the commandant of Fort Ontario. In these meetings, they probed the attitudes of the League Iroquois and the British, and sought to end hostilities with the latter, and succeeded in convincing the British of their good intentions. Speaking of "the [O]Swegachy Indian request to make peace," Johnson considered that "as they have not committed any hostilities since they assured me last year (while I was at Oswego) they would abandon the French and come to us, I am of opinion their present submission should be accepted and they be treated as part of the confederacy who are our friends." Johnson further opined that the Oswegatchies would actively support the British invasion by acting as pilots on the upper St. Lawrence. Haldimand, however, decided that it would be prudent to confine the Oswegatchie envoys until the arrival of Amherst's army at Oswego. Both the chiefs of the League Iroquois and a Kanesetake who were present at Oswego made repeated efforts to secure their release, but the Oswegatchies were held under guard until just before the departure of the British army.[31]

Ohquandageghte, Oratori, and their companions were finally permitted to leave on 5 August. They travelled back to Oswegatchie with two representatives of the League Iroquois, an Oneida and a Mohawk, and arrived on 8 August. At a council held two days later on Ile Piquet, the Mohawk and Oneida envoys invited the Kahnawakes, Kanesetakes, and Oswegatchies to "remain neutral, and allow the whites, who would soon be making peace, to fight." They assured the Canadian Iroquois that they would be well received by the British, who would be on the upper St. Lawrence within a week.[32] This proposal was accepted, and word of the results of the council passed by the League Iroquois to the British army. On 13 August, camped on an island near Fort Frontenac, Jelles Fonda, one of Johnson's subordinates, recorded, in a passage that defies modernization "in the morning I heard from our Indians that the Indians who was gone to swegatia was retorned and said whould cep themselves nuteral when we whould come there."[33]

In the meantime, the debates among the Seven Nations had tipped in favour of negotiation with the British. With British armies known to be preparing to march, representatives of "nine several Nations & Tribes of Indians inhabiting the country about Montreal" made their way to Oswegatchie.[34] There, they awaited the arrival of Amherst and Johnson. They did not wait for long.

Ohquandageghte and Oratori had returned to northeastern Kanienkeh just one step ahead of three British armies. By August the British were on the move again, and three armies were converging on northeastern Kanienkeh and Montreal. On 14 July James Murray and four thousand regulars from the garrisons of Quebec and Louisbourg set sail for Montreal, encountering only sporadic, ineffectual opposition as they ascended the St.

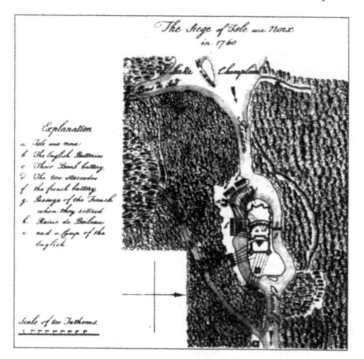

MAP 14. *The Siege of Ile aux Noix in 1760.* NMC 18292

Lawrence. By 5 September, Murray was at Longueuil; three days later his army had landed on Montreal Island and marched to within sight of the town.[35]

A second army of 3,300 regulars and provincials under Brigadier-General William Haviland assembled at Crown Point, then sailed for Ile aux Noix on 11 August 1760. The ensuing siege lasted until 28 August, when the garrison capitulated. Fort Chambly, the last French fort between the British and Montreal, surrendered on 1 September. On 5 September advance elements from Haviland's force were at Longueuil where they were met by Murray in person.[36]

Finally, on 10 August the long-awaited invasion of Canada by way of the upper St. Lawrence began when an army of ten thousand commanded by Amherst left Oswego. This force included a strong Amerindian component. A total of 1,330 League Iroquois men, women, and children had assembled at Oswego by 5 July. Of these, 706, including fifteen Oswegatchies, actually sailed with Amherst.[37]

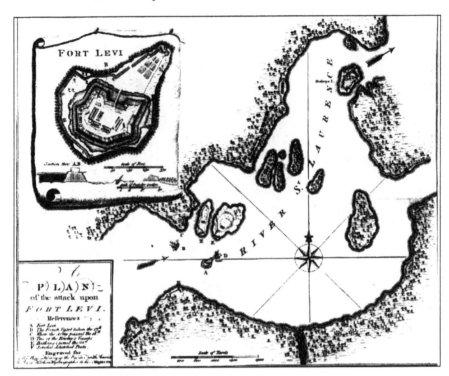

MAP 15. The siege of Fort Lévis in 1760
While this siege was in progress, the Seven Nations of Canada
were negotiating neutrality with Sir William Johnson. These negotiations took place at Amherst's headquarters, marked by the styl-
ized pavilion in the centre of a line of rectangles representing the
campsites of British regiments along the north bank of the St.
Lawrence. Île Piquet is the large island in the top right, just under
the arrow.
Plan of the attack upon Fort Levi, anon., engraver T. Kitchin. NMC
120000

In spite of the reassurances of the Oneida and Mohawk envoys, the
approach of Amherst's army provoked consternation and flight. Most of the
Akwesasnes and their Abenaki guests evacuated Akwesasne. The
Oswegatchie families who had moved to Ile Piquet forsook their temporary
homes before the British arrived. Those who remained at Oswegatchie itself
fled into the forest when the British landed there on 17 August, then re-
emerged and established amicable relations with the invaders. This cordial-
ity was not, however, enough to save the empty homes and church on Ile

Piquet. When Amerindians allied to the British landed on the island on the eighteenth, they mistook Oswegatchie homes "for the Frenchmens houses" and burned every building on the island to the ground.[38]

Oswegatchie itself was occupied by the British, who used it first as a base of operations during the siege, then as a temporary hospital. In September and early October, Oswegatchie was garrisoned by a series of British detachments of regulars and provincials who proceeded to demolish the greater part of the town. By 3 October, Jelles Fonda "found most of ... the Indian houses destroyed" and the troops "still cutting and destroying the houses for fire wood." The few buildings still standing had been taken over by Frenchmen. Only a direct request from Fonda to a senior British officer produced an order to end the destruction and expel the French. Nonetheless, when the Oswegatchies returned in October, their community lay in ruins.[39]

On the day after the landing at Oswegatchie, Amherst's army advanced to a site on the north shore of the St. Lawrence opposite Fort Lévis and invested the French outpost.[40] While siege operations were in progress, the delegates of the Seven Nations made their approach to Amherst's camp and met in council with Johnson.[41] In the course of this conference, Johnson reported, the Seven Nations "ratified a treaty with us, whereby they agreed to remain neuter on condition that we for the future treated them as friends."[42] According to the Akwesasnes, Johnson gave the Seven Nations guarantees regarding their future relationships with the British, declaring that "if the country remained in the possession of the English, we should not only enjoy the same privileges we enjoyed in the time of the French, but still more and greater, - and the usage better."[43]

Following the negotiation of this agreement, ten Akwesasnes went so far as to accompany Amherst's army to Montreal, along with thirty-six Frenchmen from the garrison of Fort Lévis who guided the British bateaux through the rapids of the upper St. Lawrence and several more who enlisted in the Royal American battalions.[44] The remainder of the Canadian Iroquois "preserved so strict a neutrality that we [the British] passed all the dangerous rapids, and the whole way without the least opposition."[45]

Like the capitulations of forts Necessity, Oswego, and William Henry, the surrender of Fort Lévis on 25 August occurred after negotiations between Europeans which took no account of the military aspirations of the Amerindians who accompanied Amherst's army. In this case, however, the large British force proved capable of protecting the French garrison, who were taken into British custody without incident. Denied the opportunity to

Passage of Amherst's Army down the Rapids of the St. Lawrence toward Montreal, by Thomas Davies, 1760. NAC C-000577

collect prisoners and matériel and having fulfilled their stated aim of seeing to the safety of the Canadian Iroquois, most of the Amerindians, including the fifteen Oswegatchies, left the army. Only 175 Amerindians continued on to Montreal after the surrender of Fort Lévis.[46]

Hostilities between the British and the Canadian Iroquois thus came to an end, but they had been replaced by a state of uneasy neutrality rather than formal alliance. Even this neutrality was apparently not considered by Amherst to extend beyond Oswegatchie, for the British continued to treat the Canadian Iroquois communities that they passed on the way to Montreal as potential adversaries. On 30 August Amherst accordingly ordered Johnson to travel ahead of the army "to hinder the Indians from joining the enemy, in which case they may be assured of being permitted to live in peace and quiet, and of receiving all the protection they can desire." Four days later the British general referred to the Akwesasnes as "the enemy's Indians."[47]

On 1 September Johnson and the fighters from Akwesasne and the Iroquois League were in Akwesasne. Johnson met in council with the ten male Akwesasnes who had remained in the town and "assure[d] them of protection on their good behavior."[48] On 6 September Johnson and Amherst reached Kahnawake, where Amerindians "promised the General, that they would observe a strict neutrality: upon which he gave orders that they should not be molested."[49]

Yet even as negotiations with Johnson were under way outside Fort Lévis, a significant contingent of Canadian Iroquois fighters remained in the field alongside the French outside Montreal. For if the Canadian Iroquois had opened lines of communication to the British, they were also careful to retain the goodwill of the French. Thus, when the last weeks of August found the French preparing to make a last stand in the Montreal area, the Canadian Iroquois responded positively to an invitation to take part.[50] By 21 August a force of 474 fighters from the Seven Nations had assembled at Fort St. Jean. With Ile aux Noix under siege by Haviland's army, the French proposed that these warriors join with 1,043 militiamen and soldiers in an operation to relieve the siege by attacking the besiegers.[51]

Rather than accepting or refusing this invitation, the Amerindians met with the French and laid out the conditions under which they would participate. First, they asked that the French provide five thousand soldiers, which was then impossible. Second, they insisted upon making their own assessment of British strength before committing themselves. They proposed that a party consisting of one warrior from each nation reconnoitre the area, then return and make their report. This would take days, and defer the moment when the Seven Nations would have to make a final decision. The Amerindians thus evaded both a direct refusal of French requests, since they did agree to fight under certain conditions, and involvement in a hopeless battle that could only poison their future relationship with the British. Their temporizing was further successful in that Vaudreuil continued to regard the Seven Nations as loyal allies, who had been temporarily intimidated by the British.[52]

The strategic procrastination continued until 24 August, when a mounted messenger arrived from Oswegatchie with word that the League Iroquois would mediate between the British and the Canadian Amerindians. The Amerindian fighters immediately left Fort St. Jean and withdrew towards Kahnawake.[53]

Five days later, during the night of 29 August, Fort St. Jean was burned and abandoned by its garrison. By 1 September most of the French forces remaining on the south shore had been ordered by Lévis to concentrate at La Prairie.

On 2 September the Canadian Iroquois accepted an invitation to meet with the French at La Prairie. The four hundred fighters who attended listened politely as Lévis proposed that the Amerindians join with the entire

French army for a final attack upon the British. But just when Lévis was certain that he had persuaded the Amerindians to join his expedition, word arrived that the British had accepted the neutrality proposed by the League Iroquois to the Canadian Iroquois. With their status changed from combatants to neutrals, the Amerindians decamped immediately: "In that instant, they dispersed and left M. de Lévis all alone, with his officers."[54]

Lévis too received word that Fort Lévis had fallen and Amherst was at the Cedars. He decided to abandon the south shore completely and withdraw to the island of Montreal. On 3 September the French evacuated their positions at La Prairie and Longueuil and crossed the river to Montreal.

With a final breach with the French effected and two British columns who were not aware of their change of status advancing on the Montreal area, the Seven Nations took steps to make contact with these armies. On 5 September a delegation of eight Canadian Iroquois and Hurons of Lorette left Kahnawake and travelled to Longueuil. There they encountered James Murray, who had come with a force of grenadiers, light infantry, and rangers to link up with the leading elements of Haviland's Lake Champlain army.

Murray's advance from Quebec had been undertaken without diplomatic preliminaries and his recorded contact with Amerindians was limited to the one encounter at Quebec in May and his possession of a an

An east view of Montreal, in Canada, by Thomas Patten, engraver, Pierre Charles Canot, 1762. NAC C-002433

Amerindian slave whom he had purchased in 1759 and would send to England as a gift for William Pitt in 1761.[55] The Seven Nations delegates, however, arrived at the same time as three League Mohawks, carrying a letter from Amherst that may have informed Murray of the agreement reached at Oswegatchie.

In any event, the envoys quickly communicated their pacific intentions and in return received a number of commitments from the British general, which were recorded in a certificate presented by Murray to the Hurons of Lorette. The Amerindians were "received upon the same terms with the Canadians" and guaranteed safe passage back to their homes, along with "the free exercise of their religion, their customs and liberty of trading with the English garrisons."[56]

Following this meeting, the Amerindian envoys returned to Kahnawake. On 6 September the fighters of the last Amerindian contingent to serve in the field alongside the French assembled on the shore of the St. Lawrence to greet Johnson. Five Kahnawakes rowed Johnson's whaleboat across the river to Montreal as British forces landed on Montreal Island.[57]

During the night of 6-7 September 1760 Vaudreuil assembled his senior metropolitan and colonial officers and officials. A last accounting of the resources left to the French made it brutally clear that further resistance was hopeless. On 8 September 1760 Vaudreuil accordingly surrendered Montreal and what remained of New France to the British.

While this larger drama was in progress outside Montreal, a series of incidents near Kanesetake and on Montreal Island revealed both the tensions that were always present beneath the surface of the alliance between the Canadian Iroquois and the French, and the uncertain status of the Amerindians' new relationship with the British. These incidents occurred at a time when the military power of the French had been neutralized and that of the British was not fully established. During this hiatus, the Amerindians of the region could act without fear of military interference from either side.

When the warriors from Kanesetake left Kahnawake after 6 September they travelled westward up the St. Lawrence River, then turned north and crossed Lac des Deux Montagnes to their homes. This route took them past the seigneurie of Vaudreuil. The French of Vaudreuil and the Amerindians of Kanesetake had lived amicably on opposite sides of Lac des Deux Montagnes for decades. They attended the same church at Kanesetake and fought side by side in a series of wars. Yet when the Amerindian-French alliance broke down, the French feared the Amerindians and the Amerindians apparently took advantage of the situation. On reaching Lac des Deux Montagnes, instead of skirting the shores of Vaudreuil, the warriors landed. Once ashore, they appropriated muskets, killed cattle, broke into homes, and generally intimidated and harassed the habitants.[58]

Within days of this incident Amherst's army passed by on the way to Montreal and the residents of Vaudreuil turned to the new British authorities for help. Vaudreuil itself was off the track of the invasion, but the neighbouring parish of St. Joseph de Soulanges had been occupied by a detachment of 150 provincials and regulars from the fourth battalion of the Royal Americans under Captain Moncrieffe.[59] Left behind by Amherst at the Cedars on 4 September, Moncrieffe was expected to pacify the area between the St. Lawrence and Lac des Deux Montagnes by collecting firearms and signatures to oaths of allegiance from the habitants. On or before 9 September some habitants from Vaudreuil brought in muskets belonging to individuals who were ill and unable to travel to the Cedars. Others arrived without any firearms at all. Questioned by Moncrieffe, they declared themselves to be victims of thefts and intimidation by the Amerindians of Kanesetake. In his report to Amherst, Moncrieffe described the habitants as "much alarm'd for fear of the Indians, their old friends [who] have killed numbers of their cattle."[60]

Village of Cedars on the St. Lawrence River, by William Henry Bartlett, 1838. NAC C-040325

CHAPTER 10

THE GOOD WORK OF PEACE, 1760–1764

Any tensions that may have been created by the incidents at Vaudreuil and Montreal Island passed quickly. On 15 and 16 September the Seven Nations of Canada met with the League Iroquois and the British to transform tentative neutrality into formal alliance at the Treaty of Kahnawake.

At this conference, the Amerindians formally brought their participation in the Seven Years' War to an end and renounced the French alliance. They would, they declared, "bury the French hatchet we have made use of, in the bottomless pit." Johnson took this metaphor further, when he symbolically took the axe and "buried the same by pulling up a large pine tree under which runs a stream of water into which I cast the axe so that it might no more be found." In the language of Amerindian diplomacy, the axe stood for war. By accepting a "French axe" from Onontio, the Seven Nations had declared war against the British. The war would continue until the axe was returned, lowered, or buried. The white pine was the "Tree of Peace." Hurling the axe into an underground river running beneath the tree further symbolized an end to war.[1]

From the defunct French alliance, the Seven Nations formally entered into alliance with the British, by "renewing and strengthening the old Covenant Chain which before this war subsisted between us, and we in the name of every nation here present assure you that we will hold fast of the same, for ever hereafter."[2] A chain of friendship represented alliance among

Vaudreuil, all was calm. The Amerindians had continued on to Kanesetake, and thus a potentially serious situation ended without confrontation and without violence. Provost's detachment was consequently withdrawn to Montreal within a few days.

A series of similar incidents occurred on the Island of Montreal. Here Amherst himself took harsher measures. He "sent several detachments into the parishes of the island to stop the domiciled Natives [of the Seven Nations] that ravaged them." One Amerindian was apprehended for breaking into a house and subsequently hanged by the British.[63]

It is extremely likely that the disturbances in Vaudreuil and Montreal Island were the result of the unauthorized actions of a very few young men who continued on their way with no intention of returning. Judging from their subsequent actions, it is certain that the Amerindians of Kahnawake had no intention of committing any act that might bring them into conflict with the British.

The British, on the other hand, proved to be more willing to stand by fellow Europeans than Amerindians. They made no attempt to obtain an Amerindian account of events at Vaudreuil, and went so far as to consider the use of military force to protect their former European enemies against Amerindians who were well on the way to becoming allies. What was more, in the midst of an intensive campaign to collect every musket in the hands of a habitant, Amherst proved willing to return some of these muskets for possible use against the Canadian Iroquois. This was a remarkable measure, given that male habitants were also militiamen, and thus French soldiers. On 14 September he authorized Moncrieffe to inform the habitants that if they cooperated with the British authorities, they would be rearmed: "You may drop a hint that as I find they do behave, I shall return a few arms to each parish, for its protection against the Indians."[64] There is no record of this remarkable proposition ever being put into effect, but Amherst's willingness to consider the idea remains a revealing example of British attitudes towards the French and Amerindians of Canada at the time of the occupation.

The relationship of the Canadian Iroquois with the British thus began with the demolition of Oswegatchie and the use of British troops to protect the French farmers of the Montreal area from their former Amerindian allies. Whatever commitments the Canadian Iroquois may have obtained at Fort Lévis, the British were proving to be possessed of a rather cavalier attitude towards Amerindian property and more inclined to display racial solidarity with fellow Europeans than sincere friendship towards Amerindians.

THE GOOD WORK OF PEACE, 1760–1764

Any tensions that may have been created by the incidents at Vaudreuil and Montreal Island passed quickly. On 15 and 16 September the Seven Nations of Canada met with the League Iroquois and the British to transform tentative neutrality into formal alliance at the Treaty of Kahnawake.

At this conference, the Amerindians formally brought their participation in the Seven Years' War to an end and renounced the French alliance. They would, they declared, "bury the French hatchet we have made use of, in the bottomless pit." Johnson took this metaphor further, when he symbolically took the axe and "buried the same by pulling up a large pine tree under which runs a stream of water into which I cast the axe so that it might no more be found." In the language of Amerindian diplomacy, the axe stood for war. By accepting a "French axe" from Onontio, the Seven Nations had declared war against the British. The war would continue until the axe was returned, lowered, or buried. The white pine was the "Tree of Peace." Hurling the axe into an underground river running beneath the tree further symbolized an end to war.[1]

From the defunct French alliance, the Seven Nations formally entered into alliance with the British, by "renewing and strengthening the old Covenant Chain which before this war subsisted between us, and we in the name of every nation here present assure you that we will hold fast of the same, for ever hereafter."[2] A chain of friendship represented alliance among

Amerindians, and the Covenant Chain was the particular alliance between the British and League Iroquois. In taking hold of the Covenant Chain, the Seven Nations formally took their place in this alliance. The Seven Nations further committed themselves to repatriate all British prisoners and provide military support to the British upon request. Henceforth the Canadian Amerindians would "be ready on all occasion to act with them [the British] against any nation which might be rash enough to quarrel with them."[3]

The Seven Nations further asked to be allowed to remain in undisturbed possession of their lands and that the military authorities prevent the sale of liquor, provide smiths and other artisans to work for Amerindians at government expense, control British merchants to ensure equitable terms of trade, and appoint English interpreters. Ad'yadarony, a Kahnawake war chief, sought an additional commitment. He asked that should any disturbances be caused by the young men of the Seven Nations, the British would come to the chiefs and allow them to resolve the matter. The response of the British to these requests was not recorded.[4]

The British, apart from assuming the normal obligations of alliance, made two specific commitment to the Seven Nations. They were henceforth to be permitted free and unrestricted passage to Albany to trade and would

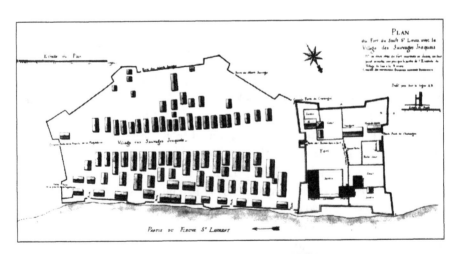

MAP 16. Kahnawake in 1754.
The caption notes that the walls of the fort on the side of the river and the town were projected, as was the town wall along the river.
Plan du fort du Sault St. Louis avec le village des sauvages Iroquois. Anon., 1754. NMC 42963

be allowed to retain their Catholic priests.[5] Overall, the Seven Nations were satisfied with the terms of the new alliance. Their speakers at the conference declared that "we have now made a firm peace with the English" as "you have now settled all matters with us & we are become firm friends."[6]

The Treaty of Kahnawake was also the occasion for a final reconciliation between the Seven Nations and the League Iroquois. Participation on opposing sides of the Seven Years' War had badly strained relations between the two groups. Now, leaders of both parties agreed to "reunite & be firm friends as heretofore" and to join together in the Covenant Chain.[7]

The Canadian Iroquois carefully adhered to the terms of their new alliance with the British. This compliance began in the weeks immediately following the Treaty of Kahnawake, when a steady stream of liberated men, women, and children were handed over to Amherst in Montreal. The Canadian Iroquois also provided assistance to British colonials seeking family members who had been taken prisoner and sold to Frenchmen.[8]

The efforts of the Amerindians of Kanesetake to comply fully with the terms of the Treaty of Kahnawake were recorded by their parish priest in a letter to Amherst. Oswegatchie refugees at Kanesetake surrendered eight prisoners to the British. Canadian Iroquois, Algonquin, and Nipissing residents immediately handed over those prisoners that they had at hand, and guaranteed that prisoners who were absent with hunting parties would be surrendered as soon as they returned from the forest. They went so far as to pursue one Amerindian who was off hunting, "in order to take away by force or by consent his prisoner in order to turn him over." Former prisoners who had been adopted into Kanesetake families, converted to Catholicism, married, and settled down as members of the community were special cases. They travelled to Kahnawake to meet with Johnson to make it clear that they were remaining behind of their own free will.[9]

What Ad'yadarony called "the Good Work of Peace" was a cumulative process that began with the first diplomatic contacts between the Canadian Iroquois and the British in 1759 and continued after the Treaty of Kahnawake. Amerindian alliances were subject to periodic renewal, and the Canadian Iroquois took care to keep their new alliance current. In 1761 the Kahnawakes and Kanesetakes reaffirmed their commitment to the agreements made at Kahnawake in 1760, and "added that they ... had firmly & unanimously resolved upon in public council that let times & events be as they would they never again would take up the hatchet against the English but would steadily mind their hunting and begged it might be recorded for the memory of us and their posterity."[10]

Grand Chief of Iroquois Warriors, by Jacques Grasset de Saint-Sauveur, engraver J. Laroque, *c.* 1796. NAC C-003161

This adherence to the new alliance went beyond words. By 1763 the Canadian Iroquois were providing the British with diplomatic and military assistance. In that year, war broke out between the British and a coalition of Great Lakes nations, all of whom had been allied with the Canadian Iroquois during the French era. Despite their former ties to the western nations, the Canadian Iroquois sided with the British. Immediately hostilities began they met at Kahnawake with Daniel Claus, Johnson's agent in Canada. There the Canadian Iroquois "unanimously agreed to send messages to the Enemy Indians, to desire them to lay down the hatchet with which, if they do not comply, the Canada Indians would declare against them."[11] Along with this diplomatic support, the Canadian Iroquois sent contingents of warriors to fight alongside the British in the west. In 1764 Johnson thanked the Kahnawakes and Kanesetakes for this assistance, provided "according to the tenor of the treaty settled with you at Cognawagey [Kahnawake] in the year 1760."[12]

British performance as allies of the Canadian Iroquois, on the other hand, was decidedly mixed. The military government did attempt to regulate trade. John Davis, a merchant working out of Fort William Augustus, discovered this the hard way. Found to be "trading there with the Indians in a most cruel and unfair manner," he was arrested and expelled from Canada.[13] The British also responded sympathetically when the Kahnawakes sought legal protection for their farmlands. The Kahnawakes had long objected to Jesuit priests going beyond their strictly religious role and alienating Kahnawake farmland to French habitants. The loss of this land posed a serious economic threat to the Kahnawakes, and when the military government was established, they lost no time in presenting their case, along with documentary evidence. In 1762 the Kahnawakes obtained a favourable decision from a court of British field officers who ordered that "the said Indians of Sault St. Louis be put in possession, and enjoy peaceably to themselves, their heirs, and other Indians that may joyn them, all these lands and income said concession may produce." Later in the British era, the Kahnawakes were unable to prevent further encroachment upon their farmland, but in 1762 they had definite grounds for optimism.[14]

Moreover, after the Treaty of Kahnawake the British were not just allies, they were also potential consumers. The occupation of Canada entailed the presence of a large garrison, possessed of significant quantities of specie. Supplying goods and services in exchange for this specie quickly became a major economic preoccupation for the Canadian Iroquois. They sold venison and fish at British outposts by the tonne and provided transportation by horse-drawn sleigh and canoe to British soldiers and officers.[15]

These encouraging developments, unfortunately for the Canadian Iroquois, were not entirely representative of British conduct. Within months of the establishment of the new alliance, the British violated both the letter and the spirit of the Treaty of Kahnawake. In January of 1761 Claus reported that the Amerindians of Canada were "living in the utmost tranquility as in the profoundest time of peace."[16] However, Canadian Iroquois soon found themselves subject to attempts to limit their freedom of movement and to physical abuse from some elements of the British garrison.

In the winter of 1760-61 the St. Lawrence valley suffered severely from wartime shortages. The Kahnawakes in particular were badly in need of ammunition and other goods that could not be obtained in Canada, but were available in New York. However, when Kahnawakes attempted to travel to Albany, they found the British authorities at Montreal had established dual policies regarding movement along the Lake Champlain corridor. British merchants were encouraged and supported in establishing trade through this area, whereas the Kahnawakes were prohibited from making any use of this route whatsoever.

Christian Daniel Claus, anon. NAC C-083514

After the surrender of Montreal the British did not treat the Lake Champlain corridor as a connection between two parts of the British empire, through which people and freight could move without restriction. Instead, the region became a military zone, separate from both Canada and New York and under the direct control of the commander-in-chief. All travel through, and settlement within, this region required the consent of the military authorities. Every person and every cargo passing north or south was stopped by the garrisons of forts George, Ticonderoga, and Crown Point. Only those possessed of a pass issued by a senior officer were allowed to continue. Smugglers were arrested, and contraband seized.[17] For the first time, a European power had asserted effective control over movement along the Lake Champlain corridor.

Amherst sought to encourage commercial traffic between Montreal and Albany along this route. The day after the surrender of Montreal he wrote to the governors of every British colony in North America, informing them of shortages of provisions in Canada and asking that they encourage entrepreneurs to take advantage of this opportunity.[18] These traders were not only invited to make use of the Lake Champlain corridor, they were subsidized by the army. Bateaux and sloops, crewed by soldiers, were made available to British merchants to carry their goods along Lake Champlain. When winter came and the lake froze, the merchants were provided with sleighs. As a result of these measures, along with economic opportunities and the enterprise of individual entrepreneurs, a flourishing traffic developed between Albany and Montreal in 1760 and 1761.[19]

Yet at the same time as the army was encouraging and assisting European entrepreneurs to travel between Canada and New York, Thomas Gage, the military lieutenant governor of Montreal, had embarked upon a deliberate campaign to eliminate the Kahnawakes from this commerce. Questioned by Claus about this policy, Gage responded that he would not tolerate what he described as "that contraband trade to be carried on as heretofore between the Albany people and Caghnaway. Indians which was their only scheme of going down." Both "an entire stranger" to the terms of the Treaty of Kahnawake and one of those "people in power" who looked upon Amerindians with an "indifferent & despiteful eye," Gage possessed the power to put this policy into action.[20] As lieutenant governor, he controlled the issue of passes for travel to Albany. These passports were freely issued to British merchants.[21] The Kahnawakes attempted to conform to British regulations, and they too applied for travel documents. The first applicants duly received passes signed by Gage. Subsequent requests, however, were rejected.

British medal awarded to those Amerindians who accompanied Amherst's army from Fort Lévis to Montreal, cast by Daniel Christian Fueter. C-001457

The Kahnawake protested, stating that "they were surprized that the road of peace opened & shown to them last fall should be barred up again." These protests were summarized by Johnson, who informed Amherst that the Kahnawakes "are a good deal surprised and concerned at not being allowed to come to trade to Albany, where they say they can have goods much cheaper than at Montreal," then added that since "they were told and promised that the road of peace & commerce should be free and open for them, they now think it hard to be debarred that liberty." Claus told Gage about the terms of the Treaty of Kahnawake, but the lieutenant governor remained inflexible.[22]

Johnson himself was "surprised General Gage will not suffer the Caghnawageys & other Inds. inhabiting there to come to Albany after making it one of ye. articles at the treaty last summer at Caghnawagey." He forwarded the Kahnawake protests to the commander-in-chief, together with his own recommendation that the New York-Canadian border be opened to Amerindians. Amherst immediately ordered Gage to cease to interfere with the movements of the Amerindians of Canada along the Lake Champlain corridor. He authorized Johnson to assure the Amerindians that "whatever promises have been made, they shall be strictly adhered to, and so long as they behave well, they shall have full liberty for a free and open trade."[23]

The question of access to Albany had thus been resolved to the satisfaction of the Canadian Iroquois, but the outbreak of war between the British and the Amerindians of the west in 1763 led to renewed attempts to control the movements of Amerindians in Canada. During that conflict, the military authorities established a pass system for Amerindians. Under this system, Amerindians who wanted to travel outside of their own communities had to apply to the military authorities for a pass for each specific journey, which they were required to present upon demand to the garrison of each British post that they encountered.

The pass system was rigorously enforced. Ohquandagehte, the Oswegatchie chief, for example, was arrested and sent as a prisoner to Montreal "for having no pass to go by The Cedars with some necessaries he purchased with his furs." Ralph Burton, who had replaced Gage as lieutenant governor of Montreal, "wrote to the [arresting] officer that he did his duty, & approved of what he had done." Even Canadian Iroquois serving alongside the British in war were not exempt from this measure. In 1764 a contingent of sixty-two Kahnawake fighters, travelling to the west to fight on behalf of the British, complained to Johnson "of their not being allowed to pass any post without a passport, and their [having] been often fired upon, which is what they have ever been strangers to, and therefore begged they might not for the future be obliged to ask for passes on every occasion." Johnson responded with a commitment to terminate this practice after the end of hostilities in the west.[24]

As well as attempts to limit their freedom of movement, the Canadian Iroquois were forced to endure violent and abusive treatment at the hands of British soldiers. For along with those Britons who established relationships of mutual civility and respect with the Canadian Iroquois, there were others who behaved more like thugs in uniform than disciplined soldiers.

Particularly notorious in this regard were the officers and soldiers of the 44th Regiment, the garrison at the Cedars, and the commandant of Fort Ticonderoga.

For the 44th, war in North America had consisted for the most part of harrowing defeats and cancelled expeditions. Like most British metropolitan and provincial units, it did not participate in a single significant victory until the last two years of the war. In the course of the Seven Years' War, the regiment took part in the Battle of Monongahela in 1755, an unsuccessful attempt to relieve Oswego in 1756, an abortive attack on Louisbourg in 1757, and the Battle of Carillon in 1758. Only in 1759 and 1760 did it take part in the successful sieges of forts Niagara and Lévis and the advance on Montreal.[25] Following the capitulation of Montreal, the soldiers of the 44th were billeted near Kahnawake.

The Kahnawakes found the 44th to be difficult neighbours. In 1761 numerous community members were assaulted, robbed, and generally abused by the soldiers of this regiment. Many of these assaults occurred when Kahnawakes driving horses and sleighs encountered soldiers marching on foot who demanded transport in these vehicles without payment. When Kahnawakes demurred, they were attacked.[26]

One such incident was described in detail by Claus. It began in April of 1761 when a number of Kahnawakes were approached by Lieutenant George Pennington of the 44th, who sought to hire them to escort a cashiered fellow officer to Crown Point. However, when the Kahnawakes met with Pennington in his quarters at La Prairie, they were unable to reach an agreement regarding their wages. At this point the lieutenant, who considered these negotiations to be "insolence," ordered a group of soldiers to bar the door. He then seized a large club and "fell beating them till he was tired." When the Kahnawakes told "him they expected no such treatment by virtue of the Treaty you [Johnson] held with them last fall, he answered them in a despisefull, unbecoming manner, that he did not pay any regard to that." Pennington sent the Kahnawakes away with a letter to the priest at Kahnawake, asking for three more Amerindians. Instead, the Kahnawakes sought redress, using Claus as an intermediary. Claus responded positively and immediately lodged a strong protest with Gage. But Gage, who had joined the 44th Regiment in 1748 and served as its lieutenant-colonel between 1751 and 1757, proved less than sympathetic. He accepted Pennington's version of the story and agreed that the Amerindians had exaggerated a minor disagreement for which they were responsible. The Kahnawakes were permitted to recover the weapons, packs, and canoes that they had been forced to leave behind, but received no further satisfaction.[27]

Claus blamed Pennington's immediate superior, Major John Beckwith, for encouraging the climate of violent hostility among the men of the 44th that produced these ugly confrontations. For not only did Beckwith refuse to attempt to moderate the behaviour of his troops, he was himself a continuous source of trouble for the Kahnawakes. On one occasion, the "strange behaviour" of this officer caused the Kahnawakes to be "so alarmed ... that they were the whole night awake & on their guard."[28]

The conduct of the 44th was not what the Canadian Iroquois expected from their new allies. Johnson shared this opinion, remarking that "This maltreatment shewn them by our troops & without provocation, [was] contrary to the assurances given them last year at the Treaty Held at Caghnawagey." Claus promised redress, and twice managed to secure severe punishment for soldiers. But he also blamed the Kahnawakes, not for provoking these incidents, but for going into Montreal where they might come into contact with British troops. In conferences with the Kahnawakes, Claus continually stressed that any future violence would be "chiefly their own fault, since they had been forewarned to avoid soldiers."[29]

Avoiding Montreal was not, however, a solution, as the Kahnawakes encountered harassment and robbery even in their fall and winter hunting camps in the southern reaches of their territory along Lake Champlain and Lake George. The most serious incidents occurred in the fall of 1762. This was a difficult time for Kahnawake families, as deer were scarce and hunting was poor. Some hunters returned to Kahnawake without killing even one deer. Others were more successful, and not only killed enough to feed their families, but managed to produce a surplus which they sold to the garrisons at forts George, Crown Point, and Ile aux Noix. At these posts they met "with the greatest civility and got full value for" their game. At Fort Ticonderoga, on the other hand, the Kahnawakes encountered a dangerously hostile commandant, Captain John Ormsby, "a very odd kind of man, rather too intimate with his bottle." With Ormsby in command, Kahnawake hunters who passed by Ticonderoga were robbed of their venison and hides and treated "in a contemptible manner."[30]

By Ormsby's standards, the treatment accorded the Canadian Iroquois was relatively benign. That officer enjoyed the dubious distinction of being one of the most truculent, least likeable commandants in British North America. During his year in command of Fort Ticonderoga, Ormsby displayed a fine impartiality as he managed to alienate fellow officers, British civilians, and a wide variety of Amerindians. In the fall and early winter of 1762 his relationships with Amerindians often ended in their arrest and confinement in the Ticonderoga guardhouse.

Ormsby first arrested an Amerindian (probably a Mohican) serving with the Massachusetts provincials for theft. No sooner had the guardhouse been vacated by the escape of this prisoner, who fled straight to Amherst to proclaim his innocence, then Ormsby filled it to capacity with other Amerindians. This time his prisoners were members of an unidentified party of hunters, whom he accused of vandalism and selling rum to the garrison. Ormsby next accused a party of League Mohawks who had visited Crown Point of the theft of twenty-six hogs. Amherst responded to Ormsby's reports of these events with considerable scepticism and orders to maintain better relations with Amerindians in the future.[31] Amherst's orders, and Ormsby's replacement later that year, did not alleviate the losses suffered at his hands by the Canadian Iroquois. However, the presence among them of John Lotteridge, Claus's deputy, may have spared them even greater trouble with Ormsby.

A third area of danger for Canadian Iroquois lay at the Cedars, where they found themselves subject to harassment and extortion by the British garrison. During the winter of 1760-61 those troops quickly gained a reputation for firing wildly at passing canoes of Kanesetakes and Kahnawakes travelling to and from hunting camps, then robbing Amerindians who were forced ashore of venison and other items. Those who protested received savage beatings from British soldiers. Three years later this abuse continued. In the last week of August 1764 several women from Akwesasne paddling in a canoe on the St. Lawrence caught sight of a British officer travelling towards the Cedars. Alarmed by the officer's erratic, aggressive behaviour, they turned away when he called out a challenge. The officer then shouted "They are Western Indians" and fired a shot which hit the head of the canoe. Less than a month after this incident, an Akwesasne family had a harrowing encounter with the garrison of the Cedars. In September of 1764, while paddling to Montreal, they were fired upon by members of the garrison and compelled to come ashore. The father, a chief who had been on his way to meet with Claus, was taken away by the garrison. He endured an uncomfortable encounter with "cursing, and swearing" soldiers who "made threatening signs at him, and, as he apprehended, abused him with ill language." Only after paying a ransom of salmon was the father released and the family allowed to proceed.[32]

Incidents such as these caused considerable concern among the Canadian Iroquois who were inclined to "suspect their new friends of intending to break their promises." This concern persisted as the British failure to adhere to the terms of the new alliance continued beyond an initial period of adjustment. In 1773 the Kanesetakes, in the presence of Kahnawakes, declared that "at the Surrender of Canada they were promised by Sir William Johnson on behalf of his Majesty to enjoy the same Privileges they did under the French government and perhaps greater, but they were now convinced of the contrary."[33]

Yet neither the British violations of the terms of the Treaty of Kahnawake between 1760 and 1764 nor the future conduct of the crown detract from the diplomatic achievement of the Canadian Iroquois in 1759 and 1760. Most of their difficulties concerned restrictions on travel imposed by a local lieutenant governor, a single regiment, and the garrisons of two small outposts, rather than a concerted imperial policy. In the years after 1764, most of meetings between Claus and the Canadian Iroquois dealt not with grievances, but the routine rituals of a working alliance: the conferring of medals, distribution of matériel, and the covering of the dead.[34]

Their new relationship with the British might have been an alliance of necessity rather than choice, but the Canadian Iroquois had managed to make the best of a very difficult, potentially catastrophic, situation. Whatever the shortcomings of the British as allies, the Canadian Iroquois had succeeded in making a peaceful transition from the French to the British era. They had converted the British invaders from dangerous and vindictive enemies into "our new Brothers."[35] In contrast, Odanak was attacked and burned after the Abenakis bluntly rejected the first British offer of neutrality in 1759 and the nations of the Great Lakes and Ohio valley were at war with the British within three years.[36] Caught between two European powers and their armies, the Canadian Iroquois acted successfully to ensure their own survival. Rather than passively await the defeat of their French allies, they turned from making war to attain personal goals and maintain their alliance with the French to practising diplomacy to secure their collective interests.

This peaceful transition was not, however, simply the product of Canadian Iroquois diplomatic skill. It was made possible both by the desire of the British to secure the Canadian Iroquois as neutrals or allies and by the status of the Canadian Iroquois communities as independent, autonomous entities.

At any time during the war the British would have been receptive to any offers from the Canadian Iroquois to remain neutral. In 1755 the British ceased their overtures only when they were manifestly rejected by the Kahnawakes. In 1759 and 1760 it was the League Iroquois and the British who took the first steps. The Canadian Iroquois had only to respond positively.

With the British willing to grant them the status of neutrals or allies and launching diplomatic initiatives to this effect in 1755, 1759, and 1760, the independence of the Canadian Iroquois gave them the freedom to respond to these initiatives when it suited their purposes. Their French neighbours were bound by their status as colonials to a relationship with the British that was predetermined by the current state of Anglo-French relations. Confronted with a successful invasion, the French in Canada had no option but surrender. For the French habitants to attain the independence enjoyed by the Canadian Iroquois would have required a revolution.

The Amerindians, on the other hand, were responsible to no one but themselves, and free to act as they saw fit to protect their interests. They used this freedom to negotiate first neutrality, then alliance, with the invaders. The British era would bring new challenges and new dangers, but the Canadian Iroquois had emerged from the Seven Years' War with their rights acknowledged and their communities intact.

NOTES

Introduction

1   The Catawbas, who lived in what is now South Carolina, had been at war with the Iroquois since the late seventeenth century. For the details of this conflict, which ended in the 1750s, see James H. Merrell, "'Their Very Bones Shall Fight': The Catawba-Iroquois Wars," in Daniel K. Richter and James H. Merrell, eds. *Beyond the Covenant Chain: The Iroquois and their Neighbors in Indian North America, 1600-1800* (Syracuse: Syracuse University Press, 1987), pp. 115-133.

2   Although Canadian Iroquois participation in the Anglo-French conflict occurred between 1753 and 1760, the "official" Seven Years' War lasted from the French and British declarations of war in 1756 until the signing of the Treaty of Paris in 1763.

3   Picquet to Beauharnois, 10 September 1746, Archives du Seminaire de St. Sulpice, Paris, vol. 4, "Pièces pour l'histoire militaire du Canada de 1750 à 1760," pièce 2, National Archives of Canada (hereafter NAC), Manuscript Group (hereafter MG) 17, A7-1, microfilm, reel C-14,014, f. 2666.

4   David Blanchard, introduction to *Narratives of the Museum of Sault St. Louis, 1667-1685* (Kahnawake: Kanienkehaka Raotitiohkwa Press, 1981), p. 7.

5   Because the Tuscaroras were admitted to the League only in 1722 or 1723, it was frequently if anachronistically labelled the Five Nations during the Seven Years' War.

6   This division of the Iroquois into Canadian Iroquois and League Iroquois follows Daniel Richter, *The Ordeal of the Longhouse: The Peoples of the Iroquois League in the Era of European Colonization* (Chapel Hill: University of North Carolina Press, 1992).

7   Lists of the Seven Nations vary slightly over time. As a result of the establishment of Oswegatchie in 1749, there were actually eight nations during the Seven Years' War, but "previously and subsequently the Eight were known as the Seven Nations of Canada. They became Seven again when the Indians of Oswegatchie merged with those of Akwesasne/St. Regis." "Descriptive Treaty Calendar," in Francis Jennings, ed., *The History and Culture of Iroquois Diplomacy: An Interdisciplinary Guide to the Treaties of the Six Nations and Their League* (Syracuse: Syracuse University Press, 1985), p. 192.

8   For the Seven Nations, see Colin G. Calloway, *The Western Abenakis of Vermont, 1600-1800: War, Migration, and the Survival of an Indian People* (Norman: University of Oklahoma Press, 1990), pp. 99, 163-164, 195; Lawrence Ostola, "The Seven Nations of Canada and the American Revolution, 1774-1783," (MA thesis, Université de Montréal, 1988); Robert J. Surtees, "The Iroquois in Canada," in Jennings, ed., *The History and Culture of Iroquois Diplomacy*, pp. 67, 70;

"Descriptive Treaty Calendar," in ibid., p. 192.

9   Claus Family Papers, NAC, MG 19, F1, vol. 23, no. 2, "Memoranda Book," microfilm, reel C-1485, ff. 69-71.

10 For examples of the extensive use of the titles Seven Nations and Seven Villages during the early British era, see "At a council held at Montreal, 14th August, 1778," British Library, additional manuscript 21,779, ff. 1, 2, 4, NAC, MG 21, microfilm, reel A-686; "Heads of a speech to the Indians of the Seven Villages of Canada," c. 1778, ibid., ff. 9-10; "A message from the Cacknawaga of Canada to the Cayuga delivered at the Cayuga village by two Cacknawaga Indians," 22 March 1779, ibid., ff. 26, 26v. For Seven Castles, see letter of General Knox, 10 February 1792, in Franklin B. Hough, *A History of St. Lawrence and Franklin Counties, New York, From the earliest period to the present time* (Albany: Little & Co., 1853; reprinted Baltimore: Regional Publishing Company, 1970), p. 193.

11 For the various European armed forces engaged in the Seven Years' War, see Fred Anderson, *A People's Army: Massachusetts Soldiers and Society in the Seven Years' War* (Chapel Hill: University of North Carolina Press, 1984); Jay Cassel, "The Troupes de la marine in Canada: men and material, 1683-1760" (Ph.D. dissertation, University of Toronto, 1987), pp. 85-100; André Corvisier, *L'Armée Française de la fin du XVIIe siècle au ministère de Choiseul: Le Soldat* (Paris: Presses Universitaires de France, 1964), pp. 147-565; W.J. Eccles, "The French forces in North America during the Seven Years' War," in *Dictionary of Canadian Biography, 1741 to 1770*, vol. III (Toronto: University of Toronto Press, 1974), pp. xv-xxiii; C.P. Stacey, "The British Forces in North America during the Seven Years' War," ibid., pp. xxiv-xxx.

12 For the details of this incident, see chapter eight.

13 For the details of this incident, see chapter three.

14 Vaudreuil to Machault, 8 June 1756, France, Archives des Colonies (hereafter AC), C11A, vol. 101, ff. 22-22v, NAC, MG 1, microfilm, reel F-101.

15 "État de ce qui a été trouvé dans le fort georges [William Henry]; qui a été détruit et rasé par les françois," Archives du Seminaire de St. Sulpice, Paris, vol. 4, pièce 18, NAC, MG 17, A7-1, f. 2823.

16 Lester A. Ross, *Archaeological Metrology: English, French, American and Canadian Systems of Weights and Measures for North American Historical Archaeology* (Ottawa: Parks Canada, 1983), pp. 54, 77; Marcel Trudel, *Initiation à la Nouvelle-France* (Montreal and Toronto: Holt, Rinehart and Winston, 1968), p. 237.

1: The Home Front

1   James Smith, *An account of the remarkable occurrences in the life and travels of Col. James Smith ... during his captivity with the Indians, in the years 1755, '56, '57, '58, & '59* (Lexington: John Bradford, 1799, reprinted Cincinnati: Robert Clarke & Co, 1870), pp. 87-88.

2   Jan Grabowski, "The Common Ground: Settled Natives and French in Montréal, 1677-1760" (doctoral dissertation, Université de Montréal, 1993), p. 273.

3   For Canadian Iroquois economic activities, see Johnson to Amherst, 18 January 1761, Great Britain, Public Record Office, War Office Papers (hereafter WO), 34, Amherst Papers, vol. 39, f. 168, NAC, MG 13, microfilm, reel B-2639; Louis Franquet,

Voyages et mémoires sur le Canada (Montreal: Éditions Élysée, 1974), p. 45; Nau to Bonin, 2 October 1735, "Lettres du père Aulneau," *Rapport de l'Archiviste de la Province de Québec* (hereafter *RAPQ*) 1926-27, p. 284; Smith, *Remarkable occurrences, passim;* Grabowski, "The Common Ground," pp. 246-273, 275-280, 302-306; Louis-Antoine de Bougainville, "Journal de l'expédition d'Amérique commencée en l'année 1756, le 15 mars," *RAPQ*, 1923-24, p. 125.

4 Gage to Amherst, 2 May 1762, wo 34, vol. 5, ff. 135-135v, reel B-2639.

5 Smith, *Remarkable occurrences*, p. 45.

6 Ibid., pp. 19-20.

7 Nau to Bonin, 2 October 1735, "Lettres du père Aulneau," p. 284.

8 Smith, *Remarkable occurrences*, p. 51.

9 Titus King, *Narrative of Titus King of Northampton, Mass.: A Prisoner of the Indians in Canada, 1755-1758*, vol. 109 of Wilcomb E. Washburn, ed., *The Garland Library of Narratives of North American Indian Captivities* (New York: Garland Publishing, Inc., 1977), p. 15. King, a captive of the Abenakis, was temporarily residing with a French family.

10 Smith, *Remarkable occurrences*, pp. 46-47.

11 "Proceedings of George Croghan esq. and treaty held with Teedyuscung & other Indians at Easton in Pensilvania [sic] in July & August of 1757, with Mr Croghan's report to Sir William Johnson on the behaviour of the Quakers and the aforesaid treaty," 22 November 1757, Great Britain, Public Record Office, Colonial Office, 5, Secretary of State, Original Correspondence, America and West Indies, vol. 1068, f. 66v, NAC, MG 11, microfilm, reel B-3005.

12 Joseph-François Lafitau, *Moeurs des sauvages amériquains, comparé'es aux moeurs des premiers temps* (Paris: Chez Saugrain, Charles Estienne Hochereau, 1724), vol. II, p. 241. This citation refers to tasks normally performed by women on campaign, which in this case were performed by young men in the absence of women. See also letter of Antoine-Denis Raudot, 1709, letter no. 33 in Camille de Rochemonteix, ed., *Relation par lettres de l'amérique septentrionale (années 1709 et 1710)* (Paris: Letouzey et Ané, 1904), p. 85. Rochemonteix incorrectly attributed this letter to Antoine Silvy.

13 The comparison with the Canadian Women's Army Corps was suggested by W.J. Eccles.

14 Daniel Claus, "Memoranda Book," NAC, MG 19, F1, Claus Family Papers, vol. 23, no. 2, ff. 69-71, reel C-1485.

15 Jean-Guillaume Plantavit de Lapause de Margon, "Relation de Mr. Poulariès envoyée à Mr. le marquis de Montcalm," *RAPQ*, 1931-32, p. 62.

16 According to Vaudreuil, this party was composed exclusively of women ["sauvagesses"]. Vaudreuil to the minister, 5 October 1759, AC, series F3, Collection Moreau de Saint-Méry, vol. 15, f. 176, NAC, MG 1, microfilm, reel F-391. According to Lévis, there were both men and women ["sauvages et sauvagesses"]. H.-R. Casgrain, ed., *Journal des campagnes du Chevalier de Lévis en Canada, de 1756 à 1760* (Montreal: C.O. Beauchemin, 1889), p. 184. Both sources, however, have women actively involved in combat with the British.

17 Daniel Claus, "Memoranda Book," MG 19, F1, vol. 23, no. 2, f. 74.

18 Vaudreuil to the minister, 5 October 1759, AC, F3, vol. 15, f. 276v. For examples of Iroquois women as combatants during the American Revolution, see Barbara Graymont, "The Six Nations Indians in the Revolutionary War," in Charles F.

Hayes, ed., *The Iroquois in the American Revolution: 1976 Conference Proceedings* (Rochester: Rochester Museum and Science Center, 1981), pp. 30-31, 34.

19 King, *Narrative*, pp. 18-19.

20 Vaudreuil to Machault, 25 September 1755, AC, F3, 14, f. 157; Doreil to d'Argenson, 29 October 1755, France, Archives de Guerre (hereafter AG), A1, vol. 3405, no. 145, f. 10; "Relation de Mr. Leduchas Capitaine au Régiment de Languedoc Infanterie, à Mr. Lamy de Chatel," 15 July 1756, AG, A1, vol. 3417, no. 182, NAC, MG 4, microfilm, reel F-666, f. 9; Williams to Johnson, March 1756, A.W. Lauber, ed., *The Papers of Sir William Johnson*, vol. IX (New York: University of the State of New York, 1939), (hereafter *Johnson Papers*, vol. IX), p. 412.

21 For smallpox epidemics, see D. Peter MacLeod, "Microbes and Muskets: Smallpox and the Participation of the Amerindian Allies of New France in the Seven Years' War," *Ethnohistory* 39, no. 1 (winter 1992), pp. 42-64.

22 Smith, *Remarkable occurrences*, p. 16.

23 Robert Eastburn, *A faithful narrative, of the many dangers and sufferings, as well as wonderful deliverances of Robert Eastburn, during his late captivity among the Indians: Together with some remarks upon the country of Canada, and the religion, and policy of its inhabitants; the whole intermixed with devout reflections* (Philadelphia: William Dunlap, 1758), reprinted in Richard Vanderbeets, ed., *Held Captive by Indians: Selected Narratives, 1642-1836* (Knoxville: University of Tennessee Press, 1973), p. 163n.

24 Bruce G. Trigger, *The Children of Aataentsic: A History of the Huron People to 1660* (Kingston and Montreal: McGill-Queen's University Press, 1976), p. 75.

25 For Eastburn's capture, see chapter two.

26 Eastburn, *A faithful narrative*, p. 164.

27 Susanna Johnson, "A Narrative of the Captivity of Mrs. Johnson," in Colin G. Calloway, ed., *North Country Captives: Selected Narratives of Indian Captivity from Vermont and New Hampshire* (Hanover: University Press of New England, 1992), p. 66.

28 Eastburn, *A faithful narrative*, p. 161.

29 Ibid., pp. 160-174.

30 King, *Narrative*, p. 17.

31 Lapause, "Relation de Mr. Poulariès," p. 62.

32 King, *Narrative*, p. 15.

33 22.5 pounds [livres] of bread and fifteen pounds of beef. When used as a measure of weight, a livre equalled 489.41 grams.

34 53 minots of maize and 340 pounds of bread. A minot, slightly larger than a bushel, was equal to 39.03 litres.

35 One half pound of vermilion, two pounds of tobacco, and one pint of spirits.

36 All of the preceding items are from "Extrait de la dépense qui a Esté fait dans les magazins du roy a Montreal tant pour les Equipments de divers petits party qui ont été sur les costs de la novelle angleterre et autres dépense a l'occasion de la guerre depuis le present Septembre 1746 jusque et compris le 31e Décembre de la d. année ainsy quil en suit," AC, C11A, vol. 86, NAC, MG 1, microfilm, reel F-86, ff. 178-183v.

37 A. de Maurés de Malartic, *Journal des Campagnes au Canada, de 1755 à 1760* (Dijon: Gaffarel, 1890), p. 218.

38 Vaudreuil to the minister, 13 October 1756, AC, C11A, vol. 101, ff. 117v-118.

39 J.G. Kohl, *Kitchi-gami: Wanderings round Lake Superior* (London: Chapman and Hall, 1860), p. 67.

40 "The Deposition of Cornelig Feeling who was taken Prisoner with John Hawl and his the Deponents Negroe in the beginning of june last by 2 Anakankos 3 Skaghtikoks and 1 Missaga Ind.," 13 October 1756, in James Sullivan, ed., *The Papers of Sir William Johnson*, vol. III (Albany: University of the State of New York, 1921), (hereafter *Johnson Papers*, vol. III), pp. 649, 650.

41 Johnson to Amherst, 22 November 1756, WO 34, vol. 39, f. 3.

42 Stoddart to Johnson, 15 May 1753, in E.B. O'Callaghan, ed., *The Documentary History of the State of New York*, vol. II, (Albany: Weed, Parsons, & Co, 1850), p. 365.

43 Jean-Nicolas Desandrouins, "Notes sur le voyage de M. Jonathan Carver dans l'amérique septentrionale, au sujet du massacre des anglois, par les sauvages, après la capitulation de Fort William Henry, en 1757," in C.N. Gabriel, *Le Maréchal de Camp Desandrouins 1729-1792, Guerre du Canada 1756-1759, Guerre de l'Indépendance américain 1780-1782* (Verdun: Renvé-Lallemant, 1887), pp. 114-117. This record of what appears to have been an unexceptionable occurrence was made by Desandrouins only to provide background for a story of the rescue of a British prisoner held by these Amerindians.

44 Canadians, on the other hand, were paid only three livres for the same work. Bougainville, "Mémoire sur l'état de a nouvelle-france," 1757, *RAPQ*, 1923-24, p. 49. When used to express monetary values, the French livre was a unit of account rather than an actual coin.

45 Duquesne to Machault, 12 June 1755 [II], AC, C11A, vol. 100, f. 24, NAC, MG 1, microfilm, reel F-100. Duquesne felt obliged to explain in some detail his decision regarding "the sum that I was forced to give to the Abenakis."

46 Lévis, *Journal*, p. 200; Gabriel, *Le maréchal de camp Desandrouins*, p. 302.

47 Cornelius J. Jaenen, *Friend and Foe: Aspects of French-Amerindian Cultural Contact in the Sixteenth and Seventeenth Centuries* (Toronto: McClelland and Stewart, 1973), p. 127.

48 These figures are averages, based upon ransoms totalling 12,686 livres for ninety-two prisoners, and payments of 1,867 livres for fifty-six scalps between September 1746 and August 1747 at Montreal. Comparable financial records for the Seven Years' War are not available, but in 1757, following the surrender of Fort William Henry, three prisoners were ransomed for 130 livres and 56 litres of brandy apiece. See "Estat des payments qui ont été ordonnés à Montréal pour les diverses dépenses faites à l'occasion de la guerre pendant les quatre derniers mois 1746 et les hui[t] premiers mois de la présente année 1747," AC, C11A, vol. 88, NAC, MG 1, microfilm, reel F-88, f. 204v; "Etat de ce qui a été trouvé dans le fort georges [William Henry]; qui a été détruit et rasé par les françois," c. August 1757, Archives du Seminaire de St. Sulpice, Paris, vol. 4, p. 2823.

49 "The Examination of Francis Beaujour a French deserter," 27 December 1755, in James Sullivan, ed., *The Papers of Sir William Johnson*, vol. II (Albany: University of the State of New York, 1922), p. 398.

50 Lapause, "Relation de Mr. Poulariès," p. 62.

51 Johnson, "A Narrative of the Captivity of Mrs. Johnson," in Calloway, ed., *North Country Captives*, p. 59.

52 "Relation de la prise et capitulation de fort georges en canada," AC, C11A, vol.

102. f. 312, \AC, MG 1, microfilm, reel F-102; Bigot to Machault, 24 August 1757, AC, F3, vol. 15, f. 59v; Vaudreuil to Machault, 15 September 1757, ibid., ff. 76v-77v.

53 See Jemima Howe, "The Captivity and Sufferings of Mrs. Jemima Howe," in Calloway, ed., *North Country Captives*, pp. 90-91. French officers were especially inclined to seek the release of British counterparts from their particular branch of the service.

54 Bougainville, "Journal," p. 304.

55 Johnson to Lords Commissioners of Trade and Plantations, 22 September 1757, CO 5, vol. 1068, \AC, MG 11, microfilm, reel B-3005, f. 58v.

56 Malartic, *Journal des Campagnes au Canada*, pp. 300-301; Calloway, *The Western Abenakis of Vermont*, pp. 178-181. See chapter nine for more details regarding this incident.

57 James Murray, *Report of the Government of Quebec and dependencies thereof*, c. 1762, \AC, MG 8, E 1, f. 60.

2: Parallel Warfare

1 See chapters three and nine.

2 "Headquarters, Camp at the Great Carrying Place [between the Hudson River and Lake George]," 21 August 1755, "Minutes of Indian Affairs, 1755-1790," vol. 1822 (Indian Records, vol. 4), ff. 86-87, \AC, RG 10, microfilm, reel C-1221.

3 Regarding baptism and autonomy, in 1757 a delegation of Oswegatchie clan mothers and chiefs informed the governor general that "in causing ourselves to be reborn in the same baptismal water that washed the Great Onontio [by which he meant the king of France], we have not renounced our liberty, [or] our rights that we hold from the Master of Life." Bougainville, "Journal," *RAPQ*, 1923-24, pp. 259-260. For the details of this incident, see chapter six.

4 Daniel K. Richter, "War and Culture: The Iroquois Experience," *William and Mary Quarterly*, 3rd ser., vol. 40, no. 4 (October 1983), pp. 529-530, 544.

5 Minutes of a conference between Sir William Johnson and a party of Kahnawakes and Kanesetakes at Johnson Hall, 14 December 1764, "Minutes of Indian Affairs, 1755-1790," vol. 1826 (Indian Records vol. 7), \AC, RG 10, microfilm, reel C-1222, p. 252. This statement was made by Tahaghtaghquisere, speaking on behalf of the Kahnawakes and Kanesetakes.

6 Louis-Léonard Aumasson de Courville, "Mémoire du Canada," *RAPQ*, 1924-25, p. 120. This portage crossed the watershed between the Mohawk and St. Lawrence basins.

7 Vaudreuil to Machault, 1 June 1756, AC, C11A, vol. 101, F-101, ff. 15v-16; Gaspard-Joseph Chaussegros de Léry, "Journal de campagne d'hiver, du 13 février au neuf avril 1756, que Gaspard-Joseph Chaussegros de Léry, ... a faite ... aux entrepôts que les anglais avaient formés pour se faciliter la conquête du Canada, ..." *RAPQ*, 1926-27, p. 373; "Instructions de M. de Vaudreuil à M. Chaussegros de Léry," 23 February 1756, in Pierre-Georges Roy, ed., *Inventaire des papiers de Léry conservés aux Archives de la province de Québec*, vol. II (Québec: Archives de la province de Québec, 1939), p. 193.

8 Vaudreuil to Machault, 1 June 1756, AC, C11A, vol. 101, F-101, f. 15; ibid., 13 August 1756, AC, F3, vol. 14, F-390, ff. 294-295; Montreuil to d'Argenson, 12

February 1756, AG, A1, vol. 3417, no. 30, ff. 1-2; Vaudreuil to Léry, 23 September 1755, *Papiers de Léry*, vol. II, pp. 192-193; "Instructions de M. de Vaudreuil à M. Chaussegros de Léry," 23 February 1756; ibid., p. 193; Léry, "Journal," *RAPQ*, 1926-27, p. 372; Bougainville, "Journal," p. 237; Robertson to Morton, 19 December, 1758, in Stanley Pargellis, ed., *Military Affairs in North America, 1748-1765: Selected Documents from the Cumberland Papers in Windsor Castle* (New York: D. Appleton-18th Century, 1936), p. 429; Courville, "Mémoire du Canada," p. 120.

9   Lapause, "Relations de la prise d'un entrepôt anglois le 27 Mars 1756 dans lequel il y avoit environ quarante milliers de poudre," *RAPQ*, 1932-33, p. 319; Léry, "Journal," pp. 372-373; Vaudreuil to Machault, 1 June 1756, AC, C11A, vol. 101, ff. 15, 16v.

10 "Instructions de M. de Vaudreuil à M. Chaussegros de Léry," 23 February 1756, in *Papiers de Léry*, vol. II, pp. 201-202.

11 On 14 June 1749 Léry noted that the French knew of this territory only through the reports of Amerindians. "Journal de la campagne que le S. de Léry, ... a faite au Détroit en l'année 1749...," *RAPQ*, 1926-27, p. 337.

12 Although the militiamen and metropolitan regulars of the expedition were elite troops, hand-picked for their ability to undergo the rigours of the season, throughout the spring Amerindians were hunting and raiding without difficulty over the same terrain and under the same weather conditions. For an assessment of Amerindian military abilities relative to those of Europeans, see Leroy V. Eid, "'National War,' among Indians of Northeastern North America," *Canadian Review of American Studies* 16, no. 2 (Summer 1985), pp. 126-128, 138-139. In his analysis of the Lake George campaign of 1755, Eid contrasts European "professional military arrogance, incompetent colonial management, and an intelligent use of their soldiers by the Indians," p. 139.

13 "Instructions de M. de Vaudreuil à M. Chaussegros de Léry," 23 February 1756, in *Papiers de Léry*, vol. II, p. 201. These instructions referred specifically to the possibility that Amerindians might elect to refuse to accompany the attack on the second warehouse after the first had been destroyed.

14 Vaudreuil to Machault, 1 June 1756, AC, C11A, vol. 101, F-101, f. 16.

15 Léry, "Journal," p. 373.

16 "Instructions de M. de Vaudreuil à M. Chaussegros de Léry," 23 February 1756, *Papiers de Léry*, vol. II, pp. 195-196; Léry, "Journal," pp. 378-380.

17 Léry, "Journal," p. 374.

18 Lapause, "Relations de la prise d'un entrepôt anglois," p. 319; Léry, "Journal," p. 377.

19 Leroy V. Eid, "The Cardinal Principle of Northeast Woodland Indian War," in William Cowan, ed., *Papers of the Thirteenth Algonquian Conference* (Ottawa: Carleton University, 1982), p. 243; Richter, "War and Culture," pp. 528-537.

20 Lapause, "Relations de la prise d'un entrepôt anglois," p. 320; Léry, "Journal," p. 387.

21 Ou8atory, Missakin, and Collière were the only Amerindians mentioned by name in French records of the expedition. For the reference to Collière, see Bougainville, "Journal," p. 260.

22 For discussions of Amerindian leadership, see Eid, "'National War,' among Indians of Northeastern North America," p. 147; Mary A. Druke, "Linking Arms: The

Structure of Iroquois Intertribal Diplomacy," in Richter and Merrell., eds., *Beyond the Covenant Chain*, p. 30; Druke, "Structure and Meanings of Leadership Among the Mohawk and Oneida During the Mid-Eighteenth Century" (doctoral dissertation. University of Chicago, 1982), pp. 132-143, 152-153, 164, 171-176, 186-188, 201-202, 266-271.

23 See chapter four.

24 Charly, "Journal de la campagne de M. de Léry, commandant du détachement que M. Le Marquis de Vaudreuil s'est déterminé d'envoyer sur les forts remplis de vivres et de munitions de guerre destinés pour l'entreprise que les anglois ont médité de faire, cette année, sur Niagara et Frontenac," in H.-R. Casgrain, ed., *Relations et journaux de different expéditions faites durant les années 1755-56-57-58-59-60* (Quebec: L.-J. Demers, 1895), p. 54.

25 Léry, "Journal," pp. 377-378.

26 Ibid., p. 382.

27 When Léry recorded these departures in his journal, he described these Amerindians as departing "in order to go to take prisoners." Ibid., pp. 379, 382, 392.

28 After leaving Oswegatchie, the allies followed the Oswegatchie River, marched up the east bank of Black Lake and the Indian River, then crossed the height of land to the Black River valley. They followed the Black River southward, then crossed a second watershed to the upper Mohawk River, where Ou8atory led the detachment to an Amerindian trail which they followed to the portage.

29 Forts Bull and Williams were named after their respective commanders, Lieutenant William Bull and Captain William Williams.

30 Lapause, "Relations de la prise d'un entrepôt anglois." p. 320.

31 "Relation de la Prise du Fort Bull," AC, C11E, Des limites et des postes, vol. 10, "Amérique du Nord: rivalité des colonies anglaises et des colonies francaises, 1689-1764," NAC, MG 1, microfilm, reel F-408, f. 200v; Léry, "Journal," p. 384.

32 Léry, "Journal," pp. 386-387.

33 Léry, "Journal de Joseph-Gaspard Chaussegros de Léry, Lieutenant des troupes, 1754-1755," *RAPQ*, 1927-1928, p. 400; Eid, "Northeast Woodland Indian War," p. 244; Richter, "War and Culture," p. 535; C.J. Jaenen, "Amerindian views of French Culture in the Seventeenth Century," *Canadian Historical Review*, 55, no. 3 (September 1974), p. 289.

34 Léry, "Journal," p. 387.

35 See chapter four.

36 "Relation de la Prise du Fort Bull," f. 201; Léry, "Journal," pp. 386-387; Louis-Guillaume de Parscau du Plessix, "Journal de la campagne de *la Sauvage*, Frégate du Roy, armée au port de Brest, au mois de mars, 1756 (écrit pour ma dame)," *RAPQ*, 1928-29, p. 219.

37 Léry, "Journal," p. 393; Johnson to Shirley, 3 April 1756, *Johnson Papers*, vol. IX, pp. 414-415; Shirley to Fox, 7 May 1756, CO 5, vol. 46, NAC, MG 11, microfilm, reel B-2111, f. 254.

38 "Relation de la Prise du Fort Bull," f. 201v; Léry, "Journal," pp. 387-88. All six of the fleeing Britons were killed.

39 Léry, "Journal," 1926-27, p. 387.

40 "Relation de la Prise du Fort Bull," ff. 200v-201, 203; Léry, "Journal," p. 387, 388, 391; Bougainville, "Journal," p. 260; Lapause, "Relations de la prise d'un

entrepôt anglois," p. 320; Malartic, *Journal des Campagnes au Canada*, p. 51.

41 Lapause, "Relations de la prise d'un entrepôt anglois," p. 320; Léry, "Journal," p. 387; Vaudreuil to Léry, 19 September 1757, *RAPQ*, 1928-29, p. 243; Léry to Vaudreuil, 21 September 1757, ibid., p. 244.

42 The four were "two French soldiers, one of the colony, and a native, [who] broke in the gate and killed the commandant who had not wanted to surrender and had killed a Native [Collière]." Malartic, *Journal des Campagnes au Canada*, p. 51.

43 Léry, "Journal," p. 387.

44 Parscau, "Journal de la campagne de *la Sauvage*," p. 219.

45 Léry, "Journal," p. 392; Eastburn, *A faithful narrative*, p. 167.

46 Vaudreuil to Machault, 1 June 1756, AC, C11A, vol. 101, f. 17v; "Extrait des nouvelles en Canada," ibid., f. 352; Léry, "Journal," p. 388.

47 "Relation de la Prise du Fort Bull," f. 202; letter of Péan, 10 April 1756, enclosed in Drucour to Machault, 19 May 1756, AC, C11A, vol. 101, f. 19v; Charly, "Journal," in Casgrain, ed., *Relations et journaux*, p. 63; Eastburn, *A faithful narrative*, pp. 154-157; Léry, "Journal," pp. 387, 392.

48 Eastburn, *A faithful narrative*, pp. 155-156.

49 "Relation de la Prise du Fort Bull," ff. 202v-203; Léry, "Journal," p. 389. French commentators agreed that the participants in this assault had been lucky. One metropolitan officer observed that it was "astonishing that the English garrison with all its grenades and all of its musket fire killed so few people." Lapause, "Relations de la prise d'un entrepôt anglois," p. 321.

50 "Relation de la Prise du Fort Bull," f. 203; Léry, "Journal," pp. 388, 391; Charly, "Journal," in Casgrain, ed., *Relations et journaux*, p. 63;

51 Whether the five prisoners taken after the storm of Fort Bull were secured by Amerindians or Frenchmen is uncertain. A further ten prisoners were obtained by a party of Amerindians that, at Léry's request, left the detachment on 8 April to reconnoitre the vicinity of Oswego. See Léry, "Journal," pp. 391, 392.

52 Picquet to Beauharnois, 10 September 1746, Archives du Seminaire de St. Sulpice, vol. 4, pièce 2, p. 2668.

53 Eastburn, *A faithful narrative*, p. 162. This "shouting" was described in more detail by another captive in 1755: "they gave the scalp halloo, as usual, which is a long yell or halloo, for every scalp or prisoner they have in possession; the last of these scalp halloos was followed with quick and sudden shrill shouts of joy and triumph." Smith, *Remarkable occurrences*, p. 7.

54 Eastburn, *A faithful narrative*, p. 161.

55 Ibid., pp. 158-162.

56 In fact, the stores at the portage had been accumulated, not to support an offensive, but to resupply the garrison of Oswego which, in the spring of 1756, was on the verge of starvation. The British had indeed been planning a spring offensive against the French posts on Lake Ontario, but this campaign was not cancelled until two months after the destruction of Fort Bull, when a council of war on 25 May concluded that only two thousand of the six thousand men needed for this enterprise could be raised. British efforts to supply the Oswego garrison were not seriously affected by the raid on the Oneida Carrying Place. In the two months immediately following the withdrawal of the French and Amerindian force from the ruins of Fort Bull (between 1 April and 25 May), two hundred whaleboat loads and five hundred bateau loads of provisions crossed the portage and continued westward to the

Lake Ontario outpost. As for the destruction of Fort Bull, when Sir William Shirley, the acting commander-in-chief of the British forces in North America, spoke of this action, he did so in the course of noting the unwillingness of the League Iroquois to protect British lines of communications to Oswego against "scalping parties of the French Indians, who have found a means to cut off a small fort and party of 25 men at one end of the Great [Oneida] Carrying Place." Shirley to Fox, 7 May 1756, CO 5, vol. 46, f. 254. See also letter of Péan, 10 April 1756, enclosed in Drucour to Machault, 19 May 1756, AC, C11A, vol. 101, f. 20; Vaudreuil to Machault, 15 June 1756, ibid., f. 28v; Bigot to Machault, 12 April 1756, AC, F3, 14, f. 234; "Copie de certificat de M. Le Marquis de Vaudreuil," enclosed in "Chaussegros de Léry, (Ch.) Joseph, Gaspard, Capitaine des troupes de la marine, servante en Canada," 1760, AC, E, Dossiers Personnels, vol. 77, NAC, MG 1, microfilm, reel F-820, f. 12; "Instructions for Capt. Williams," 12 August 1755, CO 5, vol. 46, f. 223; "Instructions for Cap. Williams," 29 October 1755, ibid., ff. 230-230v; Mercer to Williams, 24 January 1756, ibid ff. 234-234v; Mercer to Williams, 14 March 1756, ibid., f. 236; Mercer to Williams, 22 February 1756, ibid., ff. 237-237v; "At a Council of War held at the camp at Albany May 25 1756," ibid., ff. 270v-271.

57 Smith, *Remarkable occurrences*, p. 104.

58 Lapause, "Relations de la prise d'un entrepôt anglois," p. 320.

59 J.R. Miller, *Skyscrapers Hide the Heavens: A History of Indian-White Relations in Canada* (Toronto: University of Toronto Press, 1989), pp. 35-48.

3: The Ohio Valley, 1753-1755

1 Michael N. McConnell, "Peoples 'In Between:' The Iroquois and the Ohio Indians, 1720-1768," in Richter and Merrell, eds. *Beyond the Covenant Chain*, pp. 93-95; Francis Jennings, *The Ambiguous Iroquois Empire: The Covenant Chain Confederation of Indian Tribes with English Colonies from its beginnings to the Lancaster Treaty of 1744* (New York: W.W. Norton, 1984), pp. 350-353.

2 There were Abenaki families living on the banks of the Cuyahoga River in 1743, on the site of Cleveland, Ohio. See Robert Navarre, "Mémoire d'observation fait par moy Navarre du poste ou commerce le nommé françois saguin, des diverses nations qui y sont etablis et du commerce qui s'y peut faire, ..." 1743, AC, C11A, vol. 79, f. 48v, NAC, MG 1, microfilm, reel F-79; Beauharnois and Hocquart to Maurepas, 10 October 1743, ibid., ff. 44-44v. According to the Six Nations, there were twenty-seven adult male Kahnawakes and Kanesetakes living among other Mohawks in the Ohio valley in 1748. See Wilbur R. Jacobs, ed., *The Appalachian Indian Frontier: The Edmund Atkin Report and Plan of 1755* (Columbia: University of South Carolina Press, 1954; reprinted Lincoln: University of Nebraska Press, 1967), pp. 41-42. In 1749 a number of Nipissings and Abenakis were living at "Logstown" on the Ohio. Pierre-Joseph Céloron de Blainville, "Journal de la campagne que moy Céloron Ch. de L'Ordre roialle et militaire de St. Louis, Captain commandant un detachment envoyé dans la belle rivière ..." 1749, AC, F3, vol. 13, f. 335, NAC, MG 1, microfilm, reel F-389. For Kahnawakes living among the League Iroquois, Delaware, and Wyandot groups in the region, see Smith, *Remarkable occurrences*, pp. 13, 20.

3 Smith, *Remarkable occurrences*, pp. 13, 20; Journal of William Trent, 1753, CO 5, vol. 1328, f. 11v, NAC, MG 11, microfilm, reel B-4037. The Delaware-Kahnawake vil-

lage was Tullihas, located at the intersection of Mohican and Owl creeks, in what is now Coshocton County, Ohio.

4 "One cannot express," warned the governor general of New France in 1716, "to what extent the strength of England will grow if it takes possession of the rest of North America, and how formidable this strength will become in Europe." Philippe de Rigaud de Vaudreuil, "Mémoire de M. de Vaudreuil au Duc d'Orléans, Regent du Royaume," February 1716, *RAPQ*, 1947-48, pp. 291-292. See also W.J. Eccles, "The Role of the American Colonies in Eighteenth Century French Foreign Policy," in *Essays on New France* (Toronto: Oxford University Press, 1987), pp. 146-148; Eccles, *The Canadian Frontier, 1534-1760*, rev. ed. (Albuquerque: University of New Mexico Press, 1983), pp. 156-160; Guy Frégault, *La Guerre de la Conquête, 1754-1760* (Montreal: Fides, 1955), pp. 104-111.

5 W.J. Eccles has noted a similar lack of enthusiasm for involvement in French imperial ventures in the Ohio among Canadian merchants, who expected that there would be more dangers than profits for those trading in the region. Eccles, *The Canadian Frontier*, pp. 165-166.

6 Céloron "Journal de la campagne," 1749, AC, F3, vol. 13, ff. 321, 322, 322v, 329, 330; Francis Jennings, *Empire of Fortune: Crowns, Colonies & Tribes in the Seven Years War in America* (New York: W.W. Norton, 1988), pp. 16-17, 49-50; Michael N. McConnell, *A Country Between: The Upper Ohio Valley and its Peoples, 1724-1774* (Lincoln: University of Nebraska Press, 1992), p. 83, 98-100; Richard White, *The Middle Ground: Indians, Empires and Republics in the Great Lakes Region, 1650-1815* (New York: Cambridge University Press, 1991), pp. 206-207, 230-232.

7 Stoddart to Johnson, 15 May 1753, in O'Callaghan, ed., *The Documentary History of the State of New York*, vol. II, p. 365.

8 "Journal de la campagne de M de Villiers depuis son arrivé au fort Duquesne jusqu'à son retour aud. fort," enclosed in Drucourt to the minister, 6 September 1754, AC, F3, vol. 14, F-390, f. 53. I am indebted to Cornelius J. Jaenen for the translation of "maintain good relations" for "travailler aux bonnes affaires."

9 Duquesne to Contrecoeur, 18 October 1752, in Fernand Grenier, ed., *Papiers contrecoeur et autres documents concernant le conflit anglo-français sur l'ohio de 1745 à 1756* (Québec: Les presses universitaires Laval, 1952), p. 17. These forts were located on the sites of Erie and Waterford, Pennsylvania. A third fort on the route between Lake Erie and the forks of the Ohio, Fort Machault, was constructed in 1755. William A. Hunter, *Forts on the Pennsylvania Frontier, 1753-1758* (Harrisburg: Pennsylvania Historical and Museum Commission, 1960), pp. 61, 79, 136.

10 "Conseil tenû par des Sonontouans venû de la Belle Rivière," 2 September 1753, in Grenier, ed., *Papiers contrecoeur*, p. 57.

11 McConnell, *A Country Between*, p. 103.

12 Journal of William Trent, 1753, CO 5, vol. 1328, ff. 11v-12v; "Conseil tenû par des Sonontouans venû de la Belle Rivière," 2 September 1753, in Grenier, ed., *Papiers contrecoeur*, pp. 53, 57; Duquesne to Saint-Pierre, 30 January 1754, ibid., p. 99. Venango was located on the site of Franklin, Pennsylvania.

13 Duquesne to Marin, 27 August 1753, AC, C11A, vol. 99, f. 144, NAC, MG 1, microfilm, reel F-99.

14 Duquesne to Rouillé, 31 October 1753, ibid., ff. 120v-121v.

15 Hunter, *Forts on the Pennsylvania Frontier*, pp. 42-52, 97-136.

16 Duquesne to Contrecoeur, 11 May 1754, in Grenier, ed., *Papiers contrecoeur*, p. 125.

17 Dinwiddie to the Board of Trade, 18 June 1754, CO 5, vol. 1328, ff. 117, 121.

18 Léry, "Journal de Joseph-Gaspard Chaussegros de Léry, Lieutenant des troupes, 1754-1755," *RAPQ*, 1926-27, p. 358.

19 This portage formed part of an alternative route to the Ohio which was occasionally used by the French and their allies instead of the better-known portage between Fort Presqu'ile and Fort Le Boeuf.

20 Léry, "Journal ... 1754-1755," p. 359.

21 "Journal de la campagne de M de Villiers," AC, F3, 14, NAC, MG 1, microfilm, reel F-390, f. 52.

22 ibid., ff. 52-54v.

23 Varin to Bigot, 24 July 1754, AC, C11A, vol. 99, f. 493v; "Journal de la campagne de M de Villiers," f. 54v; J.C.B., *Voyage au Canada fait depuis l'an 1751 jusqu'en l'an 1761* (Paris: Aubier Montaigne, 1978), p. 87.

24 This storehouse was located at the mouth of Redstone Creek, on the site of Brownsville, Pennsylvania.

25 "Shaw Affidavit," cited in W.W. Abbot, ed., *The Papers of George Washington: Colonial Series*, vol. I (Charlottesville: University Press of Virginia, 1983), p. 158. This description of Fort Necessity is based upon "The Following is an Account of ye march of the army from Wills's Creek to Within six miles of the french fort, beginning ye 10th of June & ending ye 9th July," in Charles Hamilton, ed., *Braddock's Defeat* (Norman: University of Oklahoma Press, 1959), p. 45; "Diagram of Fort Necessity Restoration, 1954," in Hunter, *Forts on the Pennsylvania Frontier*, p. 58. The site of this outpost is now the Fort Necessity National Battlefield.

26 The allies lost one Amerindian killed and two wounded, along with two French killed and fifteen wounded during the engagement. "Journal de la campagne de M de Villiers," f. 59v; "Account by George Washington and James Mackay of the Capitulation of Fort Necessity," 19 July 1754, in Abbot, ed., *The Papers of George Washington*, vol. I, pp. 159-160.

27 Letter of Adam Stephen, *Maryland Gazette*, 29 August 1754, in "Appendix A: The Battle of Fort Necessity, July 3, 1754 [Part] I. Contemporaneous Newspaper Accounts," in Charles A. Ambler, *George Washington and the West* (Chapel Hill: University of North Carolina Press, 1936; reprinted New York: Russel & Russell, 1971), p. 215.

28 "Journal de la campagne de M de Villiers," f. 56v-59v; Varin to Bigot, 24 July 1754, AC, C11A, vol. 99, f. 493v; Léry, "Journal ... 1754-1755," p. 371; J.C.B., *Voyage au Canada*, pp. 88-91. The Virginia government failed to honour the article regarding the release of the survivors of Jumonville's escort, who were retained as prisoners in Virginia.

29 For the siege of Fort Necessity, see "Journal de la campagne de M de Villiers," f. 59v; "Relation de ce qui s'en passé le 3 juillet 1754 entre les troupes du Canada es celle de la Caroline du Sud, de la Carolinie du Nord, et de la virginie sur la rivière appellé en anglais Ohio ou belle rivière, exactement copié de la gazette de la Caroline d'une lettre ecrite par le colonel James au gouverneur de Pennsylvania," ibid., ff. 62-62v; J.C.B., *Voyage au Canada*, p. 91; "At a council of war held at Mr. Gists ju[ne] 28th 1754," in Abbot, ed., *The Papers of George Washington*, vol. I p.

155; "Account by George Washington and James Mackay of the Capitulation of Fort Necessity," 19 July 1754, ibid., pp. 159-160; letter of Washington, c. 1757, ibid., pp. 168-171; "George Washington's account of the capitulation of Fort Necessity," 1786, ibid., pp. 172-173; Report of Robert Calendar, enclosed in a letter to the Governor of Pennsylvania, 16 July 1754, *Provincial Council of Pennsylvania, from the organization to the termination of the proprietary government* (Harrisburg: Theo. Fenn & Co., 1851; reprinted New York: AMS Press, 1968, vol. 6), p. 203; Lawrence Henry Gipson, *The British Empire Before the American Revolution, Volume VI: The Great War for the Empire, The Years of Defeat, 1754-1757* (New York: Alfred A. Knopf, 1946), pp. 38-45.

30 Letter of Stobo, 29 July 1754, in *Memoirs of Major Robert Stobo of the Virginian Regiment* (Pittsburgh: John S. Davidson, 1884), p. 92; J.C.B., *Voyage au Canada*, p. 92.

31 Duquesne to Contrecoeur, 14 August 1754, in Grenier, ed., *Papiers contrecoeur*, pp. 246-247.

32 Letters of Stobo, 28 and 29 July 1754, in *Memoirs of Major Robert Stobo*, pp. 86-92.

33 The Seven Nations had agreed to send one hundred fighters to spend the winter of 1755-56 in the Ohio valley at a meeting in July 1755. Duquesne to the minister, 3 November 1754, AC, C11A, vol. 99, f. 401; "Garnisons des forts de la Bellerivière et ses dépendances qui ont hiverné en 1754," ibid., vol. 100, ff. 17, 19-19v; Duquesne to Contrecoeur, 18 July 1754, in Grenier, ed., *Papiers contrecoeur*, p. 219.

34 Hough, *History of St. Lawrence and Franklin Counties*, pp. 182-183. Hough obtained this interview from an interview with Mary Kawennitake, Atiatonharongwen's daughter. Less fortunate than his wife and son, Atiatonharongwen's father was taken prisoner during the raid on Saratoga and brought to Montreal where he became the servant or slave of a French official. Atiatonharongwen was also known as Louis Cook.

35 Contrecoeur to Vaudreuil, 21 June 1755, in Grenier, ed., *Papiers contrecoeur*, p. 365.

36 Patrick Mackellar, "A sketch of the field of battle of the 9 July upon the Monongahela, seven miles from Fort du Quesne, between the British Troops commanded by General Braddock and the French & French Indians commanded by Mons de S. Pierre, shewing the disposition of the troops when the Action began," CO 5, vol. 46, f. 135.

37 "Relation depuis le depart des trouppes de Quebec jusqu'au 30 du mois de 7bre, 1755," AG, A1, vol. 3405, no. 106, f. 2.

38 Smith, *Remarkable occurrences*, pp. 10-11.

39 "Relation depuis le depart des trouppes de Quebec jusqu'au 30 du mois de 7bre, 1755; Lapause, "Relation de l'affaire de la Belle-Rivière," *RAPQ*, 1932-33, p. 307; Stephen F. Auth, *The Ten Years' War: Indian-White Relations in Pennsylvania, 1755-1765* (New York: Garland Publishing, 1989), pp. 25-26.

40 The regulars present included thirteen officers, twenty-three cadets, and seventy-two soldiers. "Liste des officiers, cadets, soldats, miliciens, et sauvages qui composoient le détachement qui a esté [illegible] d'un corps de 2000 anglois a 3 lieues du Fort Duquesne sur le rivière Oyo et aux lequel il a eu un action le 9 juillet," 1755, enclosed in Bigot to Machault, 6 August 1755, AC, F3, vol. 14, f. 118v.

41 Harry Gordon, "Journal of Proceedings from Wills's Creek to the Monongahela:

Harry Gordon to ?," 23 July 1755, in Pargellis, ed., *Military Affairs*, p. 105. See also St. Clair to Napier, 22 July 1755, ibid., p. 103.

42 "The Journal of Captain Robert Cholmley's Batman," in Hamilton, *Braddock's Defeat*, p. 27; Gordon, "Journal of Proceedings," in Pargellis, ed., *Military Affairs*, p. 106.

43 St. Clair to Napier, 22 July 1755, in Pargellis, ed., *Military Affairs*, p. 103; "A journal of the proceedings of the Seamen (a detachment), ordered by Commodore Keppel to assist on a late expedition to the Ohio....," in Winthrop Sargent, *The History of an expedition against Fort Du Quesne, in 1755 under Major-General Edward Braddock* (Philadelphia: Lippincott, Grambo & Co., 1855), p. 384.

44 "A journal of the proceedings of the Seamen," in Sargent, *The History of an expedition*, p. 387.

45 St. Clair to Napier, 22 July, 1755, in Pargellis, ed., *Military Affairs*, p. 103.

46 "Journal of Cholmley's Batman," in Hamilton, ed., *Braddock's Defeat*, p. 28.

47 Disconcerted Britons watched as these Amerindians "divided themselves & run along our right & left flanks." Gordon, "Journal of Proceedings," in Pargellis, ed., *Military Affairs*, p. 106.

48 "Immediately they began to engage us in a half moon and still continued surrounding us more and more." "Journal of Cholmley's Batman," in Hamilton, ed., *Braddock's Defeat*, p. 28.

49 Gordon, "Journal of Proceedings," in Pargellis, ed., *Military Affairs*, p. 26.

50 "Journal of Cholmley's Batman," in Hamilton, ed., *Braddock's Defeat*, pp. 28-29.

51 "The Following is an Account of ye march of the army from Wills's Creek to Within six miles of the french fort, beginning ye 10th of June & ending ye 9th July," in ibid., p. 50.

52 "Journal of Cholmley's Batman," in ibid., p. 28.

53 "Extract of a letter from Lieutenant Dunbar - Wills Creek, 20th July 1755," in Paul E. Kopperman, *Braddock at the Monongahela* (Pittsburgh: University of Pittsburgh Press, 1977), p. 187.

54 The writer added that "there was three quarters of an hour [after being nearly encircled] before we retreated." "Journal of Cholmley's Batman," in Hamilton, ed., *Braddock's Defeat*, pp. 29-30.

55 Gage to Albemarle, 24 July 1755, in Kopperman, ed., *Braddock at the Monongahela*, p. 193.

56 Dunbar and Gage, "Inquiry into the behaviour of the troops at the Monongahela, dated Albany, 21st Novr. 1755," CO 5, vol. 46, f. 138.

57 As well as the sources previously cited, for the events of 9 July 1755 see: Contrecoeur to Machault, 20 July 1755, AC, C11A, vol. 100, f. 24v; Dumas to Machault, 19 November 1756, AC, C11A, vol. 101, NAC, MG 1, microfilm, reel F-101, f. 324; "Relation du combat du 9 juillet, 1755," AG, A1, vol. 3404, no. 189, f. 1, NAC, MG 4, microfilm, reel F-664; Mackellar, "A sketch of the Field of Battle &c, shewing the disposition of the troops about 2 a Clock when the whole of the main body had joined the advanced and working partys, then beat back from the ground they occupied as in Plan N⁰ 1," CO 5, vol. 46, f. 137; Pierre Pouchot, *Mémoires sur la dernière guerre de l'Amérique septentrionale, entre la France et l'Angleterre. Suivis d'Observations, dont plusieurs sont relatives au théâtre actuel de la guerre, & de nouveaux détails sur les moeurs & les usages des Sauvages, avec des cartes topographiques*, vol. 1 (Yverdon, 1781), pp. 37-44.

58 Vaudreuil to the minister, 5 August 1754, AC, F3, 14, f. 130; Lapause, "Relation de l'affaire de la Belle-Rivière," p. 307. For Amerindian actions after the engagement, see Contrecoeur to Vaudreuil 14 July 1755, extract enclosed in Bigot to Machault, 6 August 1755, AC, F3, vol. 14, f. 120v; "Etat de l'artillerie, munitions de guerre es autres effects, appartenants aux anglois, qui se sont trouvés sur le champ de bataille, après l'action qui s'est passée le 9 Juillet, 1755 ... outre le pillage considerable que les sauvages ont fait," ibid., ff. 116-116v; Dumas to Machault, 19 November 1756, AC, C11A, vol. 101, ff. 322-326v; "Relation depuis le depart des trouppes de Quebec jusqu'au 30 du mois de 7, 1755," ff. 1-2.

59 Patrick Mackellar, "A sketch of the field of battle of the 9 July upon the Monongahela...," CO 5, vol. 46, f. 135.

60 The allied casualties included fifteen Amerindians, three officers, two Canadians and two soldiers killed, and twelve Amerindians, two officers, and two cadets wounded. "Liste des officiers, miliciens, soldats, es sauvages, de Canada qui ont esté tué et blessé dans l'action qui s'est passé à 3 lieus du fort Duquesne...," enclosed in Bigot to Machault, 6 August 1755, AC, F3, vol. 14, f. 117.

61 Vaudreuil to the minister, 5 August 1754, ibid., f. 130; Dumas to Machault, 19 November, 1756, AC, C11A, vol. 101, f. 325v; Lapause, "Relation de l'affaire de la Belle-Rivière," p. 309; Contrecoeur to Vaudreuil, 26 July, 1755, in Grenier, ed., *Papiers contrecoeur*, pp. 399-400.

62 Auth, *The Ten Years' War*, pp. 27, 33-61, 156-194; Jennings, *Empire of Fortune*, pp. 369-41, 438-453; McConnell, *A Country Between*, pp. 119-141, 159-206.

63 Jennings, *Empire of Fortune*, pp. 407-411; Forbes to Abercromby and Amherst, 26 November, 1758, WO 34, vol. 44, f. 193, NAC, MG 13, microfilm, reel B-2661. Forbes describes the French as "being abandoned, or at least not seconded by their friends the Indians, whom we had previously engaged to act a neutral part."

4: Lake George, 1755

1 Patrick Frazier, *The Mohicans of Stockbridge* (Lincoln: University of Nebraska Press, 1992), pp. 108-109; Calloway, *The Western Abenakis*, pp. 167, 172; Bigot to Rouillé, 6 August 1750, p. 490; Phillips to La Jonquière, 4 October 1750, pp. 495-497; La Jonquière to Rouillé, 18 October 1750, pp. 492-494; La Jonquière to Rouillé, 13 October 1751, pp. 505-506; "Paroles des Abenakis de St. françois au capitaine stevens, deputé du gouverneur de Boston, en presence de Monsieur de Baron du Longueuil, Gouverneur du Canada, et des Iroquois du Sault St. Louis et du Lac Des Deux Montagnes, le 5 Juillet, 1752," pp. 510-511; Duquesne to the minister, 10 October 1754, pp. 515-518, all printed in H.-R. Casgrain, ed., *Collection de manuscrits contenant lettres, mémoires et autres documents historiques relatifs à l'histoire de la Nouvelle-France, recueillis aux archives de la province de Québec ou copiés à l'étranger* (Quebec: A. Coté, 1884), vol. III.

2 "Att [sic] a Meeting of the Comm of Indian Affairs, the 14 June, 1744," "Minutes of the Commission for Indian Affairs, Albany, 1677-1748," vol. 1820 (Indian Records, vol. 2), ff. 275v-276, NAC, RG 10, microfilm, reel C-1220. The intendant of New France said of the Kahnawakes at the beginning of the War of the Austrian Succession that "the village of Sault St. Louis [Kahnawake] inclines willingly towards neutrality." The Kanesetakes, on the other hand, had "resolved to take the offensive [against the British] if the question arises." Hocquart to Maurepas, 22 July 1744, AC, C11A, vol. 81, f. 253, NAC, MG 1, microfilm, reel F-81.

3   Calloway, *The Western Abenakis of Vermont*, p. 166.

4   Johnson to DeLancey, 15 June 1755, in James Sullivan, ed. *The Papers of Sir William Johnson, vol. I* (Albany: University of the State of New York, 1921), p. 595.

5   Smith, *Remarkable occurrences*, p. 80.

6   "Headquarters, Camp at the Great Carrying Place," 21 August 1755, Minutes of Indian Affairs, 1755-1790, vol. 1822, ff. 86-87.

7   Ibid.

8   Barthelemy Vimont, "Relation de ce qui s'est passé en la Nouvelle France, és années 1644. & 1645," 1 October 1645, in Reuben Gold Thwaites, ed., *The Jesuit Relations and Allied Documents, vol. XXVII, Hurons, Lower Canada: 1642-1645* (Cleveland: Burrows Brothers, 1896-1901; reprinted New York: Pageant Book Company, 1959), p. 261. I first encountered this citation in Mary A. Druke, "Linking Arms: The Structure of Iroquois Intertribal Diplomacy," in Richter and Merrell, eds., *Beyond the Covenant Chain*, p. 29.

9   Vaudreuil to the minister, 5 August 1754, AC, F3, 14, f. 130v.

10 The Kahnawake warnings were passed on by way of letters written by their parish priests. Duquesne to Contrecoeur, 27 April 1755, in Grenier, ed., *Papiers contrecoeur*, p. 323.

11 Among the documents were Robert Stobo's letters containing the intelligence that he gathered while a hostage at Fort Duquesne. See Vaudreuil to Machault, 5 August 1755, AC, F3, vol. 14, f. 130; Bigot to Machault, 27 August 1755, ibid., ff. 134v-135.

12 The regulars and militiamen included 150 men from the garrison of Fort St. Frédéric, 400 from an outpost at Carillon, 1,011 regulars of La Reine, Languedoc and the troupes de la marine and 1,412 militiamen. In all, the allied army mustered 3,573 effectives. See Vaudreuil to Machault, 25 September 1755, AC, F3, vol. 14, f. 148v; "Mémoire pour servir à l'instruction à Monsieur le Baron de Dieskau, Maréchal des Camps et Armées du Roy," enclosed in ibid., ff. 162-162v; "Relation de l'action qui s'est passé le 8 7bre 1755 au Lac S. Sacrement, entre un detachment françois de 1500 hommes, commandé par Mr. le Baron de Dieskau, Maréchal des camp et armées du roi, et un corps de 3000 à 3500 anglois qui étoient retranchés au dit lac," AC, F3, vol. 14, f. 183; "Relation depuis le depart des trouppes de Quebec jusqu'au 30 du mois de 7bre, 1755," AG, A1, vol. 3405, no. 106, f. 4.

13 Dieskau to Machault, 14 September 1755, AC, F3, vol. 14, ff. 144v-145; Vaudreuil to Machault, 25 September 1755, ibid., ff. 148v-149; "Relation de l'action qui s'est passé le 8 7bre 1755," ibid., f. 184.

14 Vaudreuil to Machault, 25 September 1755, ibid., ff. 149v-150; "Relation depuis le depart des trouppes de Quebec jusqu'au 30 du mois de 7bre, 1755," AG, A1, vol. 3405, no. 106, f. 6.

15 Eyre to Shirley, 10 September 1755, CO 5, vol. 46, f. 416.

16 "Relation de l'action qui s'est passé le 8 7bre 1755," AC, F3, vol. 14, f. 185.

17 Mohawk scouts had discovered the tracks of the allied army on the morning of 7 September. The teamsters sighted on the road by allied scouts were deserters from the camp at Lake George. Johnson to Shirley, 9 September 1755, CO 5, vol. 46, f. 113.

18 "Dialogue entre le maréchal de Saxe et le Baron de Dieskau aux Champs Elysées," AG, A1, vol. 3404, no. 157, f. 6. Dieskau may have been referring to the Kanesetakes as well, since he does not appear to have distinguished between the two communities in his accounts of the expedition.

19   Ibid., ff. 6-7.

20   Dieskau to Machault, 14 September 1755, AC, F3, vol. 14, f. 145; Vaudreuil to Machault, 25 September 1755, ibid., ff. 150v-151; "Relation de l'action qui s'est passé le 8 7bre 1755," ibid., 184v-186; "Dialogue entre le maréchal de Saxe et le Baron de Dieskau aux Champs Elysées," AG, A1, vol. 3404, no. 157, ff. 6-7.

21   "I ordered the Natives to fling themselves into the woods and to take them [the British] from the rear, the Canadians to take them from the sides, while with the regular troops I awaited them in front." Dieskau to Machault, 14 September 1755, AC, F3, vol. 14, f. 145v. Dieskau actually gave two versions of the deployment of the allied forces for the ambush. In the second, accompanied by a diagram, the Amerindians were in a solid block on the east side of the road, the militia on the right, and the regulars in column to the south. See "Dialogue entre le maréchal de Saxe et le Baron de Dieskau aux Champs Elysées," AG, A1, vol. 3404, no. 157, f. 8.

22   "Dialogue entre le maréchal de Saxe et le Baron de Dieskau aux Champs Elysées," ff. 7-8.

23   Vaudreuil to Machault, 25 September 1755, AC, F3, vol. 14, f. 152.

24   Claus Family Papers, NAC, MG 19, F1, vol. 23, no. 2, "Memoranda Book," microfilm, reel C-1485, ff. 69-71. A second, quite similar, account of this dialogue was preserved in Mohawk oral tradition. In this version, the Kahnawake speaker asks the League Mohawks to "Stand aside, - for our Father only makes war against the English, and does not desire to hurt any of his Children, - the Native Tribes." Carl F. Klinck and James J. Talman, eds., *The Journal of Major John Norton, 1816* (Toronto: The Champlain Society, 1970), p. 266.

25   François-Pierre de Rigaud de Vaudreuil, "Journal de la campagne de Rigaud de Vaudreuil en 1746 et de son expédition sur les terres de la nouvelle angleterre....," 20 October 1746, AC, F3, vol. 13, ff. 231v, 232v.

26   Vaudreuil to Machault, 25 September 1755, AC, F3, vol. 14, f. 152.

27   Klinck and Talman, eds., *The Journal of Major John Norton*, p. 266.

28   Pomeroy to Williams, 9 September 1755, in Louis E. de Forest, ed., *The Journals and Papers of Seth Pomeroy, sometime general in the colonial service* (New Haven: Society of Colonial Wars in the State of New York, 1926), p. 138.

29   Klinck and Talman, eds., *The Journal of Major John Norton*, p. 266.

30   Wraxall to Fox, 27 September 1755, in Pargellis, ed., *Military Affairs*, p. 139.

31   Seth Pomeroy, "Journal of Lake George Expedition," in de Forest, ed., *The Journals and Papers of Seth Pomeroy*, p. 114.

32   Johnson to Shirley, 22 September 1755, in *Johnson Papers*, vol. III, pp. 75-76.

33   "Relation de l'action qui s'est passé le 8 7bre 1755," AC, F3, vol. 14, f. 186v.

34   Dieskau to Machault, 14 September 1755, f. 145; Vaudreuil to Machault, 25 September 1755, ibid., ff. 152-153; "Relation de l'action qui s'est passé le 8 7bre 1755," ibid., ff. 186v-187; Vaudreuil to Machault, 8 June 1756, ibid., ff. 241v-244; Dieskau to Vaudreuil, 15 October 1755, ibid., f. 255; "Dialogue entre le maréchal de Saxe et le Baron de Dieskau aux Champs Elysées," AG, A1, vol. 3404, no. 157, ff. 8-9; Edna V. Moffett, ed., "James Hill - His Book," *New England Quarterly* vol. V (1932), p. 608.

35   Daniel Claus, "Memoranda Book," MG 19, F1, vol. 23, no. 2, ff. 69-71, 74.

36   Daniel Claus spoke extensively with Dieskau after the battle. He noted that the general was "convinced that part of our army was surrounded with woods, and still exposed, and without lines," and that Dieskau considered the camp to be "defence-

less" until "our line of wagons surprised him." Ibid., ff. 65, 92.

37 Pomeroy to Williams, 9 September 1755, in de Forest, ed., *The Journals and Papers of Seth Pomeroy*, p. 138.

38 "Letter from a gunner to his cousin," 10 September 1755, in E.B. O'Callaghan, ed., *Documents Relative to the Colonial History of the State of New York*, vol. VI (Albany: Weed, Parsons and Company, 1855), p. 1005; Johnson to Shirley, 9 September 1755, CO 5, vol. 46, f. 113v.

39 Dieskau to Machault, 14 September 1755, AC, F3, vol. 14, ff. 145v-146; Vaudreuil to Machault, 25 September 1755, ibid., ff. 153-153v; "Relation de l'action qui s'est passé le 8 7bre 1755," ibid., f. 187; "Dialogue entre le maréchal de Saxe et le Baron de Dieskau aux Champs Elysées," AG, A1, vol. 3404, no. 157, ff. 9-15.

40 "Relation depuis le depart des trouppes de Quebec jusqu'au 30 du mois de 7bre. 1755," AG, A1, vol. 3405, no. 106, ff. 8-9; Vaudreuil to Machault, 25 September 1755, AC, F3, vol. 14, f. 153.

41 Vaudreuil to Machault, 25 September 1755, AC, F3, vol. 14, ff. 153v-154v; Johnson to Shirley, 9 September, 1755, CO 5, vol. 46, f. 124.

42 The British lost 120 killed, 801 wounded, and sixty-two missing, mostly from the allied ambush in the morning, and two killed, eleven wounded, and five missing from their successful ambush in the afternoon. Johnson to Shirley, 9 September 1755, CO 5, vol. 46, f. 124; "Return of killed, wounded and missing in Battle of Lake George," *Johnson Papers*, vol. IX, pp. 237-238. For allied losses see "Relation de l'action qui s'est passé le 8 7bre 1755," AC, F3, vol. 14, f. 188.

43 Vaudreuil to Machault, 25 September 1753, AC, F3, vol. 14, ff. 156v-157.

44 Shirley to Robinson, 5 November 1755, CO 5, vol. 46, f. 132.

45 Letter of William Johnson, 17 January 1756, ibid., ff. 399v-400.

5: Oswego

1 Desandrouins, "Recueil et Journal des choses principales qui me sont arrives, et de celles qui m'ont le plus frappes, depuis mon départ de France," in Gabriel, *Le maréchal de camp Desandrouins*, pp. 34-35.

2 Léry, "Journal du siège du fort de Chouaguen, appartenant aux anglais, scitué dans l'Amérique septentrionale par les 43 degrés, 45 minutes de latitude, pris par les Français le 14 Août, 1756," *RAPQ*, 1926-27, p. 398.

3 This armour was made of wooden "rods cut to the same length and pressed against one another, sewn and interlaced with little cords, very tightly and neatly." G.M. Wrong, ed., Gabriel Sagard, *Sagard's Long Journey to the country of the Hurons* (Toronto: The Champlain Society, 1939; reprinted New York: Greenwood Press, 1968), p. 154.

4 See ibid., p. 154; H.P. Biggar, ed., *The Works of Samuel de Champlain*, vol. II, (Toronto: The Champlain Society, 1925; reprinted Toronto: University of Toronto Press, 1971), pp. 82-101. Champlain's account of a confrontation on the shores of Lake Champlain is the classic description of war in the northeast prior to widespread use of iron arrowheads and firearms by Amerindians. Champlain believed that his prowess with a musket terrified the Iroquois into flight. It is equally possible that, although alarmed by the noise and flash of the guns, the Iroquois followed custom and tradition in departing the field once they had suffered fatal casualties. For pre-gunpowder Amerindian warfare, see Richter, *The Ordeal of the Longhouse*,

p. 35; Brian J. Given, *A Most Pernicious Thing: Gun Trading and Native Warfare in the Early Contact Period* (Ottawa: Carleton University Press, 1994), pp. 73-80.

5   Biggar, ed., *The Works of Samuel de Champlain*, vol. II, p. 97.

6   The plain white flag was adopted by the French crown in the seventeenth century. It became a universal sign of truce or surrender among Europeans following the adoption by France of the tricolor in 1790. See René Chartrand, *Canadian Military Heritage, volume 1: 1000-1754* (Montreal: Art Global, 1993), pp. 70-71. For one example of the use of a red flag as a flag of truce by the French, see Bougainville, "Journal," *RAPQ*, 1923-24, p. 299. For French use of the Union Jack, see Brian Leigh Dunnigan, ed. and annotator, Michael Cardy, translator, *Memoirs of the Late War in North America between France and England* (Yverdon, 1781; Youngstown: Old Fort Niagara Association, Inc., 1994), pp. 148n-149n.

7   Only the sieges of Louisbourg and Quebec approached the complexity of a European siege. At Quebec in 1759 the besiegers spent most of the siege attempting to reach a point from which they could bombard the walls of the town. Once the British were in place under the walls, the garrison surrendered even before artillery could be brought to bear on the ramparts. The French commander, Jean-Baptiste-Nicolas-Roch de Ramezay, was severely reprimanded for surrendering before the British had made a practicable breach in the walls. For European siege warfare, see Christopher Duffy, *Fire and Stone: The Science of Fortress Warfare, 1660-1860* (Newton Abbot: David & Charles, 1975), pp. 90-162; J. Muller, *The Attack and Defence of Fortify'd Places* (London: J. Millan, 1747), pp. 7-142.

8   Doreil to d'Argenson, 1 September 1756, AG, A1, vol. 3417, no. 221, f. 6.

9   Vaudreuil to Machault, 13 August 1756, AC, F3, vol. 14, f. 294.

10 Patrick Mackellar, "A Journal of the Transactions at Oswego from the 16th of May to the 14 of August 1756. By Patrick Mackellar Eng'r [Engineer] en second to the expedition," in Pargellis, ed., *Military Affairs*, pp. 190, 192, 209; "Intelligence from Oswego," in letter of Loudoun, 21 August 1756, CO 5, vol. 47, NAC, MG 11, microfilm, reel B-2111, f. 185v.

11 In addition to the eighty-seven Canadian Iroquois, there were fifty-nine Abenakis, twenty-three Algonquins, and fifty-three Nipissings from the Seven Nations, along with nine Ojibwas, four Mississaugas, and twenty-three Menominees from the west. The French component of the expedition consisted of 443 men from La Sarre, 470 from Guyenne, 410 from Béarn, 137 colonial regulars and gunners, and 1,327 militiamen. See Lapause, "Mémoire et observations sur mon voyage en Canada (1755)," *RAPQ* 1931-32, p. 29; Léry, "Journal du siège," p. 403.

12 The garrison of Oswego at the time of the siege consisted of 540 men of the 50th (Shirley's) Regiment, 444 of the 51st (Pepperrell's), 140 from the New Jersey Regiment, eighteen artillerymen, one hundred seamen, and two engineers. As well, there were a number of non-combatants within the fort at the time of the siege, including 138 workers and carpenters, eighty-four women, and seventy-four servants. See Shirley to Fox, 16 September 1756, CO 5, vol. 46, f. 334; J. Barford et al., "An account of the strength of the garrison, & strength of the works at Oswego, at the time of its being invested, together with an account of the naval force at that time, & the siege of the place, in August, 1756," in Pargellis, ed., *Military Affairs*, pp. 218-219; H.-R. Casgrain, ed., *Journal du Marquis de Montcalm durant ses campagnes au Canada de 1756 à 1760* (Quebec: L.-J. Demers, 1895), pp. 103-107.

13 Hough, *History of St. Lawrence and Franklin Counties*, p. 183.

14 See MacLeod, "Microbes and Muskets," pp. 47-48.

15 This cove was described by a French officer as "un lieu propre au débarquement à un endroit nomée La Petite Anse," Bougainville, "Journal," pp. 216-217. La Petite Anse is now known as Baldwin's Bay. Dunnigan, ed., *Memoirs of the Late War*, p. 235n.

16 Léry, "Journal du siège," p. 398.

17 Desandrouins, "Recueil et Journal," in Gabriel, *Le maréchal de camp Desandrouins*, p. 50.

18 Malartic, "Relation envoyé par M. de Malartic," 4 September 1756, AG, A1, vol. 3417, no. 228, f. 3.

19 Casgrain, ed., *Journal du Marquis de Montcalm*, p. 98; Vaudreuil to d'Argenson 30 August, 1756, AG, A1, vol. 3417, no. 214, f. 10.

20 "Intelligence from Oswego," in letter of Loudoun, 21 August 1756, CO 5, vol. 47, f. 186; Mackellar, "A Journal of the Transactions at Oswego," in Pargellis, ed., *Military Affairs*, p. 212.

21 Mackellar, "A Journal of the Transactions at Oswego," in Pargellis, ed., *Military Affairs*, pp. 210-211.

22 "Journal du siège de chouaguen, commencé le 11 aôut 1756 et fini le 14," AG, A1, 3417, no. 204, ff. 8-9.

23 "Articles de la capitulation accordée aux troupes anglaises commandées par John Littlehales commandant des dtes troupes et des forts de chouaguen, par M. le marquis de Montcalm, maréchal des camps et armées du Roy général de ses troupes dans la nouvelle-France," enclosed in Vaudreuil to Machault, 1 September 1756, AC, F3, vol. 14, ff. 307-309.

24 Vaudreuil to d'Argenson, 30 August 1756, AG, A1, vol. 3417, no. 214, f. 11.

25 Eastburn, *A faithful narrative*, p. 169n; Lapause, "Mémoire et observations," p. 34; Thomas Mante, *The history of the late war in North America, and the Islands of the West-Indies, including the campaigns of* MDCCLXIII *and* MDCCLXIV *against his Majesty's Indian enemies* (London: W. Strahan and T. Cadell, 1772; reprinted New York: Research Reprints Inc., 1970), p. 72.

26 Mante, *History of the Late War in America*. p. 71; Lapause, "Mémoire et observations," p. 34; "A plan of oswego, on L. Ontario, from an actual survey made by order of his excellency major general Shirley," enclosed in letter of Shirley, 14 September 1755, CO 5, vol. 46, f. 87. See also Peter Williamson, *French and Indian Cruelty; Exemplified in the Life and various Vicissitudes of Fortune of Peter Williamson containing ... an accurate and impartial account of the operations of the* FRENCH *and* ENGLISH *forces at the siege of Oswego, where the author was wounded and taken prisoner* (Glasgow: J. Bryce and D. Patterson, 1758), pp. 59, 60.

27 Lapause, "Mémoire et observations," p. 34; Mackellar, "Journal of the transactions at Oswego," in Pargellis, ed., *Military Affairs*, p. 213.

28 "Intelligence from Oswego," in letter of Loudoun, 21 August 1756, CO 5, vol. 4, ff. 185-186v; Loudoun to Shirley, 29 August 1756, ibid., f. 230. The concern of the fugitives was not misplaced. Soldiers who took service with an enemy in time of war faced execution and Amerindians were frequently employed by the French to hunt down deserters. In January 1759 a party of Nipissings who caught two French deserters from the Berry regiment forced one to decapitate the other, then carry the head back to Fort Carillon. The second deserter was executed by the French. At Quebec in the same year a deserter from the Royal American Regiment serving

with the French army was found wounded after the Battle of the Plains of Abraham. In spite of his wounds, he was arrested, court martialled, and summarily executed. See Duquesne to the minister, 29 October 1754, AC, C11A, vol. 99, f. 239; Desandrouins, "Journal," in Gabriel, *Le maréchal de camp Desandrouins*, p. 241; Knox, *Historical Journal*, vol. 2, p. 103; Malartic, *Journal des Campagnes au Canada*, p. 217.

29 See "Intelligence from Oswego," in letter of Loudoun, 21 August 1756, CO 5, vol. 47, ff. 186-186v.

30 Mackellar, "Journal of the transactions at Oswego," in Pargellis, ed., *Military Affairs*, p. 213; Lapause, "Mémoire et observations," p. 34.

31 Mante, *History of the Late War in America*, p. 73.

32 Littlehales to Loudoun, 30 August 1756, CO 5, vol. 47, f. 419; Benzle to Hunter, 30 August 1756, ibid., f. 415.

33 Fatalities among the French comprised one militiamen and three regulars. See "Extraits des nouvelles en Canada, 1756," AC, C11A, vol. 101, f. 336v; Bigot to Machault, 3 September 1756, AC, F3, 14, p. 318; "Relation de la campagne," AG, A1, 3417, no. 222, f. 6; Casgrain, ed., *Journal du marquis de Montcalm*, p. 101. British casualties included two officers killed and three wounded, and eighteen other ranks killed or wounded. See Pritcher to Loudoun, 30 August 1756, CO 5, vol. 47, f. 407; Cheshire to Jocylyn, 30 August 1756, ibid., f. 413; Benzle to Hunter, 30 August 1756, ibid., f. 415; Littlehales to Loudoun, 30 August 1756, ibid., f. 419.

34 "Extraits des nouvelles en Canada, 1756," AC, C11A, vol. 101, f. 336v; Vaudreuil to Machault, 1 September 1756, AC, F3, vol. 14, f. 302; "Relation de l'expédition de Chouaguen, 1756," Archives du Seminaire de St. Sulpice, Paris, vol. 4, "Piéces pour l'histoire militaire du Canada de 1750 à 1760," pièce 4, NAC, MG 17, A7-1, microfilm, reel C-14,014, p. 2792; "Relation," AG, A1, 3417, no. 228, p. 6. As well as the sources previously cited, for the events of 10-14 August, 1756 see: Lotbinière to Machault, 2 November 1756, AC, C11A, vol. 101, ff. 335-337v; Montcalm, "Affaire de Chouaguen, 28 August, 1756, AG, A1, vol. 3417, no. 208, ff. 2-3; Desandrouins, "Précis des événements de la campagne de 1756 en la nouvelle France," ibid., no. 209 bis, f. 7; "Relation de la campagne," ibid., no. 222, f. 5; Broadley to Cleveland, 26 September 1756, Great Britain, Public Record Office, Admiralty 1, vol. 1487, no. 19a, f. 21, NAC, MG 12, microfilm, reel B-2607; "An Historical Account of American Affairs during the last two years, with a particular journal of the siege and surrender of Oswego," *The Gentleman's Magazine and Historical Quarterly*, 17 (1757), p. 77; Pouchot, *Mémoires*, vol. 1 pp. 70-80.

6: Fort William Henry, 1757

1 Pouchot, *Mémoires*, vol. II, pp. 226-227.

2 "Translation of Otquandageghte's Testimony from Gov Vaudreuil by Pierre Rigaud Vaudreuil, Gov. & Lieut. Gen. for the King of all New France & the Country of Louisiana &.," 29 March 1757, enclosed in Claus to Johnson, 2 June 1762, *Johnson Papers*, vol. III, p. 754.

3 "Ils se plaignent que ce chef onontagué n'est pas de la prière."

4 Bougainville, "Journal," *RAPQ*, 1923-24, pp. 259-260. See also Casgrain, ed., *Journal du marquis de Montcalm*, pp. 185-186, 187-189.

5 Vaudreuil's interference may have had its price. In 1756 sixty-six Oswegatchies had

accompanied the expedition to the Oneida Carrying Place; in 1757 only three took part in the siege of Fort William Henry.

6   Other communities of the Seven Nations presumably had to content themselves with lesser lights, like the "French Captain from Montreal" who came to Odanak in 1755 to invite the Abenakis to join Dieskau's campaign. King, *Narrative*, p. 16.

7   Montcalm to the minister of marine, 11 July 1757, AC, F3, vol. 15, ff. 30-31; Bougainville, "Journal," pp. 270-272.

8   Lapause, "Relation de Mr. Poulariès," *RAPQ*, 1931-32, p. 50.

9   Should the British strike for Quebec, Vaudreuil expected to be able to redeploy quickly troops from the Lake Champlain front in time to garrison that town. Lapause, "Mémoire de la campagne du Canada jusqu'au 20 août 1757," *RAPQ*, 1933-34, p. 190.

10 Only fifty of the British returned safely to Fort William Henry. Montcalm to Vaudreuil, 24 July 1757, AG, A1, vol. 3457, no. 85 (1757), NAC, MG 4, microfilm, reel F-721, f. 2; Lapause, "Relation de Mr. Poulariès," p. 52; Lapause, "Journal en partant de Montréal le 3 juillet 1757," *RAPQ*, 1932-33, pp. 342-347.

11 "Journal de l'expédition du fort georges, par Malartic," AG, A1, vol. 3457, no. 117, ff. 1-2; Bougainville, "Journal," pp. 282-283, 286, 289.

12 Lapause, "Journal en partant de Montréal le 3 juillet 1757," p. 345; Bougainville, "Journal," pp. 283-284.

13 Bougainville to d'Argenson, 19 August 1757, AG, A1, vol. 3457, no. 121, f. 7.

14 "Relation de l'expédition et prise du fort guillaume henry," enclosed in Vaudreuil to the minister, 18 August 1757, AC, F3, vol. 15, NAC, MG 1, microfilm, reel F-391, f. 45; Lapause, "Relation de Mr. Poulariès," *RAPQ*, 1931-32, pp. 52-53.

15 Klinck and Talman, eds., *The Journal of Major John Norton*, p. 266.

16 Bougainville, "Journal," p. 284.

17 "Journal militaire tenu par Nicolas Renaud d'Avène des Méloizes, Ch. Seigneur de Neuville, au Canada, du 8 mai 1759 au 21 novembre de la même année. Il était alors capitaine aide-major aux troupes détachées de la marine," *RAPQ*, 1928-29, p. 45. Western speakers added that they believed their own homelands to be comfortably beyond the reach of the British.

18 The 355 Canadian Iroquois consisted of 258 Kahnawakes, ninety-four Kanesetakes, and three Oswegatchies. From other members of the Seven Nations came 209 Abenakis from Odanak, Bécancour and Lake Champlain; forty-seven Algonquins from Oka and Three Rivers; fifty-three Nipissings; and twenty-six Hurons of Lorette. The 690 fighters from the Seven Nations were joined by ninety-six Abenakis, Micmacs, and Malecites; eight League Onondagas; and 931 Delawares, Foxes, Iowas, Menominees, Miamis, Mississaugas, Odawas, Ojibwas, Potawatomis, Sauks, Winnebagos, and Wyandots from the Great Lakes region. As for the French, there were 2,570 regulars of the troupes de terre, 524 from the troupes de la marine, 189 gunners and engineers, and 2,946 militiamen. See "Armée du Roy sur le Lac St.-Sacrement," enclosed in Bougainville to d'Argenson, 19 August 1757, AG, A1, vol. 3457, no. 121, f. 3.

19 Lapause, "Relation de Mr. Poulariès," p. 56.

20 Bougainville to d'Argenson, 19 August 1757, AG, A1, vol. 3457, no. 121, p. 9.

21 For the events of the allied landing and investment, see Vaudreuil to the minister, 18 August 1757, AC, F3, vol. 15, f. 40; "Relation de l'expédition et prise du fort guillaume henry," 1757, enclosed in ibid., f. 45; "Journal de l'expédition du fort

georges, par Malartic," ibid., f. 4; Joshua Frye, "A Journal of the attack of Fort William Henry by the French on the third day of August, 1757 and the surrender of it on the ninth of the same month," CO 5, vol. 888, NAC, MG 11, microfilm, reel B-3778, ff. 124v-125; Furnis to the Board of Ordnance, 26 August 1757, in William S. Ewing, ed., "An eyewitness account by James Furnis of the surrender of Fort William Henry, August 1757," in *New York History*, vol. 42, no. 3 (July 1961), pp. 309-310.

22 Casgrain. ed., *Journal des campagnes du Chevalier de Lévis*, p. 97.

23 Letter of Roubaud, 21 October 1757, in Thwaites, ed., *Jesuit Relations*, vol. LXX, p. 154. See also Furnis to the Board of Ordnance, 26 August 1757, p. 311. The fort was too small to contain the entire garrison, which consisted of 713 regulars from the 50th and 60th Regiments, thirty gunners and engineers, and 1,596 provincials from New Jersey, New Hampshire, Massachusetts, and New York. Bougainville, "Journal," pp. 304-305.

24 Bougainville, "Journal," p. 297; Lapause, "Journal en partant de Montréal le 3 juillet 1757," p. 346.

25 Vaudreuil to the minister, 18 August 1757, f. 40v.

26 "Relation de l'expédition et prise du fort guillaume henry," f. 46 See also Bougainville to d'Argenson, 19 August 1757, ff. 16-17.

27 Bougainville, "Journal," p. 299; Furnis to the Board of Ordnance, 26 August 1757, p. 312.

28 Letter of Roubaud, 21 October 1757, in Thwaites, ed., *Jesuit Relations*, vol. LXX, pp. 162, 164.

29 "Relation de l'expédition et prise du fort guillaume henry," f. 46; Letter of Roubaud, 21 October 1757, pp. 164, 166.

30 Frye, "A Journal of the attack of Fort William Henry," f. 128v.

31 Vaudreuil to the minister, 18 August 1757, f. 40v; Letter of Roubaud, 21 October 1757, pp. 164, 166; Bougainville, "Journal," p. 299.

32 Bougainville, "Journal," p. 298.

33 Furnis to the Board of Ordnance, 26 August 1757, p. 312.

34 Vaudreuil to the minister, 18 August 1757, ff. 40v-41.

35 Letter of Roubaud, 21 October 1757, p. 162.

36 Furnis to the Board of Ordnance, 26 August 1757, pp. 312-313.

37 "Relation de la prise et capitulation de fort georges en canada," AC, C11 A, vol. 102, f. 312; Vaudreuil to the minister, 15 September 1757, AC, F3, vol. 15, f. 74; Bougainville to d'Argenson, 19 August 1757, ff. 22-23; Bougainville, "Journal," p. 301; Lapause, "Mémoire de la campagne du Canada jusqu'au 20 août 1757," *RAPQ*, 1933-34, p. 193.

38 Vaudreuil to the minister, 15 September 1757, f. 74. See also Bougainville to d'Argenson, 19 August 1757, f. 22.

39 "Relation d'une expedition faitte sur les renards par un petit party de Sauvages composé de 48 hiroquois de la mission du lac des deux montagnes et de 70 huron de celle du detroit," Archives du Seminaire de St. Sulpice, Paris, vol. 4, "Piéces pour l'histoire militaire du Canada de 1750 à 1760," pièce 1, NAC, MG 17, A7-1, microfilm, reel C-14,014, ff. 2653-2654.

40 The most detailed analysis of this incident and subsequent interpretations is Ian K. Steele. *Betrayals: Fort William Henry & the "Massacre"* (New York: Oxford University Press, 1990).

41 Bougainville to d'Argenson, 19 August 1757, f. 23; letter of Roubaud, 21 October 1757, pp. 176, 178; Bougainville, "Journal," p. 301.

42 Frye, "A Journal of the attack of Fort William Henry," f. 133.

43 Desandrouins, "Notes sur le voyage de M. Jonathan Carver dans l'amérique septentrionale, au sujet du massacre des anglois, par les sauvages, après la capitulation de fort William Henry, en 1757," in Gabriel, *Le maréchal de camp Desandrouins*, p. 103.

44 Frye, "A Journal of the attack of Fort William Henry," ff. 133-133v; Bougainville, "Journal," pp. 204-377; Furnis to the Board of Ordnance, 26 August 1757, p. 313.

45 Desandrouins, "Notes sur le voyage de M. Jonathan Carver," in Gabriel, *Le maréchal de camp Desandrouins*, p. 105. For Amerindians armed with edged weapons, rather than firearms, see: Christie to Pownall, 12 August 1757, CO 5, vol. 888, f. 92; Frye, "A Journal of the attack of Fort William Henry," ibid., f. 133v; Lapause, "Relation de Mr. Poulariès," p. 62.

46 Furnis to the Board of Ordnance, 26 August 1757, p. 313.

47 Jonathan Carver, *Travels through the Interior parts of North-America, in the Years 1766, 1767, and 1768* (London: J. Walter and S. Crowder, 1778), reprinted as *Carver's Travels through North America in the Years 1766, 1767 and 1768* (Toronto: Coles Publishing Company, 1974), p. 317.

48 The remainder of the escort presumably arrived after the disturbances began. According to one British participant, Monro "hastened away, soon after the confusion began, to the French camp to endeavour to procure the guard agreed by the stipulation." Carver, *Travels through the Interior parts of North-America*, p. 325. See also Christie to Pownall, 12 August 1757, f. 92.

49 Desandrouins, "Notes sur le voyage de M. Jonathan Carver," in Gabriel, *Le maréchal de camp Desandrouins*, p. 105. The commander, a grenadier captain named de Laas, "recommended to the English to always hold together, and to follow without intervals."

50 Frye, "A Journal of the attack of Fort William Henry," f. 134.

51 Ibid.

52 Webb to Loudoun, 11 August 1757, CO 5, vol. 48, NAC, MG 11, microfilm, reel B-2112, f. 312.

53 Furnis to the Board of Ordnance, 26 August 1757, p. 314; letter of Roubaud, 21 October 1757, p. 180.

54 Lapause, "Relation de Mr. Poulariès," p. 62.

55 "Relation de la prise et capitulation de fort georges en canada, f. 312; Vaudreuil to the minister, 15 September 1757, ff. 76-77v; Bigot to the minister, 24 August 1757, f. 58v; Christie to Pownall, 12 August 1757, ff. 90-90v; Carver, *Travels through the Interior parts of North-America*, p. 316-318; Casgrain, ed., *Journal des campagnes du Chevalier de Lévis*, p. 102; Furnis to the Board of Ordnance, 26 August, 1757, p. 314; Lapause, "Relation de Mr. Poulariès," p. 62.

56 Desandrouins, "Notes sur le voyage de M. Jonathan Carver," in Gabriel, *Le maréchal de camp Desandrouins*, p. 108.

57 Ibid., p. 119; Furnis to the Board of Ordnance, 26 August 1757, p. 314; Malartic, *Journal des Campagnes au Canada*, p. 147.

58 "Etat de ce qui a été trouvé dans le fort georges [William Henry]; qui a été détruit et rasé par les françois," Archives du Seminaire de St. Sulpice, Paris, vol. 4, f.

2823. See also Vaudreuil to the minister, 15 September 1757, f. 76; Malartic, *Journal des Campagnes au Canada*, p. 146.

59 For British losses, see "Relation de la prise et capitulation de fort georges en canada," f. 312; Vaudreuil to the minister, 15 September 1757, ff. 76-77v. The allied losses consisted of five Amerindians killed and eighteen wounded, and twelve Frenchmen killed and twenty-two wounded. "Etat des soldats tués et blessés pendant le siege du fort george," AG, A1, vol. 3457, no. 93 bis, f.1.

60 Vaudreuil to the minister, 15 September 1757, ff. 76-76v, 78; "Journal de l'expédition du fort georges, par Malartic," ff. 7, 8; Bougainville, "Journal," p. 302; Malartic, *Journal des Campagnes au Canada*, p. 147; Lapause, "Relation de Mr. Poulariès," p. 62. The La Reine Brigade consisted of the metropolitan regiments of La Reine and Languedoc, and a battalion of colonial regulars.

61 "Relation de la prise et capitulation de fort georges en canada," AC, C11A, vol. 102, f. 312; Bigot to the minister, 24 August 1757, AC, F3, vol. 15, f. 59v; Vaudreuil to the minister, 15 September 1757, ibid., ff. 76v-77v; Bougainville, "Journal," p. 304. The figures cited in this chapter for prisoners taken and released are based on French sources, which were approximations. The French appear to have either underestimated the total number of captives or overestimated the number of recovered prisoners, for many prisoners remained in captivity beyond the end of the campaign. For soldiers and civilians from Fort William Henry who had not returned to British territory by the end of 1757, see Steele, *Betrayals*, pp. 133-144, 187-199.

62 Pouchot, *Mémoires*, vol. II, pp. 117-122; Johnson to Amherst, 25 July 1759, CO 5, vol. 56, part 1, NAC, MG 11, microfilm, reel B-221, f. 82v; Montcalm to Amherst, c. August 1759, H.-R. Casgrain, ed., *Lettres et pièces militaires: Instructions, ordres, mémoires, plans de campagne et de défense, 1756-1760* (Quebec: L.-J. Demers & Frère, 1891), p. 255; Amherst to Montcalm, 10 September 1759, ibid., pp. 257-258.

63 Vaudreuil had hoped that Montcalm would push on to Fort Edward after taking Fort William Henry. Nonetheless, the capture of an important fort represented a major victory.

7: Fort Carillon, 1758

1 Bougainville, "Journal," *RAPQ*, 1923-24, pp. 316, 319.

2 After consulting with C.J. Jaenen, I have translate Pouchot's "j'ai jeté mon corps" as "I staked my life." Pouchot, *Mémoires*, vol. I, pp. 127-128.

3 George R. Hamell, "The Iroquois and the World's Rim: Speculations on Color, Culture, and Contact," *American Indian Quarterly*, no. 4 (fall 1992), pp. 457, 465n.

4 Bougainville, "Journal," p. 260.

5 Pouchot, *Mémoires*, vol. I, p. 128.

6 Ibid., vol. II, p. 177.

7 Desandrouins, "Recueil et Journal des choses principales qui me sont arrivées, et de celles qui m'ont le plus frappées, depuis mon départ de France," in Gabriel, *Le maréchal de camp Desandrouins*, pp. 135-136.

8 Bougainville, "Journal," p. 316. See also Montcalm to the minister, 20 April 1758, AG, A1, vol. 3498, no. 63, f. 7, NAC, MG 4, microfilm, reel F-722.

9 Vaudreuil to the minister, 28 July 1758, AC, F3, vol. 15, ff. 112v-113; Lévis to the

minister, 17 June 1758, AG, A1, vol. 3498, no. 99, ff. 5-7; Montreuil to Cremilles, 12 June 1758, ibid., no. 99, ff. 1-2; "The Information of Taghanahiroa a principal warrior of Onondaga who has always been judged faithful to the English," 10 June 1757, CO 5, vol. 50, NAC, MG 11, microfilm, reel B-2113, f. 240; Bougainville, "Journal," p. 324; Lapause, "Mémoires et observations," *RAPQ*, 1931-32, p. 35. The French component of this force was to have been composed of four hundred regulars from the light companies of the troupes de terre, four hundred colonial regulars, and eight hundred militiamen.

10 Abercromby's army consisted of 6,367 regulars and 9,024 provincials; Montcalm's of 3,111 regulars of the troupes de terre, 150 regulars of the troupes de la marine, 250 militiamen, and fifteen Amerindians. Abercromby to Pitt, 12 July 1758, CO 5, vol. 50, f. 176; Bougainville, "Journal," pp. 386-387.

11 Colden to Halket, 17 July 1758, in C.E. Lart, ed., "Eye-Witnesses' Accounts of the British Repulse at Ticonderoga," *Canadian Historical Review*, no. 4 (December 1921), p. 363.

12 The British suffered a total of 1,944 casualties, mostly among the regulars, who lost 1,610 killed, as opposed to seven provincials. The French lost 104 killed and 273 wounded. "Relation de la victoire remporté sur les anglois le juillet 1758 par l'armée du Roy commandée par le Marquis de Montcalm," AG, A1, vol. 3498, no. 138, ff. 1-6; "État des officers, soldats tués ou blessés à la deffense des abatis près de carillon le 8 juillet 1758," ibid., no. 38 bis. f. 1; Abercromby to Pitt, 12 July 1758, CO 5, vol. 50, ff. 176-183; "Return of the killed, wounded and missing of His Majesty's troops & provincials in the action near Ticonderoga July 8th 1758," ibid., f. 184.

13 Malartic, *Journal des Campagnes au Canada*, p. 192. French reinforcements had also arrived, raising the number of Europeans in the allied army to 2,761 colonial regulars and militia, and 3,528 metropolitan regulars. Bougainville, "Journal," pp. 343-344.

14 Bougainville, "Journal," pp. 343, 345; Malartic, *Journal des Campagnes au Canada*, p. 346.

15 Hough, *History of St. Lawrence and Franklin Counties*, pp. 183, 197.

16 Abercromby to Pitt, 19 August 1758, CO 5, vol. 50, ff. 260-260v: Malartic, *Journal des Campagnes au Canada*, p. 192; Bougainville, "Journal," p. 345; Casgrain, ed., *Journal des campagnes du Chevalier de Lévis*, p. 142.

17 Desandrouins, "Journal," in Gabriel, *Le maréchal de camp Desandrouins*, pp. 199-200. This appears to have been a general sentiment among the French officers, for we find Bougainville writing in his journal: "Cruel war on their [Amerindians] part against sheep, chickens, wine, liquors and everything of that nature." Bougainville, "Journal," p. 345.

18 Montcalm to Doreil, 14 July 1758, paraphrased in letter of Doreil, 28 July 1758, *RAPQ*, 1944-45, p. 138.

19 W.J. Eccles, "Louis-Joseph de Montcalm, Marquis de Montcalm," in *Dictionary of Canadian Biography*, vol. III, pp. 458-469; Eccles, "Pierre de Rigaud de Vaudreuil de Cavagnial, Marquis de Vaudreuil," ibid., pp. 662-674; D. Peter MacLeod, "The Canadians against the French: The Struggle for Control of the Expedition to Oswego in 1756," *Ontario History* no. 2 (June 1988), pp. 143-157.

20 Bougainville, "Journal," p. 344. Bougainville was ghostwriting Montcalm's journal during this campaign, so identical sentiments occur in that document.

21 Letter of Doreil, 28 July 1758, *RAPQ*, 1944-45, p. 138. Doreil went on to ridicule

the performance of the colonial regulars and militiamen who had been present at the battle.

22 Bougainville, "Journal," p. 349.

23 Letter of Doreil, 31 July 1758, *RAPQ*, 1944-45, p. 152.

24 Malartic, *Journal des Campagnes au Canada*, p. 192; Bougainville, "Journal," p. 346.

25 "Paroles des Iroquois, Nepissingues, Algonkins, Abenakis, et Mississagués de 30 Juillet, 1758," enclosed in Vaudreuil to the minister, 4 August 1758, AC, C11A, vol. 103, NAC, MG 1, microfilm, reel F-103, f. 159

26 Ibid., ff. 159-159v. Given that these reports from the Seven Nations were sent to Versailles by Vaudreuil, who at this point had little use for Montcalm, the suspicion naturally arises that Onontio had somewhat improved the wording when he prepared his dispatches. However, in the following year, Bourlamaque said much the same thing following a disagreement with the Canadian Iroquois at Carillon, when he declared: "We know how to make war without you, what have you been good for up to now. We beat the English last year without any of you; we will do so again this year." See Desandrouins, "Journal," in Gabriel, *Le maréchal de camp Desandrouins*, pp. 280-281.

27 Malartic, *Journal des Campagnes au Canada*, p. 346.

28 "Paroles des Iroquois," ff. 159v-160.

29 Malartic, *Journal des Campagnes au Canada*, p. 194. See also "Paroles des Iroquois...," f. 160.

30 "Paroles des Iroquois...," f. 160.

31 Bougainville, "Journal," p. 347.

32 "Paroles des Iroquois...," ff. 160-161.

33 Malartic, *Journal des Campagnes au Canada*, p. 194.

34 Vaudreuil to the minister, 4 August 1758, AC, C11A, vol. 103, ff. 180v-181; Bougainville, "Journal," pp. 349-350; Casgrain, ed., *Journal des campagnes du Chevalier de Lévis* pp. 143-144; Malartic, *Journal des Campagnes au Canada*, p. 194.

35 "Réponses de M. Le Général," 30 July 1758, enclosed in Vaudreuil to the minister, 4 August, 1758, f. 159; Vaudreuil to the minister, 4 August, 1758, ibid., ff. 145-149.

36 Vaudreuil to Montcalm, 1 August 1758, cited in Montcalm to the minister, c. 6 August 1758, AG, A1, vol. 3499, no. 2, f. 2, NAC, MG 4, microfilm, reel F-723.

37 Vaudreuil to the minister, 18 August 1758, AC, C11A, vol. 103, ff. 190-190v; Abercromby to Pitt, 19 August 1758, CO 5, vol. 50, ff. 265-266; Bougainville, "Journal," p. 355; Casgrain, ed., *Journal des campagnes du Chevalier de Lévis*, pp. 144-145; Malartic, *Journal des Campagnes au Canada*, p. 197. Allied losses included two Amerindians, three soldiers, and three militiamen killed, and four Amerindians, three soldiers, and five militiamen wounded.

38 "Headquarters, Camp at the Great Carrying Place, 21 August 1755, "Minutes of Indian Affairs, 1755-1790," vol. 1822, f. 87.

8: Lake Champlain, Lake Ontario, and Quebec, 1759

1 Vaudreuil to Berryer, 5 October 1759, AC, F3, vol. 15, f. 272; Vaudreuil to Berryer, 8 November 1759, ibid., f. 360v; Bigot to Berryer, 15 October 1759, ibid., f. 335v;

"Journal des mouvemens qu'a fait le regt de Béarn [1759]," AG, A1, 3540, no. 128, ff. 33-36, NAC, MG 4, microfilm, reel F-724; Casgrain, ed., *Journal du marquis de Montcalm*, p. 501; Gabriel, *Desandrouins*, p. 278.

2   Vaudreuil to Berryer, 5 October 1759, AC, F3, vol. 15, f. 272.

3   Aegidius Fauteux, ed., *Journal du siège de Québec du 10 mai au 18 septembre 1759* (Quebec, 1922), p. 22.

4   "Genuine letter from a volunteer in the British service at Quebec (1761)," in A. Doughty and G.W. Parmelee, *The Siege of Quebec and Battle of the Plains of Abraham*, vol. V (Quebec: Dussault & Proulx, 1901), p. 16. The anonymous volunteer added that "the whole country on both sides [of] the river, for richness of soil, the various gifts of agriculture and its innumerable villages steated [sic] in the midst of plenty, may vie with the choicest vales in Great Britain."

5   Some Amerindians resented a strategy that kept the French regulars safely inside the lines while Amerindians carried the war to the enemy. On 24 July nine hundred Amerindians joined in refusing to march "because one did not attach to them a number of Frenchmen equal to their own." "Siège de Québec en 1759, copie d'après un manuscrit apporté de Londres, par l'honorable D.B. Viger," in Jean-Claude Hébert, ed., *Le siège de Québec en 1759 par trois témoins* (Québec: Ministère des affaires culturelles, 1972), p. 92.

6   James Johnson, "Memoirs of the siege of Quebec and total reduction of Canada in 1759 and 1769 by James Johnson, clerk and quarter mas'r sergeant to the 58th reg't," in Doughty and Parmelee, *The Siege of Quebec*, p. 98.

7   Vaudreuil to Berryer, 5 October 1759, AC, F3, vol. 15, f. 274v; Wolfe to Pitt, 2 September 1759, CO 5, vol. 51, NAC, MG 11, microfilm, reel B-2113, ff. 74v-75; Knox, *Historical Journal*, vol. I, p. 411; Jean-Félix Récher, *Journal du siège de Québec en 1759* (Quebec: La Société Historique de Québec, 1959), pp. 13-14.

8   "Extrait d'un journal tenu à l'armée que commandoit fut Mr. de Montcalm Lieutenant g'n'l 1759," AC, C11A, vol. 101, NAC, MG 1, microfilm, reel F-101, ff. 170v-171; Knox, *Historical Journal*, vol. I, p. 403; Récher, *Journal du siège de Québec*, p. 11.

9   Fauteux, ed., *Journal du siège*, p. 48. "Lévis had posted the Natives on the side of the falls, and the volunteers and militia a little to the rear into order to engage them [the British] and take them between two fires."

10 Marie-Joseph Legardeur de Repentigny, "Relation de ce qui s'est passé au siège de Québec, et de la prise du Canada; par une Religieuse de l'Hôpital Général de Québec: adressée à une communauté de son ordre en France," in Hébert, ed., *Le siège de Québec en 1759*, pp. 16-17. This viewpoint was presumably that of wounded participants in the battle who were treated at the hospital. A British observer expressed a similar opinion, recording that the retreating soldiers were "greatly intimidated, with a view of the enemy's unapproachable works, and the great number of men already lost before the work was begun, as well as the cruelty of the savages." Johnson, "Memoirs of the siege of Quebec," in Doughty and Parmelee, *The Siege of Quebec*, vol. V, p. 90.

11 Vaudreuil to Berryer, 5 October 1759, AC, F3, vol. 15, f. 278; Saunders to Pitt, 5 September 1759, CO 5, vol. 51, ff. 38v-39; Wolfe to Pitt, 2 September 1759, ibid., ff. 76-80; Knox, *Historical Journal*, vol. I, pp. 449-456; Lévis to Belle Isle, 2 August 1759, H.-R. Casgrain, ed., *Lettres du Chevalier de Lévis concernant la guerre du Canada (1756-1760)* (Montreal: C.O. Beauchemin & Fils, 1889), p. 229.

12 "Mémoire sur la campagne de 1759, depuis may jusqu'au 7bre," AG, A1, vol. 3540, no. 99, f. 12.

13 Renaud, "Journal militaire," *RAPQ*, 1928-29, p. 52.

14 Récher, *Journal du siège de Québec*, p. 43.

15 In addition to the seventy-one Canadian Iroquois, there were nineteen "Wolves" (Delawares or Mohicans), fifteen Mississaugas, and five Hurons, along with 261 colonial regulars and 820 militiamen. Given that they were accompanied by François Piquet, the resident Sulpician priest at Oswegatchie, some of the Canadian Iroquois were likely from that community. "Relation de la campagne de M. le Chevalier de la Corne a Chouaguen, en 1759," Casgrain, ed., *Relations et journaux*, p. 214; Lapause, "Relation de M. Poulariès," *RAPQ*, 1931-32, p. 90.

16 William Amherst, "Col. Amherst's Journal," CO 5, vol. 56, part 1, NAC, MG 11, microfilm, reel B-221, ff. 68-68v; Knox, *Historical Journal*, vol. I, pp. 493-496.

17 The allies had lost ten killed, twenty wounded and four deserters. The British lost three killed and fourteen wounded. See Vaudreuil to Berryer, 30 October 1759, AC, F3, vol. 15, ff. 345v-346; William Amherst, "Col. Amherst's Journal," ff. 68-68v; Knox, *Historical Journal*, vol. I, pp. 493-496; Lapause, "Relation de M. Poulariès," pp. 90, 92; "Relation de la campagne de M. le Chevalier de la Corne," pp. 215-218.

18 Lapause, "Relation de M. Poulariès," pp. 94-95. Work on Fort Lévis began on 29 August, when two hundred regulars and militiamen arrived at the site. The fort was constructed on what is now called Chimney Island. See also Lapause, "Mémoire et réflexions politiques et militaires sur la guerre du Canada depuis 1746 jusqu'à 1760," *RAPQ*, 1933-34, pp. 157-158; Lévis, *Journal*, pp. 191-192, 195-203; Dunnigan, ed., *Memoirs of the Late War*, p. 238n.

19 "Campagne de 1759," AC, F3, vol. 15, f. 247; Desandrouins, "Journal," in Gabriel, *Le maréchal de camp Desandrouins*, pp. 283-284; "Troupes campées à l'Ile-aux-Noix," c. August 1759, in H.-R. Casgrain, ed., *Lettres de M. de Bourlamaque au maréchal de Lévis* (Quebec: L.-J. Demers & Frère, 1891), p. 16. French forces in the Lake Champlain region included 1,376 metropolitan regulars, 417 colonial regulars, and 1,230 militiamen.

20 "Campagne de 1759," f. 247; "Instructions pour M. de Bourlamaque Brigadier des armées du Roy," 20 April 1759, AC, F3, vol. 15, ff. 364-368v; Desandrouins, "Journal," pp. 283-284; Lapause, "Relation de M. Poulariès," pp. 90, 92, 94; Lapause, "Mémoire et réflexions politiques et militaires sur la guerre du Canada," p. 157.

21 Renaud, "Journal militaire," pp. 30-51.

22 Ibid., pp. 44-45; Frazier, *The Mohicans of Stockbridge*, p. 131; William Amherst, "Col. Amherst's Journal," f. 66.

23 Renaud, "Journal militaire," p. 45.

24 Ibid., pp. 44-45. Joseph was among those rangers who escaped the Kahnawake pursuit. His presence was revealed by Captain Jacob Naunauphataunk, a Stockbridge Mohican serving as an officer in Rogers' Rangers, who had commanded the scouting party and was among the prisoners.

25 Desandrouins, "Journal," pp. 280-281.

26 Ibid.

27 Desandrouins, "Journal," pp. 283-284.

28 "Col. Amherst's Journal," f. 71. For the British landing, see also Bourlamaque to Berryer, 19 October 1759, AC, F3, vol. 15, f. 354v; Desandrouins, "Journal," p. 290;

Renaud, "Journal militaire," p. 51.

29 "Col. Amherst's Journal," ff. 70v-72; Knox, *Historical Journal*, vol. I, pp. 502-506. Amherst's total force in the region numbered 6,537 regulars and 4,039 provincials. "Army for Lake George as the totals of the numbers are at present officers included," 19 June 1759, CO 5, vol. 55, part 2, f. 109, NAC, MG 11, microfilm, reel B-221.

30 The Rivière à la Barbue is now known as Putnam's Creek. Dunnigan, ed., *Memoirs of the Late War*, p. 163n.

31 Desandrouins, "Journal," p. 292.

32 Gabriel, *Le maréchal de camp Desandrouins*, p. 291; Renaud, "Journal militaire," p. 51.

33 There were 278 metropolitan and colonial regulars, 120 militiamen, and one Nipissing named Outchik in the garrison of Fort Carillon during the siege. Gabriel, *Le maréchal de camp Desandrouins*, p. 291; Renaud, *RAPQ* 1928-29, p. 51.

34 Desandrouins, "Journal," pp. 293-295.

35 Renaud, "Journal militaire," p. 52.

36 "Col. Amherst's Journal," ff. 72-76; Amherst to Pitt, 5 August 1759, CO 5, vol. 56, part 1, ff. 77-81; Desandrouins, "Journal," pp. 283-284, 290-299; Knox, *Historical Journal*, vol. I, pp. 501-512.

37 Amherst to "the present commandant of the Fortress and dependent forts of Crown point and those that shall hereafter succeed him as such," 24 November 1759, WO 34, vol. 52, NAC, MG 13, microfilm, reel B-2666, f. 9.

38 Amherst to Pitt, 22 October 1759, CO 5, vol. 56, part 2, NAC, MG 11, microfilm, reel B-221, ff. 24-25.

39 This statement was made at a conference held to resolve conflicting Kahnawake and Abenaki claims in the Lake Champlain valley. "Ind Speech to the Governours [sic] of N. York & Quebec delivered on Isle a la Mote[sic] in Lake Champlain 9. Sept. 1766." Superintendents's Office Correspondence, 1755-1830, vol. 1828 [Indian Records, vol. 9], NAC, RG 10, microfilm, reel C-1222, f. 86. During the campaign of 1757 other Amerindian nations deferred to the Canadian Iroquois as "originally proprietors of this region." Bougainville to d'Argenson, 19 August 1757, AG, A1, vol. 3457, no. 121, f. 7.

40 Lapause, "Mémoire et observations sur mon voyage en Canada," *RAPQ*, 1931-32, pp. 94-95.

41 La Corne to Lévis, 17 August 1759, H.-R. Casgrain, ed., *Lettres de Divers particuliers au Chevalier de Lévis* (Quebec: L.-J. Demers & Frère, 1895), pp 205-206; ibid., 10 August 1759, Casgrain, ed., p. 203.

42 "L'armée du Roy sur le Lac St. Sacrement," in Bougainville to d'Argenson, 19 August 1757, AG, A1, vol. 3457, no. 121, f. 3.

43 Mante, *The History of the Late War in North-America*, pp. 307-308.

44 William Johnson, "Journal of Niagara Campaign," 26 July-14 October 1759, *Johnson Papers*, vol. XIII, pp. 133, 142.

45 Ibid., pp. 142, 150.

46 Ibid., pp. 155, 155-156.

47 Haldimand to Amherst, 19 May 1760, WO 34, vol. 38, f. 102, NAC, MG 13, microfilm, reel B-2656.

48 "Instructions for Captain Quinton [or Kinton] Kennedy of His Majesty's 17th Regiment of Foot," 8 August 1759, WO 34, vol. 38, f. 79-79v.

49 For the Kennedy affair, see Vaudreuil to Berryer, 5 October 1759, AC, F3, 15, f. 282; Amherst to Pitt, 22 October 1759, CO 5, vol. 56, part 2, ff. 1v-2, 13; Amherst to Pitt, 11 December 1759, CO 5, vol. 57, part 1, ff. 5v-6v, NAC, MG 11, microfilm, reel B-2171; Jeffery Amherst, "Journal, 1760," f. 37, NAC, MG 18, L4, British officers, Amherst Family, vol. 015/8, microfilm, reel A-1826; Vaudreuil to Lévis 26 August 1759, in H.-R. Casgrain, ed., *Lettres du marquis de Vaudreuil au Chevalier de Lévis* (Québec: L.-J. Demers, 1895), pp. 89-90; Bigot to Lévis, 26 August 1759, in Casgrain, ed., *Lettres de l'intendant Bigot au Chevalier de Lévis* (Québec: L.-J. Demers, 1895), pp. 49-50; Vaudreuil to Moncton, 13 October 1759, in Casgrain, ed., *Lettres et pièces militaires*, p. 267; Bernier to Lévis, 31 August 1759, in Casgrain, ed., *Lettres de divers particuliers*, p. 46; Fauteux, ed., *Journal du siège de Québec*, p. 59; Frazier, *The Mohicans of Stockbridge*, pp. 132-133, 137, 140.

50 Narrative of Elvine Obomsawin Royce, in Gordon M. Day, "Rogers' Raid in Indian Tradition," *Historical New Hampshire* 17 (June 1962), p. 11.

51 The relationship between the Mohicans and the Abenaki was very complicated. Day suggests that the Mohican raider was a relative of a family that had been given refuge at Odanak. Ibid., p. 11.

52 Narratives of Theophile Panadis and Elvine Obomsawin Royce, ibid., pp. 9-13.

53 Renaud, "Journal Militaire," p. 85.

54 Robert Rogers, *Journals of Major Robert Rogers: Containing an Account of the several Excursions he made under the Generals who commanded upon the Continent of NORTH AMERICA, during the late War* (London: J. Millan, 1765; reprinted Ann Arbor: University Microfilms, Inc., 1966), p. 158n; Lapause, "Mémoire et observations sur mon voyage en canada," p. 103.

55 "Extrait d'un journal tenu à l'armée que commandoit fut Mr. de Montcalm Lieutenant g'n'l 1759," AC, C11A, vol. 101, f. 207.

56 For the raid on Odanak, see Amherst to Pitt, 22 October 1759, CO 5, vol. 56, part 2, f. 13; Amherst to Pitt, 16 December 1759, CO 5, vol. 57, part 1, ff. 5v-7; Bourlamaque to Lévis, 27 September 1759, in Casgrain, ed., *Lettres de Bourlamaque*, p. 47; Lévis, *Journal*, pp. 223-224; Malartic, *Journal des Campagnes au Canada*, pp. 300-301; Renaud, "Journal Militaire," pp. 75, 79, 84-85; Rogers, *Journals*, pp. 144-158; Calloway, *The Western Abenakis*, pp. 175-181; Day, "Rogers' Raid," pp. 9-13; Frazier, *The Mohicans of Stockbridge*, p. 136.

57 "An Account of the action which happened near quebec, 13th September, 1759," in Pargellis, ed., *Military affairs*, p. 438. See also "Journal des faits arrivés à l'armée de quebec capital dans l'amérique septentrional pendant la campagne de l'année 1759 par m. de Soligné," AC, C11A, vol. 101, f. 289v; Vaudreuil to Berryer, 5 October 1759, AC, F3, vol. 15, f. 287.

58 Townshend to Pitt, 20 September 1759, CO 5, vol. 51, f. 90v.

59 Knox, *Historical Journal*, vol. II, pp. 98-99.

60 James LeMoine, *The Scot in New France: An Ethnological Study* (Montreal: Dawson Brothers, 1881), p. 29.

62 Knox, *Historical Journal*, vol. II, p. 116.

62 James Murray, "Report of the Government of Quebec and dependencies thereof," c. 1762. NAC, MG 8, E 1, f. 60.

9: Lake Ontario and the St. Lawrence Valley, 1760

1 "Conseil Secrete tenu à Montréal par les Onneyouts, Kaskaronenk, Goyog8in, adressés à nos domiciliés, le 23 8bre, 1754," enclosed in Duquesne to the minister, 31 October 1754, AC, C11A, vol. 99, f. 37v.

2 Lapause, "Relation de Mr. Poulariès," *RAPQ*, 1931-32, p. 52. A second version of this statement is in Bougainville, "Journal," *RAPQ*, 1923-24, p. 284.

3 John Butler to Johnson, Fort Stanwix, 24 April 1760, in Milton W. Hamilton, ed., *The Papers of Sir William Johnson*, vol. X (Albany: University of the State of New York, 1951), pp. 140-141.

4 "At a Meeting of the Deputies of the 6 Confederate Nations," 13-14 February 1760, CO 5, vol. 58, ff. 149-149v, NAC, MG 11, microfilm, reel B-2172.

5 Lapause, "Relation des affaires du Canada depuis le 1 Xbre 1759 au...[21 May 1760]," *RAPQ*, 1933-34, p. 144; Casgrain, ed., *Journal des campagnes du Chevalier de Lévis*, p. 257; Malartic, *Journal des Campagnes au Canada*, p. 307; Hough, *History of St. Lawrence and Franklin Counties*, p. 183. Apart from the Oswegatchies, French records do not identify the Amerindian fighters in this campaign.

6 D. Peter MacLeod, "Treason at Quebec: British espionage in Canada during the winter of 1759-1760," *Canadian Military History* 2, no. 1 (Spring 1993), pp. 49-62.

7 "Monthly Return of His Majestys Forces in the River St. Lawrence under the command of Brig Gen James Murray Quebec 24 April 1760," enclosed in Murray to Pitt, 25 May 1760, CO 5, vol. 64, f. 103, NAC, MG 11, microfilm, reel B-2175; James Murray, "Journal of the Expedition against Quebec in the year One thousand Seven Hundred and fifty Nine and from the surrender being the 18 day of Sep 1759 to the 17 May 1760, also a journal resum'd from the 18 May to the 17 Sep following...," James Murray Papers, NAC, MG 23, G II 1, series 4, vol. 1, ff. 95-97, microfilm, reel C-2225; Casgrain, ed., *Journal des campagnes du Chevalier de Lévis*, pp. 263-268; C.P. Stacey, *Quebec, 1759: The Siege and the Battle*, rev. ed. (London: Pan Books, 1973), pp. 165-169.

8 Vaudreuil to Belle Isle, 29 June 1760, AG, A1, 3574, no. 68, f. 1, NAC, MG 4, microfilm, reel F-725; Malartic, *Journal des Campagnes au Canada*, p. 315.

9 Henry Hamilton, "Reminiscences," 1792, NAC, Henry Hamilton Papers, MG 23, G II 11, f. 92.

10 "Allons mes enfants marchez." Henry Hamilton, "Reminiscences," f. 91. I first encountered a reference to this incident in René Chartrand, *Canadian Military Heritage, volume II: 1755-1871* (Montreal: Art Global, 1995), p. 208n.

11 Casgrain, ed., *Journal des campagnes du Chevalier de Lévis*, p. 281.

12 Malartic, *Journal des Campagnes au Canada*, p. 326.

13 Lapause, "Journal de l'entrée de la campagne 1760," *RAPQ*, 1933-34, p. 206.

14 Casgrain, ed., *Journal des campagnes du Chevalier de Lévis*, p. 285.

15 This passage occurs in a postscript, dated "Since I wrote the above." Murray to Pitt, 25 May 1760, CO 5, vol. 64, f. 23v, NAC, MG 11, microfilm, reel B-2175.

16 Benoît-François Bernier, "Evenements en Canada depuis le mois d'octobre 1759 jusqu'au mois de Septembre 1760," AG, A1, 3574, no. 112, f. 3.

17 Amherst to Johnson, 2 June 1760, WO 34, vol. 38, f. 115. See also Amherst to Haviland, 11 June 1760, ibid., vol. 52, f. 47.

18 "The governor said by his interpreter 'Jamais.' The Indian by the same interpreter returned 'Oh toujours Jamais!' The event justified the Indians' sarcastic remark." Hamilton, "Reminiscences," f. 95.

19 Pouchot, *Mémoires*, vol. II, p. 250.

20 Guichart to Amherst, 22 September 1760, WO 34, vol. 83, ff. 79-79v, NAC, MG 13, microfilm, reel B-2684; Pouchot, *Mémoires*, vol. II, pp. 200-206, 240, 247, 250-251; ibid., vol. III, p. 88. Ile Piquet is now known as Galop Island; Toniata as Grenadier Island, in Leeds country, Ontario. Dunnigan, ed., *Memoirs of the Late War*, p. 238n, 273n.

21 Haviland to Amherst, c. June, 1760, WO 34, vol. 51, f. 47, NAC, MG 13, microfilm, reel B-2666.

22 When the Oswegatchies did receive requests for assistance between May and August they kept the warriors at home while making non-committal responses that satisfied the French. Pouchot, *Mémoires*, vol. II, pp. 227-228, 239-240.

23 "Examinations taken by the order of Colonel Haldimand & opinion thereupon at Fort Ontario 17th May 1760 by the following officers. Capt [Walter] Rutherford [60th], Capt Strechy [artillery], Capt [Marcus] Prevost [60th], Capt [Thomas] Sowers [engineer]," WO 34, vol. 39, ff. 145-145v.

24 Johnson to Amherst, 7 March 1760, WO 34, vol. 38, f. 99. Two months later, he referred to the Kahnawakes as "our enemys." Johnson to Lotteridge, 10 May 1760, ibid., vol. 39, f. 142.

25 Amherst to Johnson, 23 February 1760, ibid, vol. 38, f. 97.

26 Pouchot, *Mémoires*, vol. II, pp. 236-237. See also Jennings, *Empire of Fortune*, pp. 415-416, 419.

27 Pouchot, *Mémoires*, vol. II, p. 248. Pouchot, recording this statement in his journal, added in a footnote that "Cela fut vrai."

28 Ibid., pp. 178-182, 192-194.

29 Johnson to Amherst, 10 June 1760, WO 34, vol. 39, f. 157v. Ohquandageghte was baptized as Pierre Otkuentaguette, and married Cécile Seuentcaien on 10 May 1760. Pouchot, *Mémoires sur la dernière guerre*, vol. II, pp. 193-193, 200; Dunnigan, ed., *Memoirs of the Late War*, p. 263n.

30 Johnson to Amherst, 26 June 1760, *Johnson Papers*, vol. III, p. 262.

31 Ibid., pp. 262-263; Johnson to Haldimand, 4 July 1760, ibid., pp. 264-265; Pouchot, *Mémoires*, vol. II, pp. 225-226, 239-240. Haldimand probably ordered the detention of the envoys after the British learned of private meetings between Ohquandageghte and the Onondagas, at which the negative implications of a British conquest of Canada were discussed. "Journal of Jelles Fonda," 29 June-23 October 1760, *Johnson Papers*, vol. XIII, p. 168.

32 Pouchot, *Mémoires*, vol. II, pp. 254-255.

33 "In the morning I heard from our Indians that the Indians who was gone to Oswegatchie was returned and said [that they] would keep themselves neutral when we would come there." "Journal of Jelles Fonda," *Johnson Papers*, vol. XIII, p. 169.

34 Johnson to Pitt, 24 October 1760, ibid., vol. III, p. 272.

35 Jeffery Amherst, "Extracts of my journal," NAC, MG 18, L4, British officers, Amherst Family, vol. 014, f. 96, microfilm, reel A-1826; Murray, "Journal of the Expedition against Quebec...," NAC, James Murray Papers, MG 23, G II 1, series 4, vol. 1, ff. 122-170, microfilm, reel C-2225; Knox, *Historical Journal*, vol. II, pp. 466-522.

36 Amherst to Haviland, 12 June 1760, WO 34, vol. 52, f. 53; Casgrain, ed., *Journal des campagnes du Chevalier de Lévis*, pp. 297-301; Mante, *History of the Late War*, pp. 340-341.

37 See the "Return of the Men, Women & Children of the Six Nations of Indians, under the command of Sir William Johnson, Bart. at Oswego, August 5 1760, WO 34, vol. 39, f. 158; "Embarkation Return of His Majesty's Forces under the Command of Major-General Amherst from the Camp at Fort Ontario, 9th of August 1760," CO 5, vol. 59, part 1, f. 123, NAC, MG 11, microfilm, reel B-2173.

38 Amherst, "Journal, 1760," L4, vol. 015/8, ff. 20, 41. During the siege of Fort Lévis, Île Piquet was occupied by British forces, who erected a battery mounting three twenty-four pounders, two twelve-pounders, and one ten-inch mortar. See Amherst to Pitt, 26 August 1760, CO 5, vol. 58, f. 144v; Amherst, "Journal, 1760," ff. 14, 20; "Journal of Jelles Fonda," *Johnson Papers*, vol. XIII, pp. 170, 172; Knox, *Historical Journal*, vol. II, pp. 542-543, 553.

39 "Journal of Jelles Fonda," *Johnson Papers*, vol. XIII, pp. 171-172. Fonda's phrasing is often imprecise, and it is possible that the British detachment had merely stood by as the Frenchmen demolished Oswegatchie. What is clear is that the town of Oswegatchie was virtually destroyed during the British occupation. For the use of Oswegatchie as a hospital, see Jeffery Amherst, "Journal, 1760," f. 39.

40 The site occupied by the main body of Amherst's army, then known to the French as Pointe à l'Ivrogne, is now called Tuttle Point. Pouchot, *Mémoires*, vol. II, p. 265; ibid., vol. III, p. 90; Dunnigan, ed., *Memoirs of the Late War*, p. 303n.

41 Johnson is vague about the exact date of the meeting, noting only that "on our arrival at Fort Levi[s] deputies came from the before mentioned nations," who were "the several nations & tribes of Indians inhabiting the country about Montreal." Johnson to Pitt, 24 October 1760, *Johnson Papers*, vol. III, p. 273. This implies that the delegation arrived on 18 August and the conference extended over 18-19 August.

42 Ibid.; Knox, *Historical Journal*, vol. II, p. 533.

43 "Sir William Johnson received the following complaint of the Indians of Aughquisasne, transmitted to him by Dan Claus Esq, Dep Agent for Canada, bearing the date 8 Septem 1764," "Minutes of Indian Affairs, 1755-1790," vol. 1826 [Indian Records, vol. 7], f. 184, NAC, RG 10, microfilm, reel C-1222.

44 "Return of such Indians as proceeded with the Army under the command of His Excellency General Amherst, from Fort William Augustus to Montreal," 13 September 1760, WO 34, vol. 39, f. 159v; Pouchot, *Mémoires*, vol. II, p. 284.

45 Johnson to Pitt, 24 October 1760, *Johnson Papers*, vol. III, p. 273. Johnson added that he had "by that means made those Indians our friends by a peace, who might otherwise have given us much trouble." See also "Journal of Warren Johnson," 29 June 1760-3 July 1761, ibid., vol. XIII, pp. 188-190.

46 The British considered this withdrawal to be an act of treachery, provoked by Amherst's refusal to allow his allies to plunder Fort Lévis. Amherst to Alexander Murray, 17 September 1760, WO 34, vol. 20, f. 13v; Amherst to Johnson 22 February 1761, ibid., vol. 38, f. 138v; "Return of such Indians as proceeded with the Army under the command of His Excellency General Amherst, from Fort William Augustus to Montreal," 13 September 1760, ibid., vol. 39, f. 159v; Amherst to Haviland, 26 August 1760, ibid., vol. 52, f. 81; "Journal of Warren Johnson," *Johnson Papers*, vol. XIII, pp. 188-190; Pouchot, *Mémoires*, vol. II, p. 284.

47 Amherst to Johnson, 30 August, 3 September 1760, WO 34, vol. 38, ff. 122, 123.

48 Amherst to Pitt, 8 September 1760, CO 5, vol. 59, part 2, f. 96v, reel B-2173. When writing to the resident priest at Akwesasne, Amherst declared that "tant qu'ils restront tranquilles chez eux & qu'ils éviteront toutes hostilités il ne seront point molesté dans leurs habitations." Amherst to "Prêtre au village de Asquesashna," 3 September 1760, WO 34, vol. 85, f. 80, NAC, MG 13, microfilm, reel B-2685.

49 Mante, *History of the Late War in North-America*, p. 310.

50 Even in the late summer, some French leaders continued to hope that if their frontier forts could hold out, it was at least possible that they might be able to retain control of the Montreal area for another year. Bigot to Belle Île, 29 August 1760, AC, F3 vol. 16, f. 112v, NAC, MG 1, microfilm, reel F-392; Casgrain, ed., *Journal des campagnes du Chevalier de Lévis*, p. 297. They were convinced that the Canadian Iroquois would support them in this effort. When the governor general assembled a force to defend the upper St. Lawrence, "he also hoped that a large number of Natives would travel to that area." "Suittes de la campagne de 1760 en Canada," AG, A1, vol. 3574, no. 129 bis, f. 4.

51 "Relation de la suite de la campagne de 1760, depuis le 1 juin jusqu'à l'embarquement des troupes pour la France," [unsigned], in Casgrain, ed., *Relations et journaux*, pp. 252-253; Roquemaure to Lévis, 21 August 1760, 10:00 p.m., in Casgrain, ed., *Lettres de Divers Particuliers*, pp. 124-125.

52 Vaudreuil to Machault, 29 August 1760, AC, F3, 16, f. 117v.

53 "Mais ce projet ne put avoir lieu parce qu'au moment de son exécution les sauvages ayant eu la nouvelle que ceux des *cinq* nations se portoient pour médiateur entre eux et les anglois, ils abbandonnent le camp et se retirerent chex eux." "Suittes de la campagne de 1760 en Canada," AG, A1, vol. 3574, no. 129 bis, f. 5.

54 Ibid., ff. 7-8; Casgrain, ed., *Journal des campagnes du Chevalier de Lévis*, pp. 301-302; Roquemaure to Lévis, 1 September 1760, 10:00 p.m., in Casgrain, ed., *Lettres de Divers Particuliers*, pp. 131-132.

55 Murray to Pitt, 11 May 1761, Letters to and From General Murray, 1759-1789, MG 23 G II 1, series 1, vol. 3, f. 100. Murray described his captive as "a true Indian boy dressed in the fashion of his own country." In a chilling display of European racism, Murray went on to equate the young man with an example of Quebec's colourful local handicrafts, using "curiosity" or "curious" to describe each item. "I hope such a curiosity will prove agreeable to your self or Lady Esther. The boy has lived with me near two years appears to be of a very mild disposition, and remarkably quick and docile ... I take the liberty to beg that Lady Esther will accept of a working basket a sample of the Nuns' performance on bark as this kind of work is by many esteemed curious..."

56 "Copy of a certificate granted by Gen Murray to the Huron Indians. 5 Sept: 1760," in "From Mrs. Murray, of Bath," *Report of the Work of the Archives Branch for the year 1910* (Ottawa: Government Printing Bureau, 1911), pp. 50-51. See also "Journal of the Expedition against Quebec..." NAC, James Murray Papers, MG 23, G II 1, series 4, vol. 1, f. 164, microfilm, reel C-2225; Amherst, "Journal, 1760," MG 18, L4, vol. 015/8, f. 45; Knox, *Historical Journal*, vol. II, pp. 515-517.

57 "Journal of Warren Johnson," *Johnson Papers*, vol. XIII, pp. 188-190, 202.

58 Moncrieffe to Amherst, 9 September 1760, WO 34, vol. 83, ff. 16-16v; Moncrieffe to Amherst, 13 September 1760, ibid., ff. 43-43v; "Captain Moncrieffe's orders to Ensign Prevost for the protection of Vaudreuil," Moncrieffe to Ensign Prevost of the 4th Battalion of the Royal Americans, 12 September 1760, enclosed in ibid., f. 46; Amherst to Moncrieffe, 14 September 1760, WO 34, vol. 85, f. 98; Bougainville,

"Mémoire sur l'état de la nouvelle-france [1757]," *RAPQ*, 1923-24, p. 67.

59 Amherst, "Journal, 1760," f. 44.

60 Moncrieffe to Amherst, 9 September, 1760, WO 34, vol. 83, f. 16.

61 Ibid., ff. 16-16v.

62 "Captain Moncrieffe's orders to Ensign Prevost for the protection of Vaudreuil," 12 September 1760, WO 34, vol. 83, f. 46. See also Amherst to Moncrieffe, 9 September 1760, ibid., vol. 85, f. 83. As Provost departed, Moncrieffe continued to receive habitants who came in twos and threes to make their peace with the military authorities. Some of these habitants informed Moncrieffe that they had been unable to come to the Cedars before "As they have Escaped [f]rom the Indians." Moncrieffe to Amherst, 13 September 1760, ibid., vol. 83, ff. 43-43v.

63 Malartic, *Journal des Campagnes au Canada*, p. 353.

64 Amherst to Moncrieffe, 14 September 1760, WO 34, vol. 85, f. 98. The search for firearms was so intense that Moncrieffe sent an officer "to look in each house, and pick up any arms that they may have." The weapons thus collected were sent to Amherst in Montreal. Moncrieffe to Amherst, 13 September 1760, WO 34, vol. 83, ff. 43-43v.

10: The "Good Work of Peace," 1760-64

1 Indian Conference, 16 September 1760, *Johnson Papers*, vol. XIII, p. 164; "Extract from the minutes of proceedings between Sir Wm. Johnson Bart, and the Six Nations and Indians of Caghnawaga in Canada &c," 7 September 1763, WO 34, vol. 39, f. 411v. The Tree of Peace was "uprooted to bury the hatchet, to cast the weapons of war into the underground stream that carries off [the] pollution of war, and then the tree of peace is replanted." William N. Fenton, "The Lore of the Longhouse: Myth, Ritual and Red Power," *Anthropological Quarterly*, 48, no. 3 (July 1975), p. 143. For Amerindian diplomatic metaphors, see also Claude Charles Le Roy de la Potherie, "Termes et expressions des sauvages," in *Histoire de l'Amérique Septentrionale*, vol. III (Paris: Jean-Luc Nion, François Didot, 1722; reprinted Ann Arbor: University Microfilms, 1969), non-paginated, pp. v-vi, viii; "Glossary of Figures of Speech in Iroquois Political Rhetoric," in Francis Jennings, William N. Fenton, Mary A. Druke, David R. Miller, eds., *The History and Culture of Iroquois Diplomacy: An Interdisciplinary Guide to the Treaties of the Six Nations and Their League* (Syracuse: Syracuse University Press, 1985), pp. 118, 122.

2 Indian Conference, 16 September 1760, p. 163.

3 Indian Conference, 26 February 1765, "Minutes of Indian Affairs, 1755-1790," vol. 1826, f. 263. See also Claus to Johnson, 19 March 1761, *Johnson Papers*, vol. III, p. 362; Indian Conference, 16 September 1760, pp. 163-164.

4 Ibid., pp. 164-166.

5 Johnson to Claus, 1 May 1761, Claus Papers, vol. 14, f. 43, NAC, MG 19, F1, microfilm, reel C-1481; Indian Conference, 16 September 1760, pp. 163, 165. No account of Johnson's speeches on 15 September have survived. Consequently, there is no record of British commitments beyond those for which the Seven Nations thanked Johnson on the second day of the meeting or to which subsequent references were made.

6 Indian Conference, 16 September 1760, pp. 164, 163.

7   Ibid., p. 164. The League Iroquois would have preferred an even closer relationship with the Canadian Iroquois. In 1773 they asked the Kahnawakes to "look upon themselves for the future as one body wth. those of the 6 nats." The Kahnawakes made a non-committal reply. Daniel Claus, Journal, 17 June-27 July, 1773, Claus Papers, vol. 21, part 1, f. 18, NAC, MG 19, F1, microfilm, reel C-1483.

8   Jeffery Amherst, "Journal, 1760," entry of 22 September 1760, f. 13, NAC, MG 18, L4, 015/9, microfilm, reel A-1826; Claus to Johnson, 6 November 1760, Claus Papers, vol. 1, f. 14.

9   Guichart to Amherst, 22 September 1760, WO 34, vol. 83, ff. 79-79v.

10 Claus to Johnson, 18 March 1761, Claus Papers, vol. 1, f. 34.

11 Johnson to Amherst, 25 August 1763, WO 34, vol. 39, f. 394v.

12 "Indian Proceedings," 2-16 December 1764, "Minutes of Indian Affairs, 1755-1790," vol. 1826, f. 250. See also "Journal of Indian Affairs," 2-14 June 1764, "Minutes of Indian Affairs," f. 120.

13 Claus to Johnson, 30 September 1761, *Johnson Papers*, vol. III, pp. 546-547.

14 "Translation of the sentence of the court of field officer at Montreal held by order of his excellency Major General Gage for the trial of the dispute between the Indians, & Jesuits concerning the lands at Sault St. Louis," c. 1762. "Minutes of Indian Affairs, 1755-1790," vol. 1825 [Indian Records, vol. 6], f. 184, NAC, RG 10, microfilm, reel C-1222. See also "Copy of a Conference held by his Excell Major General Gage in the presence of Capt. Danl Claus Depy Agt of Indian affairs with four chiefs of Caghnawaga, or Sault St. Louis, deputies in behalf of the whole nation," 30 January 1762, ibid., ff. 180-182; Gage to Amherst, 16 March 1762, WO 34, vol. 5, f. 70v.

15 Gage to Amherst, 2 May 1762, WO 34, vol. 5, ff. 135-135v; Claus to Johnson, 9 April 1761, *Johnson Papers*, vol. III, p. 376; Lotteridge to Johnson, 12 December 1762, ibid., pp. 969-970.

16 Claus to Johnson, 19 January 1761, Claus Papers, vol. 1, f. 18.

17 Those arrested were British merchants transporting alcohol and gunpowder without authorization. See Amherst to Wrightson, 27 June 1761, WO 34, vol. 50, f. 214, NAC, MG 13, microfilm, reel B-2665; Wrightson to Amherst, 9 September 1761, ibid., f. 78; Amherst to Wrightson, 20 September 1761, ibid., f. 225; Amherst to Wrightson, 20 July 1761, ibid., f. 219.

18 Amherst added that this shortage of provisions threatened his ability to support a garrison in Canada. "Copy [of a] Circular letter from General Amherst to the gov of the Continent from Cape Breton to Georgia Inclusive, dated Camp of Montreal 9 Sept. 1760, Acquainting them with the entire reduction of Canada ... Capitulation, &ca.," CO 5, vol. 59, ff. 145-145v. See also Bernard to Amherst 27 September, 1760, CO 5, vol. 59, part 2, f. 113.

19 Haviland to Amherst, 27 February 1761, WO 34, vol. 51, f. 110v; Haviland to Amherst, 3 April 1761, ibid., f. 113v; Haviland to Amherst, 16 May 1761, ibid., f. 124; Amherst to the Officers Commanding at Fort George, Ticonderoga, & Crown Point, 25 September 1760, WO 34, vol. 52, f. 89; Henry N. Muller, "The Commercial History of the Lake Champlain-Richelieu River Route, 1760-1815" (doctoral dissertation, University of Rochester, 1969), pp. 10-11.

20 Claus to Johnson, 9 April 1761, Claus Papers, vol. 1, ff. 42-43; ibid., 26 February 1761, *Johnson Papers*, vol. III, p. 348; ibid., 1 December 1761, Claus Papers, vol. 1, ff. 64-65.

21 Haviland to Amherst, 3 April 1761, WO 34, vol. 51, f. 113v.

22 Claus to Johnson, 9 April 1761, Claus Papers, vol. 1, ff. 42-43; Johnson to Amherst, 23 April 1761, WO 34, vol. 39, f. 178.

23 Johnson to Claus, 1 May 1761, Claus Papers, vol. 14, f. 43; Amherst to Johnson, 7 May 1761, WO 34, vol. 38, f. 147. See also Johnson to Claus, 11 June 1761, Claus Papers, vol. 14, f. 50. Ironically, even as their right to travel to Albany was confirmed, the Kahnawakes, who had dominated the carrying trade for the past century, found themselves relegated to the margins of this trade by British entrepreneurs. The removal of inter-European borders had removed the obstacle that prevented more heavily capitalized European merchants from entering the trade directly, and eliminated demand for the Kahnawakes as carriers.

24 "Sir William Johnson received the following complaint of the Indians of Aughquisasne, transmitted to him by Dan Claus Esq, Dep Agent for Canada, bearing the date 8 Septem 1764," "Minutes of Indian Affairs, 1755-1790," vol. 1826, ff. 183-184; "Journal of Indian Affairs," 2-14 June 1764, "Minutes of Indian Affairs, 1755-1790," vol. 1826, f. 120.

25 Thomas Carter, *Historical Record of the Forty-Fourth or the East Essex Regiment* (Chatham: Gale & Polden, 1887), pp. 8-19; Mante, *History of the Late War in North America*, p. 100.

26 Claus to Johnson, 26 February 1761, *Johnson Papers*, vol. III, p. 349; Claus to Johnson, 1 December 1761, Claus Papers, vol. 1, f. 64.

27 Claus to Johnson, 9 April 1761, *Johnson Papers*, vol. III, p. 376; Claus to Johnson, 1 May 1761, Claus Papers, vol. 1, ff. 46-47.

28 Claus to Johnson, 1 May 1761, Claus Papers, vol. 1, ff. 46-47.

29 Johnson to Claus, 20 May 1761, ibid., ff. 48-49; Claus to Johnson, 1 December 1761, ibid., ff. 64-65. See also Claus to Johnson, 30 March 1761, ibid., f. 38-39.

30 Claus to Johnson, 27 October 1761, ibid., f. 58; Lotteridge to Johnson, 12 December 1762, *Johnson Papers*, vol. III, pp. 969-970.

31 Ormsby to Amherst, 6 September 1762, WO 34, vol. 50, f. 110; Ormsby to Amherst, 13 October 1762, ibid., ff. 111-112; Ormsby to Amherst, 28 October 1762, ibid., f. 113; Ormsby to Amherst, 17 November 1762, ibid., f. 115; Ormsby to Amherst, 15 November 1762, ibid., ff. 116-116v; Ormsby to Amherst, 4 January 1763, ibid., f. 122; Ormsby to Amherst, 31 January 1763, ibid., f. 123.

32 "Sir William Johnson received the following complaint of the Indians of Aughquisasne, transmitted to him by Dan Claus Esq, Dep Agent for Canada, bearing the date 8 Septem 1764," "Minutes of Indian Affairs, 1755-1790," vol. 1826, ff. 183-184. See also "At a meeting with the Deputys of the Cauchenewagoes, Canasedagoes, and other nations of Indians living in Canada, at Albany, June 28th, 1761," WO 34, vol. 39, f. 195.

33 Claus to Johnson, 1 December 1761, Claus Papers, vol. 1, f. 65; "Memorandum for Sir W 1773 during my stay in Canada," 19 June-27 July 1773," ibid., vol. 21, f. 26.

34 See, for example, Daniel Claus, Journal, 19 August 1767- 8 July 1768, ibid., ff. 4-22.

35 Indian Conference, 16 September, 1760, p. 165.

36 Auth, *The Ten Years' War*, pp. 156-194; Jennings, *Empire of Fortune*, pp. 438-453; McConnell, *A Country Between*, pp. 159-206.

BIBLIOGRAPHY

ARCHIVAL SOURCES

National Archives of Canada

Manuscript Groups

MG 1 Archives des Colonies
C11A, Correspondance générale, Canada
    vol. 79, reel F-79
    vol. 86, reel F-86
    vol. 99, reel F-99
    vol. 100, reel F-100
    vol. 101, reel F-101
    vol. 102, reel F-102
    vol. 103, reel F-103
C11E, Des limites et des postes
    vol. 10, reel F-408
E, Dossiers Personnels
    vol. 77, reel F-820
F3, Collection Moreau de Saint-Méry
    vol. 13, reel F-389
    vol. 14, reel F-390
    vol. 15, reel F-391
    vol. 16, reel F-392
MG 4 Archives de la Guerre
A1, Correspondance générale, opérations militaire
    vol. 3404, reel F-664
    vol. 3405, reel F-665
    vol. 3417, reel F-666
    vol. 3457, reel F-721

vol. 3498, reel F-722
vol. 3499, reel F-723
vol. 3540, reel f-724
vol. 3574, reel F-725

MG 8 Documents relatifs à la nouvelle-france et au Québec (xviie-xxe siècles)
E 1, Régime militaire

James Murray, "Report of the Government of Quebec and dependencies thereof"

MG 11 Colonial Office Papers
CO 5, Original Correspondence, Secretary of State, America and West Indies

vol. 46, reel B-2111
vol. 47, reel B-2111
vol. 48, reel B-2112
vol. 50, reel B-2113
vol. 51, reel B-2113
vol. 55, part 2, reel B-221
vol. 56, part 1, reel B-221
vol. 56, part 2, reel B-221
vol. 57, part 1, reel B-2171
vol. 58, reel B-2172
vol. 59, part 1, reel B-2173
vol. 59, part 2, reel B-2173
vol. 64, reel B-2175
vol. 888, reel B-3778
vol. 1068, reel B-3005
vol. 1328, reel B-4037

MG 12 Great Britain, Public Record Office, Admiralty, London
vol. 1487, reel B-2607

MG 13 Great Britain, Public Record Office, War Office Papers
WO 34 Amherst Papers

vol. 5, reel B-2639
vol. 20, reel B-2648
vol. 38, reel B-2656
vol. 39, reel B-2657
vol. 44, reel B-2661
vol. 50, reel B-2665
vol. 51, reel B-2666
vol. 52, reel B-2666
vol. 83, reel B-2684
vol. 85, reel B-2685

MG 17 Archives religieuses

A7-1, Église Catholique, Archives du Seminaire de St. Sulpice, Paris
vol. 4, reel C-14,104

MG 18 Pre-conquest papers

L4, British officers, Amherst Family
vols. 014, 015, reel A-1826

MG 19 Fur Trade and Indians

F1, Claus Family Papers
vol. 1, reel C-1478
vol. 14, reel C-1481
vol. 21, reel C-1483
vol. 23, reel C-1485

MG 21 Transcripts from papers in the British Library

Sloane and Additional Manuscripts, Haldimand Papers
additional manuscript 21,779, reel A-686

MG 23 Late Eighteenth-Century Papers

G II 1, James Murray Papers
series 1, "Letters to and From General Murray, 1759-1789," vol. 3,
reel C-2225
series 4, "Murray's Journals," vol. 1, reel C-2225

G II 11, Henry Hamilton Papers
"Reminiscences," 1792

Record Group

RG 10 Records Relating to Indian Affairs

Records of the Superintendent's Office

Minutes of the Commission for Indian Affairs, Albany, 1677-1748 vol. 1820
(Indian Records, vol. 2), reel C-1220

Minutes of Indian Affairs, 1755-1790
vol. 1822 (Indian Records, vol. 4), reel C-1221
vol. 1825 (Indian Records, vol. 6), reel C-1222
vol. 1826 (Indian Records, vol. 7), reel C-1222

Superintendents's Office Correspondence, 1755-1830
vol. 1828 (Indian Records, vol. 9), reel C-1222

PRINTED PRIMARY SOURCES

Abbot, W.W., ed. *The Papers of George Washington: Colonial Series.* vol. 1.
Charlottesville: University Press of Virginia, 1983.

Ambler, Charles A. *George Washington and The West.* Chapel Hill: University of North Carolina Press, 1936, reprinted New York: Russel & Russell, 1971.

J.C.B. *Voyage au Canada fait depuis l'an 1751 jusqu'en l'an 1761.* Paris: Aubier Montaigne, 1978.

Biggar, H.P., ed. *The Works of Samuel de Champlain*, vol. II. Toronto: The Champlain Society, 1925; reprinted Toronto: University of Toronto Press, 1971.

Calloway, Colin G. ed. *North Country Captives: Selected Narratives of Indian Captivity from Vermont and New Hampshire.* Hanover: University Press of New England, 1992.

Casgrain, H.-R., ed. *Collection de manuscrits contenant lettres, mémoires et autres documents historiques relatifs à l'histoire de la Nouvelle-France, recueillis aux archives de la province de Québec ou copiés à l'étranger.* vol. 3. Québec: A. Coté, 1884.

— . *Collection des manuscrits du maréchal de Lévis.* 12 vols. Montréal and Québec, 1889-1895.

— . vol. 1, *Journal des campagnes du Chevalier de Lévis en Canada, de 1756 à 1760.* Montréal: C.O. Beauchemin, 1889.

— . vol. 2, *Lettres du Chevalier de Lévis concernant la guerre du Canada (1756-1760).* Montréal: C.O. Beauchemin & Fils, 1889.

— . vol. 4, *Lettres et pièces militaires: Instructions, ordres, mémoires, plans de campagne et de défense, 1756-1760.* Québec: L.-J. Demers & Frère, 1891.

— . vol. 5, *Lettres de M. de Bourlamaque au maréchal de Lévis.* Québec: L.-J. Demers & Frère, 1891.

— . vol. 7, *Journal du Marquis de Montcalm durant ses campagnes au Canada de 1756 à 1760.* Québec: L.-J. Demers, 1895.

— . vol. 8, *Lettres du marquis de Vaudreuil au Chevalier de Lévis.* Québec: L.-J. Demers, 1895.

— . vol. 9, *Lettres de l'intendant Bigot au Chevalier de Lévis.* Québec: L.-J. Demers, 1895.

— . vol. 10, *Lettres de Divers particuliers au Chevalier de Lévis.* Québec: L.-J. Demers & Frère, 1895.

— . vol. 11, *Guerre du Canada: Relations et journaux de différentes expéditions faites durant les années 1755-56-57-58-59-60.* Québec: L.-J. Demers, 1895.

Carver, Jonathan. *Travels through the Interior parts of North-America, in the Years 1766, 1767, and 1768.* London: J. Walter and S. Crowder, 1778; reprinted as *Carver's Travels through North America in the Years 1766, 1767 and 1768.* Toronto: Coles Publishing Company, 1974.

De Forest, Louis E., ed. *The Journals and Papers of Seth Pomeroy, sometime general in the colonial service.* New Haven: Society of Colonial Wars in the State of New York, 1926.

Doughty, Arthur George, and G.W. Parmelee, eds., *The Siege of Quebec and Battle of the Plains of Abraham*, vol. V. Quebec: Dussault & Proulx, 1901.

Dunnigan, Brian Leigh, ed. and annotator, and Michael Cardy, translator, Pierre Pouchot, *Memoirs of the Late War in North America between France and England*. Yverdon, 1781; reprinted Youngstown: Old Fort Niagara Association, 1994.

Eastburn, Robert. *A faithful narrative, of the many dangers and sufferings, as well as wonderful deliverances of Robert Eastburn, during his late captivity among the Indians: Together with some remarks upon the country of Canada, and the religion, and policy of its inhabitants; the whole intermixed with devout reflections.* Philadelphia: William Dunlap, 1758; reprinted in Richard Vanderbeets, ed., *Held Captive by Indians: Selected Narratives, 1642-1836.* Knoxville: University of Tennessee Press, 1973.

Ewing, William S., ed. "An eyewitness account by James Furnis of the surrender of Fort William Henry, August 1757," in *New York History* 42, no. 3 (July 1961), pp. 307-316.

Fauteux, Aegidius, ed. *Journal du siège de Québec du 10 mai au 18 septembre 1759.* Québec: published by the editor, 1922.

Franquet, Louis. *Voyages et mémoires sur le Canada.* Montréal: Éditions Élysée, 1974.

Gabriel, C.N. *Le Maréchal de Camp Desandrouins 1729-1792, Guerre du Canada 1756-1759, Guerre de l'Indépendance américain 1780-1782.* Verdun: Renvé-Lallemant, 1887.

Gentleman's Magazine and Historical Quaterly, vol. 17 (1757).

Grenier, Fernand, ed. *Papiers contrecoeur et autres documents concernant le conflit anglo-français sur l'ohio de 1745 à1756.* Québec: Les presses universitaires Laval, 1952.

Hamilton, Charles, ed. *Braddock's Defeat.* Norman: University of Oklahoma Press, 1959.

Hébert, Jean-Claude ed. *Le siège de Québec en 1759 par trois témoins.* Québec: Ministère des affaires culturelles, 1972.

Hill, James, "James Hill - His Book," Edna V. Moffett, ed., printed as "The Diary of a private on the first Crown Point Expedition," *The New England Quarterly* 5, no. 3 (July 1932), pp. 602-618.

Jacobs, Wilbur R. ed. *The Appalachian Indian Frontier: The Edmund Atkin Report and Plan of 1755.* Columbia: University of South Carolina Press, 1954; reprinted Lincoln: University of Nebraska Press, 1967.

King, Titus. *Narrative of Titus King of Northampton, Mass.: A Prisoner of the Indians in Canada, 1755-1758*, vol. 109 of Wilcomb E. Washburn, ed.,

The Garland Library of Narratives of North American Indian Captivities. New York: Garland Publishing, 1977.

Knox, John. *An Historical Journal of the Campaigns in North America for the Years 1757, 1758, 1759, and 1760....* vol. II. London: W. Johnston and J. Dodsley, 1769; reprinted Arthur G. Doughty, ed., Toronto: The Champlain Society, 1915.

Kohl, J.G. *Kitchi-gami: Wanderings round Lake Superior.* London: Chapman and Hall, 1860.

Lafitau, Joseph-François. *Mœurs des sauvages amériquains, comparées aux mœurs des premiers temps.* Paris: Chez Saugrain, Charles Estienne Hochereau, 1724.

Lart, C. E., ed. "Eye-Witnesses' Accounts of the British Repulse at Ticonderoga," *Canadian Historical Review* 2, no. 4 (December 1921), pp. 360-363.

Le Roy de la Potherie, Claude Charles. *Histoire de l'Amérique Septentrionale,* vol. III. Paris: Jean-Luc Nion, François Didot, 1722; reprinted Ann Arbor: University Microfilms, 1969.

Malartic, Anne-Joseph-Hippolyte de Maurés de. *Journal des Campagnes au Canada, de 1755 à 1760.* Dijon: Gaffarel, 1890.

Muller, J. *The Attack and Defence of Fortify'd Places.* London: J. Millan, 1747.

Mante, Thomas. *The history of the late war in North America, and the Islands of the West-Indies, including the campaigns of* MDCCLXIII *and* MDCCLXIV *against his Majesty's Indian enemies.* London: W. Strahan and T. Cadell, 1772; reprinted New York: Research Reprints, 1970.

Norton, John. *The Journal of Major John Norton, 1816.* Carl F. Klinck and James J. Talman, eds., Toronto: The Champlain Society, 1970.

O'Callaghan, E.B., ed. *The Documentary History of the State of New York,* vols. I and II. Albany: Weed, Parsons, and Company, 1850.

— . *Documents Relative to the Colonial History of the State of New York,* vol. VI. Albany: Weed, Parsons and Company, 1855.

Pargellis, Stanley, ed. *Military Affairs in North America, 1748-1765: Selected Documents from the Cumberland Papers in Windsor Castle.* New York: D. Appleton-18th Century, 1936.

Pouchot, Pierre, *Mémoires sur la dernière guerre de l'Amérique septentrionale, entre la France et l'Angleterre. Suivis d'Observations, dont plusieurs sont relatives au théatre actuel de la guerre, & de nouveaux détails sur les moeurs & les usages des Sauvages, avec des cartes topographiques,* 3 vols. Yverdon, 1781.

Rapport de l'archiviste de la province de Québec, 1923-24, "La mission de M. de Bougainville en France en 1758-1759," pp. 1-70; "Le journal de M. de Bougainville," pp. 202-393.

— , 1924-25, Louis-Léonard Aumasson de Courville, "Mémoire du Canada," pp. 202-393.

— , 1926-27, "Lettres du père Aulneau," pp. 261-330; "Les journaux de campagne de Gaspard-Joseph Chaussegros de Léry," pp. 331-405.

— , 1927-28, "Journal de Joseph-Gaspard Chaussegros de Léry, Lieutenant des troupes, 1754-1755," pp. 355-430.

— , 1928-29, "Journal militaire tenu par Nicolas Renaud d'Avène des Méloizes, Cher, Seigneur de Neuville, au Canada, du 8 mai 1759 au 21 novembre de la même année. Il était alors capitaine aide-major aux troupes détachées de la marine," pp. 29-86.

— , 1931-32, Jean-Guillaume Plantavit de Lapause de Margon, "Mémoire et observations sur mon voyage en Canada," pp. 3-125.

— , 1932-33, "Les 'mémoires' du Chevalier de la Pause," pp. 305-391.

— , 1933-34, "Les 'papiers' La Pause," pp. 67-231.

— , 1944-45, "Lettres de Doreil," pp. 3-171.

— , 1947-48, "Correspondance entre M. de Vaudreuil et la cour (suite)," pp. 135-139.

Récher, Jean-Félix. *Journal du siège de Québec en 1759.* Québec: La Société Historique de Québec, 1959.

Report of the Work of the Archives Branch for the year 1910. Ottawa: Government Printing Bureau, 1911, "From Mrs. Murray, of Bath," pp. 50-55.

Rochemonteix, Camille de, ed. *Relation par lettres de l'amérique septentrionale (années 1709 et 1710).* Paris: Letouzey et Ané, 1904.

Roy, Pierre-Georges, ed. *Inventaire des papiers de Léry conservés aux Archives de la province de Québec,* vol. II. Québec: Archives de la province de Québec, 1939.

Sagard, Gabriel, *Sagard's Long Journey to the country of the Hurons.* G.M. Wrong, ed., Toronto: The Champlain Society, 1939; reprinted New York: Greenwood press, 1968.

Sargent, Winthrop, ed. *The History of an expedition against Fort Du Quesne, in 1755 under Major-General Edward Braddock.* Philadelphia: Lippincott, Grambo and Company, 1855.

Smith, James. *An account of the remarkable occurrences in the life and travels of Col. James Smith ... during his captivity with the Indians, in the years 1755, '56, '57, '58, & '59.* Lexington: John Bradford, 1799; reprinted Cincinnati: Robert Clarke & Co, 1870.

Stobo, Robert. *Memoirs of Major Robert Stobo of the Virginian Regiment.* Neville B. Craig, ed., Pittsburgh: John S. Davidson, 1884.

Sullivan, James, et. al., eds. *The Papers of Sir William Johnson,* 15 vols.

Albany: University of the State of New York, 1921-65.

Thwaites, Reuben Gold, ed. *The Jesuit Relations and Allied Documents: Travels and Explorations of the Jesuit Missionaries in New France, 1610-1791*, vols. XXVII, LXX, Cleveland: Burrows Brothers, 1896-1901; reprinted New York: Pageant Book Company, 1959.

Williamson, Peter. *French and Indian Cruelty; Exemplified in the Life and various Vicissitudes of Fortune of Peter Williamson containing... an accurate and impartial account of the operations of the FRENCH and ENGLISH forces at the siege of Oswego, where the author was wounded and taken prisoner.* Glasgow: J. Bryce and D. Patterson, 1758.

SECONDARY SOURCES

Anderson, Fred. *A People's Army: Massachusetts Soldiers and Society in the Seven Years' War.* Chapel Hill: University of North Carolina Press, 1984.

Auth, Stephen F. *The Ten Years' War: Indian-White Relations in Pennsylvania, 1755-1765.* New York: Garland Publishing, 1989

Blanchard, David. Introduction to *Narratives of the Museum of Sault St. Louis, 1667-1685.* Kahnawake: Kanienkehaka Raotitiohkwa Press, 1981, pp. 1-25.

Calloway, Colin G. *The Western Abenakis of Vermont, 1600-1800: War, Migration, and the Survival of an Indian People.* Norman: University of Oklahoma Press, 1990.

Carter, Thomas. *Historical Record of the Forty-Fourth or the East Essex Regiment.* Chatham: Gale & Polden, 1887.

Cassel, Jay, "The Troupes de la marine in Canada: men and material, 1683-1760." Ph.D. dissertation, University of Toronto, 1987.

Chartrand, René. *Canadian Military Heritage, volume I: 1000-1754.* Montreal: Art Global, 1993.

— . *Canadian Military Heritage, volume II: 1755-1871.* Montreal: Art Global, 1995.

Cook, Peter Laurence. "Symbolic and Material Exchange in Intercultural Diplomacy on Canada's Western Frontier, 1703-1725," paper read at the Seventh Fur Trade Conference, St. Mary's University, Halifax, 26 May 1995.

— . "French-Amerindian Diplomacy on New France's Western Frontier, 1703-1725," MA thesis, University of Ottawa, 1993.

Corvisier, André. *L'Armée Française de la fin du XVIIe siècle au ministère de Choiseul: Le Soldat.* Paris: Presses Universitaires de France, 1964.

Day, Gordon M. "Rogers' Raid in Indian Tradition," *Historical New Hampshire,* 17 (June 1962), pp. 3-17.

Dixon, C.W. *Smallpox*. London: J. & A. Churchill, 1962.

Druke, Mary A. "Linking Arms: The Structure of Iroquois Intertribal Diplomacy," in Daniel K. Richter and James H. Merrell, eds., *Beyond the Covenant Chain: The Iroquois and their Neighbours in Indian North America, 1600-1800*. Syracuse: Syracuse University Press, 1987, pp. 29-40.

— . "Structure and Meanings of Leadership Among the Mohawk and Oneida During the Mid-Eighteenth Century." Ph.D. dissertation, University of Chicago, 1982.

Duffy, Christopher. *Fire and Stone: The Science of Fortress Warfare, 1660-1860*. Newton Abbot: David & Charles, 1975.

Eccles, W.J. *The Canadian Frontier, 1534-1760*, rev. ed. Albuquerque: University of New Mexico Press, 1983.

— . "The Role of the American Colonies in Eighteenth Century French Foreign Policy," in *Atti de I Congresso Internazionale de Storia Americana, Genovo, 29 Maggio 1976* (Genova, 1978), pp. 164-173; reprinted in Eccles, *Essays on New France*. Toronto: Oxford University Press, 1987, pp. 144-155.

— . "Louis-Joseph de Montcalm, Marquis de Montcalm," in *Dictionary of Canadian Biography, volume III, 1741 to 1770*. Toronto: University of Toronto Press, 1974, pp. 458-469.

— . "Pierre de Rigaud de Vaudreuil de Cavagnial, Marquis de Vaudreuil," in *Dictionary of Canadian Biography, volume IV, 1771 to 1800* (Toronto: University of Toronto Press, 1979), pp. 662-674.

— . "The Battle of Quebec: A Reappraisal," in Alf Andrew Heggoy, ed., *The French Colonial Historical Society, Proceedings of the Third Annual Meeting*. Athens, Georgia: French Colonial Historical Society, 1978, pp. 70-81; reprinted in Eccles, *Essays on New France*. Toronto: Oxford University Press, 1987, pp. 125-133.

Eid, Leroy V. "'National War,' among Indians of Northeastern North America," *Canadian Review of American Studies* 16, no. 2 (Summer 1985), pp. 125-154.

— . "The Cardinal Principle of Northeast Woodland Indian War," in William Cowan, ed., *Papers of the Thirteenth Algonquian Conference*. Ottawa: Carleton University, 1982, pp. 243-250.

Fenton, William N. "The Lore of the Longhouse: Myth, Ritual and Red Power," *Anthropological Quarterly*, vol. 48, no. 3 (July 1975), pp. 131-147.

Frégault, Guy. *La Guerre de la Conquête, 1754-1760*. Montréal: Fides, 1955.

Frazier, Patrick. *The Mohicans of Stockbridge*. Lincoln: University of Nebraska Press, 1992.

Gipson, Lawrence Henry. *The British Empire Before the American Revolution*, *volume VI: The Great War for the Empire; The Years of Defeat, 1754-1757.* New York: Alfred A. Knopf, 1946.

Given, Brian J. *A Most Pernicious Thing: Gun Trading and Native Warfare in the Early Contact Period.* Ottawa: Carleton University Press, 1994.

Grabowski, Jan. "The Common Ground: Settled Natives and French in Montréal, 1677-1760." Doctoral dissertation, Université de Montréal, 1993.

Graymont, Barbara. "The Six Nations Indians in the Revolutionary War," in Charles F. Hayes, ed., *The Iroquois in the American Revolution: 1976 Conference Proceedings.* Rochester: Rochester Museum and Science Center, 1981, pp. 25-36.

Harris, R. Cole, ed. *Historical Atlas of Canada, volume 1, From the Beginning to 1800.* Toronto: University of Toronto Press, 1987.

Hopkins, D.R. *Princes and Peasants: Smallpox in History.* Chicago: University of Chicago Press, 1983.

Hough, Franklin B. *A History of St. Lawrence and Franklin Counties, New York, From the earliest period to the present time.* Albany: Little & Co., 1853; reprinted Baltimore: Regional Publishing Company, 1970.

Hunter, William A. *Forts on the Pennsylvania Frontier, 1753-1758.* Harrisburg: The Pennsylvania Historical and Museum Commission, 1960.

Jaenen, Cornelius J., "Amerindian views of French Culture in the Seventeenth Century," *Canadian Historical Review* 55, no. 3 (September 1974), pp. 261-291.

— . *Friend and Foe: Aspects of French-Amerindian Cultural Contact in the Sixteenth and Seventeenth Centuries.* Toronto: McClelland and Stewart, 1973.

Jennings, Francis. *Empire of Fortune: Crowns, Colonies & Tribes in the Seven Years War in America.* New York: W.W. Norton, 1988.

— . *The Ambiguous Iroquois Empire: The Covenant Chain Confederation of Indian Tribes with English Colonies from its beginnings to the Lancaster Treaty of 1744.* New York: W.W. Norton, 1984.

Jennings, Francis, William N. Fenton, Mary A. Druke, David R. Miller, eds. *The History and Culture of Iroquois Diplomacy: An Interdisciplinary Guide to the Treaties of the Six Nations and Their League.* Syracuse: Syracuse University Press, 1985.

Kopperman, Paul E. *Braddock at the Monongahela.* Pittsburgh: University of Pittsburgh Press, 1977.

LeMoine, James. *The Scot in New France: An Ethnological Study.* Montreal: Dawson Brothers, 1881.

MacLeod, D. Peter. "Treason at Quebec: British espionage in Canada during the winter of 1759-1760," *Canadian Military History* 2, no. 1 (spring 1993), pp. 49-62.

— . "Microbes and Muskets: Smallpox and the Participation of the Amerindian Allies of New France in the Seven Years' War," *Ethnohistory* 39, no. 1 (winter 1992), pp. 42-64.

— . "The Canadians Against the French: The Struggle for Control of the Expedition to Oswego in 1756," *Ontario History* 80, no. 2 (June, 1988), pp. 143-157.

McConnell, Michael N. *A Country Between: The Upper Ohio Valley and its Peoples, 1724-1774*. Lincoln: University of Nebraska Press, 1992.

— . "'Peoples In Between:' The Iroquois and the Ohio Indians, 1720-1768," in Daniel K. Richter and James H. Merrell, eds. *Beyond the Covenant Chain: The Iroquois and their Neighbors in Indian North America, 1600-1800*. Syracuse: Syracuse University Press, 1987, pp. 93-114.

Merrell, James H. "'Their Very Bones Shall Fight:' The Catawba-Iroquois Wars," in Daniel K. Richter and James H. Merrell, eds., *Beyond the Covenant Chain: The Iroquois and their Neighbors in Indian North America, 1600-1800*. Syracuse: Syracuse University Press, 1987, pp. 115-133.

Miller, J.R. *Skyscrapers Hide the Heavens: A History of Indian-White Relations in Canada*. Toronto: University of Toronto Press, 1989.

Muller, Henry N. "The Commercial History of the Lake Champlain-Richelieu River Route, 1760-1815." Doctoral dissertation, University of Rochester, 1969.

Ostola, Lawrence. "The Seven Nations of Canada and the American Revolution, 1774-1783." MA thesis, Université de Montréal, 1988.

Richter, Daniel K. *The Ordeal of the Longhouse: The Peoples of the Iroquois League in the Era of European Colonization*. Chapel Hill: University of North Carolina Press, 1992.

— . "War and Culture: The Iroquois Experience," *William and Mary Quarterly*, 3rd ser., vol. 40, no. 4 (October 1983), pp. 528-559.

Ross, Lester A. *Archaeological Metrology: English, French, American and Canadian Systems of Weights and Measures for North American Historical Archaeology*. Ottawa: Parks Canada, 1983.

Stacey, C.P. *Quebec, 1759: The Siege and the Battle*. rev. ed. London: Pan Books, 1973.

Steele, Ian K. *Betrayals: Fort William Henry & the "Massacre"*. New York: Oxford University Press, 1990.

Trigger, Bruce G. *The Children of Aataentsic: A History of the Huron People to 1660*. Kingston and Montreal: McGill-Queen's University Press, 1976.

Trudel, Marcel. *Initiation à la Nouvelle-France*. Montreal and Toronto: Holt, Rinehart and Winston, 1968.

White, Richard. *The Middle Ground: Indians, Empires and Republics in the Great Lakes Region, 1650-1815*. New York: Cambridge University Press, 1991.

Wilkins, Charles. "The Mythic White Pine is in trouble," *Canadian Geographic* 114, no. 5 (September/October, 1994), pp. 58-66.

Wise, S.F. "Thomas Gage," in *Dictionary of Canadian Biography, volume III, 1741 to 1770*. Toronto: University of Toronto Press, 1974, pp. 278-282.

Index